The Truth Shall Set You Free

Confessions of a Pastor's Wife

Barbara Barnett

WinePress Publishing Mukilteo, WA 98275

The Truth Shall Set You Free
Copyright © 1996 by Barbara Barnett

Published by WinePress Publishing
PO Box 1406
Mukilteo, WA 98275

Cover by **DENHAM**DESIGN, Everett, WA

All rights reserved. No part of this publication may be reproduced, stored in a retrieval system or transmitted in any way by any means, electronic, mechanical, photocopy, recording or otherwise, without the prior permission of the publisher, except as provided by USA copyright law.

Some testimonies and experiences in the narrative are actual quotes taken from tapes, including statements by the pastor. Dialogue is recounted from the author's memory. Conversations are sometimes abbreviated, but the information is accurate. There is nothing in the text about the misconduct of the pastor that hasn't been revealed, at least to some extent through the news media. The names of some individuals have been changed or deleted.

Unless otherwise noted, Scripture quotations are from the *King James Version of the Bible*.

Printed in Canada on recycled paper.

Library of Congress Catalog Card Number: 96-61549
ISBN 1-883893-67-4

Contents

Preface v
Introduction ix

1. Tear-washed eyes 11
2. A Country Girl Meets Jesus 15
3. Me, Marry a Preacher's Son? 35
4. Beginning Our Journey
   Together in God's School 61
5. Tests of Our Faith in God's
   Healng and Forgiveness 85
6. Discerning God's Leading 97
7. Charismatic Explosion 109
8. One Door Closed, Another Opened 131
9. "Pastor, Please Let Me Give" 157
10. A Dream Comes True 167
11. A Vision From God 185
12. Bible College Tests, Not All On Paper . 199
13. Blessed by Men of God 225
14. "Satan, I Declare War on You!" 249
15. Who is the Son? 269
16. From Glory to Glory, We Shall Behold Him 281
17. What Is This Love?—Ecstasy and Agony . 305
18. Angels Unawares, Holy and Unholy 329

19. A Dozen Red Roses 359
20. The Scapegoat 385
21. "Pastor, Please Practice What You Preach" 407
22. Shattered Dreams—Shattered Lives 423
23. Oh, Donald, Donald! 439
24. The Flawed Diamond 461

Appendix 471
End Notes 477

Preface

Community Chapel and Bible Training Center, born by the Spirit of God, grew from one family to a congregation of about four thousand. On the crest of the mightiest move of God the Chapel had ever known, the church crumbled. The Chapel's shame was broadcast around the world (*60 Minutes, New York Times, Time, etc.*) Having labored with the pastor, as his wife, for 23 years of ministry, I have been commissioned by the Spirit of the Lord to reveal what really happened.

When Jesus asked me to write this book for Him, He put within my mind what He wanted included, how I was to write it, and why He wanted it written. He told me:

"My people need to know what I did and what I wanted to do at the Chapel. I am going to pour my love on my universal Body to prepare my Bride for her soon-coming Bridegroom. I want them to know what happened at the Chapel so they can benefit from both what was right and what was wrong, so they will have an advantage over the devil that you did not.

"Don't preach or teach. Just tell the story of what I have done in your life and at the Chapel—including visions, dreams, and your experiences with angels and demons. The people need to know what the devil did, too, so don't be concerned about what people will think of you, just write it."

Now you would think after the Lord spoke so plainly to me I would sit right down and begin writing. I didn't. I meant to. I even tried to. I told Jesus I would. Yet every time I tried, I was battled by the devil until one day two years later, I attended a meeting where Ruth Heftlon (a prophetic minister) called me out of the congregation and, not knowing who I was, spoke these words:

"What I saw was this: that there's a new dimension of soaring in the Spirit that God is leading you into. I see God is bringing a prophetic release into your spirit beyond anything you've ever known. You're going to be able to describe the vision and declare the Word of the Lord in such picturesque words, that which God has given you in measure. You're going to find a fullness, instead of a little dab of paint here and there. It's going to be the full picture coming forth for the body of Christ. And it's going to bring such an excitement into your own spirit. It's the day you've waited for!"

Later, she interrupted her own sermon to speak in tongues and say: "There's somebody here tonight . . . to whom God is saying, 'I've told you to write the vision.' If you're one of those people God's been speaking to about 'writing the vision' He's already given you, you better get on with it and 'write the vision.' And as the Scripture says, 'Write it plainly that he that readeth it may be able to run'" (Habakkuk 2:2).

I left the meeting knowing in my heart that Jesus had indeed commissioned me to tell His story and mine, as we have walked together these 62 years.

In the course of writing this book, two distinct things happened. Both were from the Lord. The first one happened shortly after I started the manuscript. Telling certain aspects of my life were too painful, and I had decided to leave them out. Then Jesus spoke to me while I was worshipping Him in prayer.

As the song *I Am the Bread of Life,* by John Michael Talbot, played, instantly I saw Jesus, hanging naked on the cross. He said, "It was painful for me to be exposed to the world, but it was the only way I could become the Bread of Life. Are you willing, for My sake, to lay your life bare so others can feed on you—even the vultures?" I laid on my face and wept until I became willing to say "yes."

Toward the end of the second re-write of this book, I was crying out to the Lord, "Jesus, don't let me say anything You don't want said. I want every page to be anointed."

Again, He spoke to my heart, "You do your job, and I'll do Mine."

My prayer for you, dear pilgrim, is that Jesus and His love will be more real to you when you lay the book down than when you first picked it up. And to the pastors for whom this book is primarily intended, I will be beholden to the Lord if even one of you profits by hearing the wonderful things Jesus allowed me to experience, and by His lessons as a result of my own weaknesses and failings.

Introduction

This story actually had its beginning when Jesus was nailed to the cross. It was there—when His side was pierced and out gushed blood and water—that His church, His bride and helpmate, was born.

Come with me on an incredible journey into the spiritual realm, where angels and demons compete for the ones He died for. Witness how Jesus called over four thousand members of His body together one-by-one from all walks of life. Step by step, day by day, month by month, He clothed them with His grace and fed them from His Word, all the while Satan worked underground to "deceive, if possible, the very elect" (Matthew 24:24) and devour them (Revelation 12:4) before Jesus could have the darling of His heart. You'll learn how much our Creator respects His creation, because He never interferes with the human will—the choice is ours.

Chapter One

Tear-washed Eyes

*"...and my eyes will bitterly weep,
and flow down with tears, because the
flock of the Lord has been taken captive."
(Jeremiah 13:17)*

Late in the afternoon of August 5th, 1993, exactly 44 years from when I stood in the Barnett mansion and became Mrs. Donald Barnett, I went to the mailbox and pulled out a letter from my lawyer. Suspecting what it contained, I put it in my car and drove to Alki Beach which stretches for miles along Puget Sound's coast, directly across the bay from Seattle's skyline.

Sitting on the concrete bulkhead with the salt water lapping at my feet, I held the letter in my hands and stared across the water at the Smith Tower where we went on our honeymoon 44 years ago. It's now dwarfed by the skyscrapers which have arisen around it, but it's still special to me. Before the sun set, I opened the envelope and read: "As of 2:30 p.m. on August 3rd, your marriage has been dissolved." My tears mixed with the sea at my feet. I felt Jesus so real it was as if He hugged me. I sensed that somehow angels gathered up my tears to store them in a bottle (Psalm 56:8).

I sat alone, with the distinct aroma of the sea enveloping me, and watched the lights come on across the bay. My mind went back to almost a year ago when I had ventured to go to a church service in North Seattle. It was as hard for me to go alone as it had been to go in a grocery store and shop for only me after I'd moved out of the parsonage and into an apartment. The speakers in the North Seattle church were Rick Joyner and Paul Caine. My hunger to know about their relationship with Jesus overruled my pain.

I was standing at the bookcounter, when a minister, well-known in Seattle, approached me. "Sis Barnett," he said, "I want you to know that I consider you and your husband to be pioneers in what God did in the charismatic movement in Seattle." I clenched my teeth in an effort to keep the well of tears that had been stored up in my heart for twenty-four years from gushing out. He took my hand and added, "I have the highest respect for you, in spite of all that has happened. I want to meet with you, and do what I can to restore you."

I never heard the ministers preach that night; I was too full of emotion to listen. I wondered, *Would my life be different today if these ministers would have accepted and supported us back then? Now it's too late. Dare I even hope that Brother — will give me love and support now when I'm more alone than ever, as he says he will?*

Before I left the beach to face my unknown future, I prayed, "Jesus, thank You for always being with me. I know I can trust Your commitment to me. You have proven to me that Your Word is above Your Name (Psalm

138:2). I would never want to go back to the relationship I had with You before You sent us Your mighty baptism of love."

The lights of Seattle blurred as I reflected on the lights in the kingdom of God who had come to Him: from my first new convert, the little black girl who gave her heart to Jesus in the Bible club when I was sixteen, to the thousands God had rescued from the devil's grip since Community Chapel was founded. "Jesus," I continued, "Please don't let the devil get one of them back. And Jesus, show me what caused the flaw in my love for my husband that has put me here today—my marriage gone, my home lost, my ministry taken, and our church dissolved."

Suddenly, I heard a song, written by one of the Chapel's musicians years ago, being sung in my mind:

The mercy of the Lord is all around me.
The mercy of the Lord is my defense.
His love and His compassion surround me.
The mercy of the Lord is my defense.

And my mind drifted back to 1931.

I saw that for our entire lives both my ex-husband, Don, and I had been in God's school preparing us for the day in 1966 when the Chapel would be born and develop.

"Perhaps my mother wouldn't have given her heart to Jesus if the circumstances were different when I was born," I mused...

Chapter Two

A Country Girl Meets Jesus

"Suffer the little children to come unto Me and forbid them not, for such is the kingdom of heaven."
(Matthew 19:14)

One week before Christmas in 1931, in an upstairs bedroom of a boarding house in Lava Hot Springs, Idaho, I entered the world, joining my two older brothers. Immediately after my arrival, my mother went downstairs and helped my father prepare the evening meal for our boarders. The Great Depression was underway, and my family didn't escape.

Mamma heard about Jesus soon after my birth, and she surrendered her life to Him, inspiring a dramatic change in her life. She went directly to the mirror and wiped off her bright red lipstick–a symbol of worldliness in those days. She found a church home to which she took all of us children regularly, even though many times it meant walking as far as three miles each way.

THE TRUTH SHALL SET YOU FREE

My earliest encounter with Jesus was at three years old. We had just moved to Boise, and my two brothers were in the same crib, one at each end, both covered with chicken pox. Mamma, pregnant with my little brother, was standing over them with a hand on each child, praying for Jesus to heal them. Just when one boy stopped crying, the other began. She hadn't noticed my runny nose and feverish brow as I squatted on the bare brown wood floor, hugging my knees and crying in a sing-song rhythm.

Discovering a pox on my knee, I stood straight up, clutching my skirt in an effort to hold it away from my knee. I wailed above the whimpering of my brothers, "Mamma, tell Jesus to take it away!" After feeling my forehead for fever and looking at my knee, Mamma prayed. As soon as we opened our eyes, the pox was gone! I never got another one. Mamma hugged me and laughed because Jesus had made Himself real to me.

In the years that followed, I saw the Lord—because of Mamma's faith—provide for us. During the Great Depression, Daddy, unable to find work was gone for long periods of time. Mamma found herself alone with four children and running out of food. She put the last of the raisins on the stove, which also served to heat the one-room laundry house that was our home. We called it "the little round house" because it was ten feet in diameter. It sat back on an alley and was just big enough to hold our only bed, a rocking chair, and the stove with a stool beside it on which sat a basin of water.

Gathering up my crying, hungry baby brother, Lee, Mamma sat in the rocker and sang a song we had heard every day for a week. "Hurry up, raisins, and cook, for

A COUNTRY GIRL MEETS JESUS

Mamma's little Lee is hun - ger - y. Hurry up, raisins, and cook." Realizing Lee wasn't going to fall asleep this time, she said, "Okay, everyone line up. It's time for raisins."

My two brothers and I scrambled off the bed and stood in front of the stove. We were thankful Mamma "found" some coal the previous night, when she went out into the dark after we were in bed and walked across town to the railroad tracks, climbed up on a box car and lifted out a couple chunks of coal. It felt good to be warm in the below-zero weather.

"One for you," Mamma counted, as she put a spoonful of raisins in each mouth. "Now, chew and chew to make them last a long time," she added.

"Mamma," Teddy, my oldest brother, moaned after he swallowed, "I'm still hungry." Mamma gave him the last spoonful.

I asked, "Mamma, what about you? You didn't get any."

"It's okay, honey. I'm not hungry. Come here, and let's thank Jesus for giving us raisins." We three tots hugged Mamma around her legs as she held Lee. "Jesus, we thank You for giving us raisins to eat...." She was interrupted by a loud knock on the door.

Teddy shouted, "I'll get it!"

Mamma said, "No, I will."

Hoping it was Daddy, she flung open the door. Wide-eyed, we beheld our neighbor lady who lived in a big house on the street and who made no effort to hide her hatred for us, shaking, with a kettle of beans in her hands.

"Here, take these," she shouted and shoved the kettle at Mamma. "I was about to throw them in the garbage when a Power came over me and said, 'Don't throw those away! Take them over to the round house and give them to the lady with those kids.' I hate this feeling! I want to get rid of it. Here!"

With that she turned and was gone before Mamma could give her back the kettle. As soon as the door shut behind her retreating figure, we all began dancing and cried, "Thank you, Jesus, for sending us food!"

On two other occasions during the Depression, the Lord miraculously supplied our food. One time a box of groceries was left on our doorstep. Included in the package was a single light bulb. How did the Giver know that our only light bulb had burned out that very day?

> *A simple trust in God as my Provider was being planted in my heart.*

By the time I was ready to enter second grade, we had moved into a two-room house on an acre of land, and my only sister had joined us. That summer, Mamma's faith really paid off for me.

We children ran barefoot. Since money was scarce, shoes were saved for school. One day my little brother, Lee, and I attempted to build a table from the end of an orange crate which had a knot in it. Teddy grabbed the hammer and threatened, "I'm going to knock that knot out."

"No," I cried, "You'll ruin our board! It's going to be a table."

"Ah, you can't make a table," he chided, as he lifted the hammer over his head with both hands.

I slid my left foot over the knot and screamed, "No!"

It was too late—the hammer was already on its way. The knot was saved, but my toe was not.

Mamma caught me as I screamed and hopped around the yard. A puddle of blood formed in the dirt as she held my foot and prayed in tongues, crying almost as hard as I. She carried me into the house. Finding a freshly laundered white sheet, Mamma tore it into strips and wrapped it around my toe. She put me in bed with a mound of pillows holding my foot high into the air.

The next day, the bandage was stuck to my toe and had to be soaked off. Of course, I cried the whole time. Mamma prayed. One look at my toe made me throw up. "Teddy," Mamma directed, "Get that book for Barbara." He held the book open on my lap so I couldn't see my toe. Twice a day, we went through the same ritual.

Teddy felt so bad that for two weeks he worked to build the table. When he had it just right, he brought it in and placed it by my bed. He smiled and said, "It's a little wobbly, but it can hold your new coloring book and crayons."

To repay him, I smiled back and offered, "You can color one of the pictures, if you want to."

He knelt by the table and happily paged through the book. It was a special treat to have crayons and a coloring book. My Sunday School teachers, as soon as they heard about my toe, came right over with the gift and prayed for me.

After two weeks, the doctor came to examine my toe. He spoke to Mamma in hushed tones, making it clear that the toe must come off or I would lose my entire foot. The red streak extending up my ankle confirmed blood poisoning; the wounded flesh was putrid, it smelled awful. Mamma, however, refused the amputation. She declared she would believe Jesus to heal me and save my toe. The Epsom salt soaks were increased to six times a day, and my foot was kept elevated above my head. Mamma prayed for healing of that toe during every soak session.

Every week, my Sunday School teachers faithfully visited and agreed with us in prayer. How important those visits were to me! Their presence each week reinforced my faith that my toe was being healed by Jesus. I didn't attend school until December that year, wearing a big soft slipper on one foot–but my toe was saved, and my foot is normal today.

> *These caring Sunday School teachers left a lasting impression which helped shape my own teaching ministry.*

It was an exciting day when we moved into a big house with two bedrooms upstairs, on five acres. Daddy worked as a cook at a cafe in Boise. Later he acquired a small cafe on main street, which he owned and operated until he retired. He worked seven days a week, rarely taking a day off. I can remember going some place with Daddy only three times during my entire childhood. It was also a special treat when he attended church with us.

My fondest memories of my father are of being alone with him in our pasture. I followed him out to the edge of the irrigation ditch. We sat on the bank and breathed in the smell of the pasture as the water flooded it and soaked the earth, me hugging my knees and Daddy chewing on a toothpick that was always in his mouth. Not a word was spoken, but I loved just being with Daddy.

> *The absence of a relationship with my father undoubtedly influenced my opinion of myself. Was I so starved for affection I let men abuse me?*

My first promise to the Lord was made when my baby brother, Buddy, was seven months old. Two other children came to live with us. Mamma agreed to raise her cousin's youngest children when his wife was permanently institutionalized. The addition of a two-year-old boy and infant girl brought our family up to eight children. Since the baby, Sandy, was only five months old, it was like having twins in the family.

It was my job to watch by their crib at nap time until Sandy got accustomed to her new home. I stood and looked at her baby blue eyes wide with fear. Patting her, I prayed as I wiped the tears off my cheeks, "Jesus, it must feel awful to lose a mother. Please come into Sandy's heart like you did mine. I will be the best sister to her that I can." I was, too, until when she was seven years old her father put her brother and her in the same Catholic boarding school their three older sisters had attended. It broke my heart.

Mamma would have taken in all five children, if their father would have allowed it. She always had room in her heart for one more. Through her example, I acquired a desire to nurture and care for God's children. She dedicated the last twenty-five years of her life to her daycare, where she took care of as many as twenty-five children a day. One young man who asked to be a pallbearer at her funeral declared, "I wouldn't be alive today if Grandma hadn't taken care of me when I was a baby; she saved my life." As a baby, he had a heart condition which required constant care after surgery.

Mamma also taught me how to pray. Not by telling, but by doing. When I was eight years old, I watched Mamma fold a mountain of clothes as she spoke to my brother, Teddy, about Jesus. Sensing the Holy Spirit's presence, she sat down and invited us to gather around her knees so she could pray for Jesus to come into our hearts.

I'll never forget that day. I was born-again as I accepted Jesus as my Savior, and He gave me my first vision of Himself. Tears streamed down my face. I whispered, "Jesus," over and over as I saw a beautiful brightness—*shekinah* glory, we called it—surrounding Jesus as He moved toward me. I knew I wanted Him in my life forever. That picture is as clear to me now as it was when I first saw Him. When the Lord gives an experience of Himself, it doesn't fade, for He is beyond the realm of time.

I was an extremely shy girl and never raised my hand in class, nor spoke even when the teacher called on me. At recess I'd go outside and stand behind a bush next to the building until the bell rang.

I had a stubborn streak, too. After I'd walked over a mile to school in below zero weather, I was so cold that ice formed on my face. I'd push right past the hall monitors and go inside, even though no one was allowed into the school until the bell rang.

> *Surely my shyness and stubbornness gave the devil an advantage.*

World War II was a fearful time for me. The nights found me praying to Jesus to take the airplanes away that flew over our farm. Of course, Daddy kept his ear glued to the radio, which meant everyone had to be quiet. Like every other town, we had blackout drills and ration stamps for food, along with rubber, metal, and grease drives for the war effort.

We had plenty of sugar, a precious commodity, because of the cafe, but soap was hard to come by, so Daddy made his own. We had a victory garden, as fresh produce in the stores was scarce. We raised cattle, pigs, and chickens to provide meat for the cafe and our family.

> *Fear got an awful foothold in my life.*

Mamma hadn't understood why I tagged after her all day when Pearl Harbor was bombed. When I refused to let go of her skirt even long enough for her to use the outhouse her patience ran out. She yanked my dress above my head, imprisoning my arms and rendering me powerless to defend my bottom, and spanked me.

I was so scared I couldn't eat. I flung myself on my bed feeling Jesus probably had more important matters than to help me. That night, it was if He entered my room. I felt His presence. He never spoke a word. I only saw His face, yet the look in His eyes said it all. I felt I was the only person in the whole world—His full attention was on me. He was devoted to being whatever I needed Him to be. He stayed there, looking at me, curled up on the bed, until that message was imprinted on my spirit and soul. Then His face faded, but the message of His personal love has never left me. It has kept me from condemnation through all my sin and mistakes.

> *A warm feeling floods over me when I remember it was because of World War II that my prayer life began.*

Mamma took me to the intercessory prayer meetings she and two other ladies had for the men overseas. One lady's husband worked as a cook on a warship. I learned how God uses prayer even to chart the course of ships. I became a part of the unity in prayer experienced by the ladies. One time our intercession changed direction every three minutes; it was so specific we timed it. The cook's wife received a letter from her husband. He wrote, "We were in the war zone and would have been sunk if we hadn't changed directions every three minutes." The Lord intervened because one cook's wife was praying.

I wasn't surprised when, years later after I was married, God used me to intercede for my own beloved brother, Jim. He joined the army at age eighteen and was taken prisoner in the Korean War. Many times I was awakened in the middle of the night sobbing. I'd slip out of bed so as not to awaken my husband and kneel at the couch. It became such a common occurrence that when my husband found I was gone, he knew where I was. Sometimes the intercession would last a couple of hours, sometimes only fifteen minutes. One day the intercession stopped. When the prisoners were released, we learned that Jim had been taken out and shot because of his faith in God.

Another lady's husband was on Wake Island with a construction crew when Pearl Harbor was bombed. Clarine didn't hear from her husband for four long years. Unlike the servicemen's wives who had the government to inform them of the whereabouts of their loved ones, she had no way of receiving word from him. But she knew he was alive because of what we experienced in prayer.

The Lord used him in the lives of men stranded on that island—not just by his words, but by his life. Years later as my husband was witnessing to a man at Boeing where he worked, the man recalled the time when during the war he, too, was stranded on Wake Island. He said, "There was a certain 'preacher' who astounded everyone because he put our welfare above his own. Food was scarce, and men were starving; but Mr. Johnson would never take anything for himself until everyone else had something to eat. Many times there wasn't any left for him, but God always sustained him. I know God is real, because of the life of that man on Wake Island."

To occupy her time, Clarine started a "Bible Club" for children across the tracks in Boise. Together with

THE TRUTH SHALL SET YOU FREE

Mamma, they began holding meetings once a week. The children were so hungry for Jesus that it grew to twice a week with separate classes for the preschoolers, which I got to teach. Soon we started another Club in an area of Boise called Garden City. That's where I had the privilege of winning my first little girl to the Lord. What a joy it was to see Jesus transform her, to watch her little black face light up with the glory of God! When she sang, she was always a few words behind the rest of us, but she never failed to finish the song.

Seeing their children change, parents started coming. Clarine's house became a soul-saving station. When her husband walked in the door one day, joy rang out and praise to Jesus for keeping him. He had a congregation waiting for him to be their pastor! A church was born as a result of those Bible Clubs.

> *Back then, I suppose I witnessed more for my own sake rather than the Lord's. It was so fun watching those children being transformed by God's Spirit—I probably did it for me more than for Jesus.*

* * *

Oh, how I longed to receive the baptism of the Holy Spirit and to pray in tongues! I went forward at every altar call since my vision of Jesus when I was eight years old. It wasn't until I was sixteen that I was filled. One of my Sunday School teachers always stayed and prayed with me no matter how long I stayed at the altar—and I was usually the last one to leave. Little did that teacher know what a lasting impact she was making on me by her faithfulness and how it would affect my own ministry in the future.

Many times the devil battled me. When I prayed to be filled with the Holy Spirit; I got terrible nosebleeds. My nose never bled at any other time. The Lord used my future husband to get me delivered. Don had come to Boise to attend the Bible college founded by my pastor a few years earlier. After witnessing my problem, Don came over to where I was praying and said, "You don't need to put up with this any longer." He took me to the pastor and they rebuked the devil. I haven't had one nosebleed since.

> *With this blatant attack of the devil, I should have realized he was on my trail to stop my spiritual growth, but I didn't stop and consider it.*

What a glorious day it was for me when Jesus baptized me in His Holy Spirit! I should say what a glorious three days, since it was that long before I could again speak in English. It was the fall of 1948. Mamma packed her car full, and we went to the special Camp Meeting held at Brother Rohan's church in Caldwell. Even though his new church wasn't finished, he opened it for these services because God was beginning to move in what was later called the "Latter Rain."

THE TRUTH SHALL SET YOU FREE

The sawdust on the floor and the bleachers for seats were no hindrance for the Spirit of God. I had been distracted during the service. I was sixteen, and there was a new batch of men in town to attend Bible college, but when the minister gave the altar call for those who wanted to be filled with the Holy Spirit, my girlfriend and I rushed forward.

Already the sawdust floor was full of people hungry for God. I was wearing my most prized possession, a full-circle black skirt—a gift from my two older brothers. I tried to sit down carefully so as not to get it crushed or full of sawdust. But when I witnessed my friend being filled, I got desperate. I told the Lord, "I want You more than anything." I no longer cared about my clothes or what happened. I just wanted Jesus to fill me with His Holy Spirit.

I had already experienced every gimmick known to man to try to get the Holy Ghost, including fingers in my mouth and wiggling my tongue. No one had told me that I was to do the speaking and the Holy Spirit would give the utterance. (Acts 2:4).

I found myself thrown back on the floor by the power of the Holy Spirit, and my arms shot up in the air. I felt the Spirit of God come and immerse me in Him. I became unaware of anyone else in the room or even where I was. I opened my mouth and began to speak. The words were in a new language. I lay there under the power of God for well over four hours. I found myself speaking in first one language and then another. At one point I heard my mother's voice speak a sentence in tongues, then I would speak a sentence. Our spirits were conversing, although our minds didn't understand the words. This went on for some time. Sometimes we laughed and sometimes we cried.

When I finally opened my eyes, I was shocked to see a circle of people standing around me. It was 3:00 a.m. They helped me to the car, since I couldn't walk because the power of God still lingered. The day was breaking by the time we had delivered our carload to their respective homes. I woke up after a few hours' sleep, still speaking in tongues. It wasn't until the following day that I spoke again in English.

My life changed dramatically. In school, the teacher asked for someone to volunteer to a debate on evolution versus creation. My hand shot up. Everyone was shocked! My teacher chose me. I had two weeks to prepare. On the day of the speech, the mayor was one of the judges. I got a standing ovation. Of course, I had God on my side.

A new wave of God's Spirit was beginning to roll in over Boise valley just as William Branham, the world-renown man of God with a powerful healing ministry, had predicted a few years earlier. I attended his meetings in the senior high school auditorium on the two occasions he came to Boise in the early forties.. His ministry had a lasting impact on my life. The power of God was so profound in the meetings I wept through them. I wanted to fall at the feet of Jesus and worship Him. I yearned for the power of God in my own life.

As a young girl, I almost wished I had a physical ailment so I could get prayed for and have an excuse to be close to Brother Branham. My girlfriend's mother had that opportunity, as she was dying in the hospital. They brought her on a stretcher to the meetings and put her backstage. After his sermon, Brother Branham went through the backstage to come down in front to pray for the sick. As he started down the steps, the angel that accompanied him stopped at her side. We didn't know why Brother Branham took so long to come down in front, until we saw my friend's mother dancing across the platform in her nightgown with her arms raised shouting and praising God. She was completely healed!

Not only did I see the power of God manifest, but also the power of Satan. Late one afternoon, as crowds gathered outside the auditorium, waiting for the doors to open for the evening service, a teenage girl I knew began to have a manifestation of demons. Suddenly, she swelled up until she was head and shoulders above everyone. The hideous smirk on her face is one I'll never forget as she cackled and jeered. Some men decided to remove her, but with her arm she swept them aside like straw. Everyone then decided to leave her alone and let Brother Branham deal with her.

Compelled by demons, during the service, she rushed toward Brother Branham to stop the service. He never said a word to her. He was a very small, frail person, but he just stood there and watched her run towards him. His eyes filled with compassion. When she reached him, she fell at his feet as though dead. Quietly he told us, "Close your eyes. The demons are going to leave her in the form of a huge spider. It is important for you to be obedient and keep your eyes closed. If you are curious to see the devils, they will be looking for another 'house' and can come to those who are disobedient." Believe me, my eyes were squeezed shut so tight that after he said we could open them because the demons were gone, I kept mine closed a little longer just to be sure.

On Brother Branham's second visit to Boise, the Lord gave him a word for my pastor. He predicted that our church would overflow because of the move of God's Spirit coming soon. We would need to build a new sanctuary very quickly which would fill up immediately. He also stated that the church would empty just as quickly if the pastor wasn't honest and forthright in all his dealings.

It was shortly after my baptism that the Spirit of the Lord descended on our congregation of 150 members. The young people were drawn by the Spirit of God to the basement prayer room after the youth service prior to the Sunday evening worship service. We prayed for hours. In fact, that prayer room was seldom empty for months and months. Neither was the kitchen, because we had services three times a day, and Mamma took charge of cooking meals for everyone. No one wanted to leave, so we fed them right there. Daddy even came and helped when he could.

People who worked in town spent their lunch hours at church. Farmers took care of their animals and hurried back. Out went the service format of three songs, a prayer, testimonies, offering and announcements, a special song and then the sermon. These were replaced by a heavenly visitation of spontaneous singing in the Spirit that could last for hours. It got labeled "the heavenly choir." People got saved or filled with the Holy Spirit right in the service. Healings and messages from God in tongues and interpretation or prophecy were common.

Ministers received revelation in the Word, got up and preached spontaneously.

My brother, Jim, showed up at a service with his buddy. Jim was backslidden, along with my oldest brother, Teddy. Mamma made a mistake when they were in their early teens. The task of taking us all to Sunday evening service got to be too much for her. She wanted one service where she didn't have to keep track of eight kids. She started leaving all of us home Sunday evenings, except on occasions when she would take one. When Teddy and Jim begged to go, and she refused, they became bitter and said, "You just wait. There will come a day when she will beg us to go to church." They rebelled against God. It took the Korean War to bring Jim back to the Lord, and Teddy came back to God on his deathbed with cancer at age thirty-five.

Jim and his buddy's intention in coming to the meeting that night was to make fun of it. The Spirit of the Lord smote them as they stood. We heard a loud thump as they both hit the floor, stiff as boards, and the ushers carried their rigid bodies out. When God's power lifted off them, they returned to the service with reverent attitudes.

> *I learned a valuable lesson through my mother's mistake. My husband and I took our three children to every service we attended together.*

God sent gifted teachers to us like Brother Huckstra, Brother Baxter, and Brother Erikson, who were begged not to stop until one service melted into the other, so we had church around the clock. When people got hungry, they slipped downstairs, ate, and quickly returned to the service. Likewise, when the Spirit of the Lord came upon Mamma in the kitchen, she went upstairs, stood behind the piano so no one could see her soiled apron, and spoke forth a message in tongues. Then she returned to her duties in the kitchen. Brother Huckstra gave an account of one such time in his book.

The most significant aspect of this great wave of God's Spirit (which became known as the Latter Rain Revival) was the teaching. The five gift ministries and the nine gifts of the Spirit were restored to the church. We saw the rebirth of body ministry, as ministers and the congregation alike were free to step to the pulpit and minister as they felt led by the Holy Spirit, rather than adhering to a planned schedule. I witnessed people whom I knew were too bound to give a testimony or witness stand under the power of God and preach the Gospel. We were completely amazed with the awesome transformations. Relatives and sinners came to Jesus.

We had to knock out a wall to accommodate the crowds. The new sanctuary that Brother Branham spoke of was quickly built. It held 500 people, giving us a seating capacity of nearly 800. It was filled in no time. But our beloved pastor did step into the trap the devil laid for him. As a result, within a few more years, the church building became an empty shell, with only a handful of people remaining. The congregation split and scattered. But the impact of that mighty move of God's Spirit had a lasting effect on everyone who experienced it, including me and the man who became my husband.

Chapter Three

Me, Marry a Preacher's Son?

"Through thy prophets I get understanding: therefore I hate every false way. Thy Word is a lamp unto my feet and light unto my path."
(Psalm 119:104,105)

Don's childhood was different from mine in the natural, but not spiritually. He was a young boy, the second of four, when his father accepted a position with Weyerhaeuser and moved his family to Tacoma from Pullman, Washington. We called Don's father, Dad Barnett. Along with his four-year sweetheart and bride, Edna, a first-grade teacher, Dad Barnett dedicated his life to the service of Jesus.

Dad loved to recount stories of how he learned about Jesus from his mother. He was especially fond of one experience the family had in the early 1900's. In a little schoolhouse, he heard his mother speak in tongues and his little brother sing in the Spirit, the words and melody given by God. Even though Dad led a wild life in college, when he and Mom made a commitment to the Lord, it was one hundred percent. They determined to trust God for everything. Each time they saw a truth in the Word of God, they embraced it. God's provision to heal was no exception. They chose to never go to a doctor again, nor take as much as an aspirin for pain. Dad used to tell me, "Honey, if I take an aspirin for this pain, I may miss what God is trying to teach me. If He wanted my pain gone, He would cause it to go."

Dad had a hunger for God's Word, coupled with a brilliant mind which could add four columns of figures in his head at once. He became a profound Bible scholar and teacher. Given his compassion for souls, it is not surprising that he started a church and built the building himself. Studying the Word with the Holy Spirit as his guide, Dad discovered what Charles Colson, in his book *Born Again,* described as "the essence of Christianity." On page 125, Mr. Colson wrote, "The central thesis of Lewis' book (*Mere Christianity* by C. S. Lewis) and the essence of Christianity is summed up in one mind-boggling sentence: *Jesus Christ is God* (see John 10:30). Not just a part of God, or just sent by God, or just related to God. *He was* (and therefore, of course, is) *God.*[1]

Dad also understood prophecy like few other men of his time. His unique ability to put Scripture together and make difficult passages plain made him the favored speaker in a fellowship of churches.

Mom Barnett was completely devoted to the Lord and her family. The top student in her class, she skipped one grade and she was always increasing her knowledge of the Bible and the world around her. She left her teaching career to raise her family, but she shared all she learned from personal study with her boys which gave them an advantage over their peers. She was a fastidious housekeeper, and in the thirty-seven years I knew her, there was never anything out of its place unless it was in use. Our relationship was close and dear. She had as much influence in my life as an adult as my own mother did when I was a child. Don said of his mother, "I can't remember her ever doing anything wrong."

> *Looking back now, I can see how Don's opinion of his mother influenced me. I once asked Mom, "Why do you let Dad blame you for everything, when in some cases it couldn't possibly be your fault—like when he forgets and leaves his lunchbox at work?" She answered, "Because he couldn't bear it if he thought I knew he did something wrong. Honey, I don't mind; he needs to believe that I think he's perfect."*
>
> *This concept, fueled by indoctrination into the traditional Pentecostal churches which held strict lines for women regarding authority and submission, shaped my thinking which led me to make wrong choices without realizing it.*

Mom encouraged and supported her sons in their own individual interests and pursuits. Mom and Dad themselves were ardent antique collectors. Many times they involved the boys in restoring the treasures picked up at rummage or garage sales and auctions. Mom became an expert in old lace and had one of the most extensive collections in the Northwest. Their parents' many col-

THE TRUTH SHALL SET YOU FREE

lections—from guns to thimbles—had an effect on the boys. Bob collected American Indian artifacts, Joe collected dogs, but Don was thoroughly fascinated with World War II and its machinery.

Don made model airplanes and played war games with toy soldiers for hours. He followed every detail of the war with unusual interest. He knew every kind of airplane, tank, and weapon used by the United States as well as its enemies. The war's influence in Don's young life carried over into his adulthood and ministry. His goal was to have a body of believers that resembled Alexander the Great's powerful army.

Don's other fascination was little girls. He had his first emotional involvement with a little girl in third grade. Although she probably never knew it, she broke his heart when in fourth grade she moved to another school.

> *Was this because he didn't have any sisters, or did his problem start way back here? I just don't know.*

Unfortunately, Don began to develop a "middle kid" complex and, feeling insecure, even questioned whether or not he was adopted. Perhaps some of the reasons for this was because of the strong authoritarian role his father played in his life. He ruled his household with a razor strap. You didn't question Dad; you simply obeyed, or else. He never raised his voice. He didn't have to. The fear of the razor strap was always present.

Don told of the time he did something after getting permission from his mother. He didn't tell her that his father had already forbade him to do it. When he came home, his father ordered him to get the razor strap. Don argued, "Mother gave me permission to do it." Dad told him, "I'm not whipping you for disobeying your mother. I'm whipping you for disobeying me."

Don's recollections of the razor strap incidents were always the same. Dad held one hand and Don ran around the outer circle shouting, "I won't, Daddy! I won't, Daddy!" as the razor strap was applied to the seat of learning.

Possibly the second reason for Don's insecurities was his parents couldn't support Don's interests the way they could Bob and Joe's. It was easy to pick up an Indian book for Bob or a dog statue for Joe at garage sales, but no one was selling model airplanes, so Don felt he wasn't loved as the others. Thirdly, Bob was "studying" and Joe was "too little," so Don got stuck with more chores—or so it seemed to him. Criticism rather than praise is easy to find with the job done by a child, so Don feared he could never please his father.

> *I saw this root of fear grow and take many forms until it ruled Don's life. One way he tried to beat it was in striving for excellence. I wonder how my choices nurtured it?*

Don's family enjoyed outings such as picnics together, and his father took the boys fishing and hunting at every opportunity. Dad was a small man who expressed a lot of love and affection, too.

The Barnetts were faithful to have family devotions every night with their boys, which included singing, Bible study, and prayer. If you ever heard Dad pray, you know his prayers could last as long as a church service. These times didn't have a negative influence on Don as he always spoke fondly of them. In fact, his pulpit ministry resembled his father's, and his prayers from the pulpit were profound and edifying to his listeners.

After a few years in Tacoma, Don found himself living in an old mansion in what is now the historical section of the city. For just a few thousand dollars his parents bought the old home, built in the late 1800's. It was badly in need of repair. The whole family was commissioned to the task of removing the ivy that had overtaken the house. Of course, Kenneth, Don's baby brother, was exempt as the muscle-destroying disease called Progressive Muscular Dystrophy prevented him from being able to participate to any great extent. Trusting God for Kenneth's healing was the greatest test of their faith the Barnetts endured, even though Don saw the healing power of Jesus work in the Barnett household in unprecedented ways. Their testimonies could fill a book.

For instance, Don witnessed the drowning of his younger brother when Joe was only two years old. When no life was found in him, Dad wrapped him in a blanket, carried him home, got in bed with him, and prayed. The little blonde boy started breathing again and soon was out playing with his brothers.

And when Bob got a mastoid through water in his ear while swimming at the YMCA, his parents learned there was no medical history of anyone living over thirteen days without an operation. Although Bob's head had a massive swelling behind his ear and he was delirious with pain and fever, they believed God. On the thirteenth day, the Lord revealed to Dad while he was at work that his son was healed. When he shared the news with a co-worker, he was asked if he had received a phone call with the news. Dad answered, "No, we don't have a phone. I know because God just told me." When he arrived home, Bob met him at the door, completely healed! He had even been outside playing ball.

When Don was in the ninth grade, his father, brother, and a neighbor contracted urimic poisoning from eating a bad lemon pie. The neighbor was rushed to the hospital, but he died. Mom and the boys held on to God. At one point, the only way she could get any food into Joe was by praying, "In the name of Jesus," as she held the spoon to his mouth. His mouth would open, she'd put the spoonful of food in, and his mouth would clamp shut again. She continued the process with each bite.

Joe's fever broke, and he began his recovery; but not so with his father. Dad lost his mind and became weaker and weaker. Don carried him up and down the stairs. Then, one afternoon as two lady prayer warriors came to watch Dad so Mom could get a rest, Dad's body fell off the couch. He testifies that he experienced his soul leaving his body. He saw it lying on the floor and he knew it was dead. Believing him to be dead, the ladies picked up his body and placed it back on the couch before they went upstairs to notify Mom.

Dad said he found himself returning to his body. When his eyes opened he was in his right mind, completely healed! The Lord gave Dad a vision of the ministry He had for him. He quit his job and went into the full-time ministry as an evangelist and teacher. Leaving his family at home, he was gone for weeks at a time as he traveled up and down the West Coast, winning the lost and teaching and preaching in churches. It wasn't long, however, until Dad started his own church in Tacoma.

As Kenneth's physical condition grew worse, his faith grew stronger. When he had an opportunity to go to William Branham's meetings in Portland, he told his teacher in the special school he attended, "I won't be back, because God is going to heal me." He even took a new pair of shoes, as he was sure he would walk again. But, for reasons of His own, God chose not to heal Kenneth. The heartbreaking disease only served to draw Kenneth into a deep and wonderful relationship with his Savior. As he went to be with Jesus in November of 1950, his face shone like an angel's, and he spoke in tongues. His bent legs straightened for the first time; he exclaimed, "It's so beautiful!" as he slipped into that eternal heavenly realm to suffer no more.

> *Following Kenneth's death, Don harbored doubts and fears about what is God's will regarding healing. He has studied the subject thoroughly.*

The eldest Barnett son, Bob, was baptized in the Holy Spirit with the evidence of speaking in tongues at age sixteen. He lost all interest in his Indian collection. In fact, he was so hungry for God's Word that finishing high school had no meaning. He knew God was calling him into a full-time ministry. He persuaded his parents, both with college degrees, to give him permission to go to Bible college. He moved to Boise and enrolled in the college at my church. I was twelve when I saw Bob in our young people's meeting. I told Mamma, "I wish I was older, because I would like to marry him." I didn't know he had a brother who was just a year and a half older than I.

* * *

I saw Don for the first time when he came to Boise to be his brother's best man. Bob had fallen in love with Louise and courted her during his four years of Bible college. When Don came to Bible college, he made a decision that he wasn't going to date. His time was devoted to his job at the "Y" and studying the Bible, because God had answered a prayer he had prayed when he was fourteen years old.

That prayer came about because of the monthly meetings of the fellowship of churches to which Don's father belonged. The whole family attended the power-packed services where one minister made the comment that the Word of God meant more to him than daily food. To an active fourteen-year-old who loved to eat, this seemed impossible. Don prayed, "Lord, if it's possible, make Your Word more precious to me than my daily food." God's answer set the course of his life—and mine.

> *That simple request, prayed with all sincerity has brought Jesus more pleasure, joy, and honor than any other single aspect of Don's life. As I write this, tears escape from my eyes and they seem to wash away all the loneliness I endured while, hour after hour apart from me, my husband studied the Word.*

THE TRUTH SHALL SET YOU FREE

With amazement, I watched Don stick with his no-dating policy until the spring of 1949. But I got my first boyfriend, a tall, handsome blonde student named Stanley. He had just arrived to attend Bible college from a farming community a hundred miles away. I heard him sing at a church fellowship and was deeply affected. When I contacted him with an invitation to our farm for the hayride we had every fall, he asked, "Will you be my date?" I could hardly believe it—my first real date! That was the beginning of a whirlwind romance that lasted only four months.

Stan taught me how to kiss, that is, if we need to be taught that sort of thing. He told me he had read a book on the subject, so we sat on the couch at his uncle's home one Sunday afternoon and, hiding behind the newspaper, practiced. My brothers and father didn't trust my new boyfriend. They said he bragged about the farm chores he could do and wasn't truthful. Our dating ended shortly after he attempted to reach into my blouse and I stopped him. I was afraid of what petting would lead to. Not because my parents had talked to me—sex just wasn't a subject that was talked about—but because of what I had experienced with my oldest brother.

Ever since Teddy was twelve years old, he tried to sexually molest me. It happened when we were playing *Kick the Can*. The next day Jim came to me and said, "Teddy took your panties off yesterday, didn't he?"

"How do you know?" I asked, defensively.

"He told me."

"Well, I didn't want him to," I defended.

Jim warned, "Barbara, you mustn't let him ever touch you again, because he could make you have a baby." I didn't question his wisdom.

ME, MARRY A PREACHERS SON?

After that, I tried never to let myself be alone with Teddy; if I was, I had to fight him off. My parents never knew about my plight. So, when my boyfriend tried to touch my breasts, I stopped him. It cost me our relationship. A few days later, on my birthday, Stan told me he wasn't going to date me any longer. I was devastated; my family was relieved. I pined away until spring when Elizabeth Whittel (whose mother had been healed in William Branham's meetings years before) invited the young people to a fellowship after the evening service. As all of us were walking to her home, Don came up behind me as we approached her front steps and said, "Remember, we are going steady tonight."

What?! This man, whom every girl in the church wanted? Wavy black hair! Perfect physical condition! Immaculate dresser! And the son of a minister! Why me? There were lots of girls in the church prettier than I. I was just a little country hick.

That night when I got home, I woke up my little sister. "Don't tell a single soul," I whispered, "but I think I'm going to marry Don Barnett." When he hitchhiked (no young person owned a car in those days) out to the farm, my whole family liked him. My little sister, Ola, ran up the gravel road when she saw him coming and hung on his arm. We had a hard time getting any time to ourselves, so I stayed in town after Sunday morning services so we had the afternoons together. I rode back out to the farm with Mamma when the evening service closed.

Being a YMCA resident, Don wasn't allowed to have a female guest in his room, but guests were permitted in the game room on the second floor. We started going to the game room so Don could teach me how to play chess.

It wasn't long before we were on the couch involved in heavy petting. Afterward, I felt terrible and laid awake at night talking to the Lord about it, trying to figure out why I wasn't able to resist it. Since my brother, Jim, had given me a warning, I wouldn't let my brother touch me the many times he tried to force me. Was it because my first boyfriend had rejected me when I refused his caresses, and I was afraid if I lost Don for the same reason that I'd never get another chance to get married?

At age seventeen, I just didn't know what was wrong with me. I knew Jesus loved me regardless of my sins. He had proven that to me with the experiences I'd had with Him in prayer. I could never doubt His love. At any rate, I'd give it to the Lord, accept His forgiveness, and go on determined not to be tricked into doing it again.

One day when Don came down the road to our home, everyone knew why he was coming but me. Ola jumped up and down and rushed out to meet him. He had a hard time getting away from her long enough to give me the ring she knew he had in his pocket. Mamma made Ola stay in the house while Don took me out in the front yard under a tree and asked me to be his wife. We held each other and kissed while everyone watched through the window.

Don wanted to take me to Tacoma to meet his parents and have his father marry us in their home. Mamma was a little disappointed. She argued, "It would be better if you're married before you travel together alone." However, we had no money for the kind of weddings that were the norm for the church in Boise, so the decision was made.

* * *

ME, MARRY A PREACHERS SON?

Nervous is hardly adequate to describe how I felt about meeting Don's parents. Don had told me about the wonderful old mansion full of antiques, but I had never lived in a house with an indoor bathroom. In the summer, I took my baths in the creek that ran through our farm, and in the winter we filled the washtub with water and it became a bathtub. I wasn't used to toilets that flushed. I'd never been more than fifty miles from home. Once Daddy took us for a drive to Lowell Lake—that was the largest body of water I had ever seen.

I decided there was no point in finishing out the school year. My parents were struggling financially; I needed to get a job to help out. Jim had joined the army and was gone. Teddy had married Zelda and was cooking at the cafe. Besides, I needed some clothes for the trip. I only had two dresses, one I'd made in Home Economics class; but I still had my cherished full-circle, black skirt.

I found a job at the Purity Bakery wrapping bakery products and waiting on the public for $.50 an hour. It was hard work and I worked long hours without any extra pay, but I was proud of my $15-a-week paycheck.

Don accepted a new job, too. He began working at the Nampa Health Club teaching both wrestling and judo which he learned from the owner. He went to Bible college in the mornings and found a ride to Nampa, thirty miles away, where he worked afternoons and evenings. It was a rough schedule, but the farm was halfway between college and work. Sometimes he stopped off either coming or going, so we'd have some time together. As soon as college was out, we planned to take the train to Tacoma. Mamma tried one more time to convince us that we could get married in a little ceremony after the

Friday evening service, but Don was set on his father being the minister.

Don took a leave of absence from the health club, as business was slow in the summer. We left on the 10:00 p.m. train without the $150 Don's boss owed him, but his boss promised he would get it in the mail in a few days. All we had was my last paycheck.

As the train neared Tacoma at 2:00 in the afternoon, Don cautioned, "Now, don't get all emotional over my home. I don't want my folks to think you are some giddy girl too immature to be my wife. And don't 'ooh' and 'ahh' over everything like you've never seen anything before in your life. I don't want them to think I'm marrying somebody out of my class, you know what I mean?"

"Okay, I'll remember," I quivered. "You give me a signal by rubbing your nose if I do anything wrong, okay?"

At the famous old train station with a dome ceiling, a porter took Don's large, old trunk and tied it on the back of a taxi. Don ordered the driver, "Take the waterfront route."

As we approached a huge old castle made of red brick with turrets overlooking the bay, Don exclaimed, "That's my high school."

"Wow!" I whispered in awe.

Pointing a finger up the hill, he shouted, "There! Up there on the corner—that's my house!" He looked at me and grinned. I didn't have any trouble with getting too emotional; I was too scared.

"Could we go in the back door?" I managed to squeak. "I'd feel more comfortable going into the kitchen first."

"Sure," Don replied, patting my hand and smiling. He knew I loved to hear him say the word "sure" because he has a unique way of pronouncing "r's." He hated his speech impediment, but I didn't. "Driver," he ordered, "Pull around to the alley, please."

Don jumped out before the cab even stopped at the concrete steps leading to the back yard, about twenty feet south of the old coach house. He helped me out of the cab and, leaving the driver to untie the trunk, ushered me to the back porch.

Don didn't hold down his own excitement to be home after being gone (eight months) for the first time in his life. He flung open the back door after using the antique iron knocker to signal his arrival.

Drying her hands, Mom stood at the home's original kitchen sink, which was the first thing visible from the back door. She was a gentle lady with her wavy graying hair combed back into a row of neat curls at the base of her neck.

"Hi, honey," she said, as Don scooped her up into his arms and turned her toward me. Her greeting to me was the same as it was to Don, "Hi, honey." Instantly I felt accepted as one of the family. "At last I have a daughter," she laughed, squeezing my hand.

Don took me on a tour of the house, opening every drawer and closet. I thought, *Poor Mom. If there was anything she wanted to conceal, it would certainly get exposed.* I soon learned that the basement and the attic were as organized as the rest of the home. When the boys were small, even their wooden blocks were placed in alphabetical order before being returned to the shelf.

Mom did all the baking and sewing, and she darned all their socks. Even the two large, braided rugs gracing the hardwood floors were made by Mom from worn-out jeans she tore into strips. Dad supported the family doing gardening, because he didn't take any wages from the offerings received from his church. He wasn't home when we arrived.

When we went upstairs, Mom followed us into Bob's room and announced, "This will be your room, Barbara." It was the most impressive bedroom—other than the master suite—with a view of the bay out the three front leaded glass windows. It also housed some of their most treasured antiques, including Dad's gun collection. The closet was full of very old gowns made with rare lace and satin. It took hours to see everything.

I was anxious to get to Don's room, because lying in his bed was Kenneth. Completely unable to move by himself, he acted as excited to see me as I was to meet him. He hadn't had a conversation with a girl close to his age for years. The only women in his life were the friends of his mother who came to visit. After Don introduced me, he quickly pulled the toy bubble gum machine out of his suitcase and said, "Now you're a businessman, Kenneth. You can operate your own store." A broad grin covered Kenneth's face as he watched his brother fill the machine with the brightly colored gum balls.

"I get to be your first customer," I giggled, producing a penny to put in the slot.

"You'll make plenty of money off of Joe and his buddies," chimed Don, as he searched his pockets for another coin.

I had a hard time holding back the tears, seeing how excited Kenneth was over his new gift. Don jumped up on the bed and pretended to get a judo hold on Kenneth, and the two brothers laughed together. I thought, *It must have been really hard for Kenneth when Don left for Bible college. I don't want him to think he's being replaced in Don's heart by me. I'm going to give Kenneth as much attention as possible while we are here.*

Kenneth's room became the central meeting place. Don and I ate most of our meals there to keep Kenneth company. Don gave him quizzes about the Bible and other subjects. His mind was sharp even though his little body was twisted out of shape.

Kenneth never complained or asked for help. He would lay in a cramped position for hours without letting us know he needed to be moved. I made it a habit to ask him, "How can I make you more comfortable, Kenneth?" When I asked him if there was anything he needed, the answer was always, "No."

Don was eager to show me Tacoma. Two weeks flew by as we explored all the places Don loved as a child.

When Don's paycheck didn't arrive, Dad suggested, "Don, come and work for the gardening company. They have plenty of work." When I learned Don owed his parents some money from loans, I encouraged him to work with his father. I assured him, "I'll be just fine with Kenneth and Mom."

I became anxious to get our wedding date set. It didn't seem as important to Don. Was it because he was enjoying having me here in his home, being a part of his family, to need a marriage relationship? Or was he having second thoughts about my being the right girl for him? He had told me he always thought he would marry a girl much prettier than I, that I really wasn't pretty enough for him. I thought, *What will I do if I have to go back to the farm unmarried—no one will want me now.*

Before we left Boise, Don had convinced me that the Bible, in the Old Testament, said if a man was going to marry a woman, it was all right to have intercourse with her. I trusted his knowledge of the Bible over mine, so once, when the health club was closed, I surrendered my virginity. Afterwards, I began sobbing uncontrollably. I had never cried like that before. The sobs came from deep within. I cried all night. By morning I knew I would never allow it to happen again, even if God did say it was okay. Later, Don said he didn't remember telling me the Old Testament says it's okay and if he did say it, he lied.

> *Do you suppose my insecurities—more than Don's then immature knowledge of the Bible—caused me to let this happen? I just don't know.*

I was worried. Feeling very insecure, I went to Don, "Can we go some place where we can talk?"

"Sure," Don responded. "Wright Park is just a few blocks from here, and I want to show it to you anyway. It's like a museum of trees—hundreds of them, all labeled, with no two trees alike." As we walked toward the park, he continued, "Wait until you see the conservatory; it's one of the finest in the nation. Mom loves to come over here and walk through it, because they change the flowers every season."

"Oh, good," I said. "Maybe she and I can walk over here when you are working with Dad."

As we settled down under a big oak tree, Don said, "I'm really pleased at the way my folks have accepted you.

ME, MARRY A PREACHERS SON?

You don't have any problem calling them Mom and Dad, do you?"

"Not at all," I answered. "It's easy, because they're real 'down home' folks. Besides, they just accepted me like a daughter right from the start."

"Here, lie on my arm," he said, lying back with his hands under his head. His biceps were like rocks.

"Your arms are harder than the ground," I kidded as I snuggled in close to his side.

"Joe likes you, too, huh?" Don asked.

"Oh yeah, he and I get along great," I answered. "I like Joe. We could be buddies. He's real, you know what I mean? He doesn't mind if I see him covered in grease and sweaty. He tells it like he sees it, too. He doesn't pretend. He accepts me, too—the way I look and act, I mean. Yeah, I feel fine around Joe."

My fingers nervously twirled the hair on Don's chest through his open v-neck shirt. I changed the subject. "Honey, I've been nervous lately, because—well, I was thinking that maybe you're having second thoughts about marrying me, like maybe I'm not everything you want. You know, I'm not pretty enough or smart enough—stuff like that."

"Well, Jean, [Don always called me by my middle name]" Don sighed, "It's true that I always dreamed of marrying a beautiful girl. I always dated the prettiest girls in high school. Beauty is something that I'm really attracted to; maybe it's because I notice curves and lines more than most people. When I was in second grade and the teacher had us draw a hand, I was the only kid who posed my left hand out in front of me so I could study the lines as I drew. Maybe it's because I'm an artist, but I notice things about the female shape and I know what's attractive and what isn't. If it is, it really affects me. It seems that I get affected more than other people. Shape is important to me, that's all."

He ran his finger down my nose. "Take your nose, for instance. I really like the shape of your nose.

"But, I probably never would find 'the perfect girl,' he mused. "I'll admit I wasn't attracted to you at first, because you weren't pretty enough for me. Then I saw you in that dress at Elizabeth's, and that's what did it." Gently pressing my hand, he added, "You've really tried hard to please me, and that makes me love you. You've already stopped saying 'he don't' and 'ain't'; I'm really proud of you. I asked you to marry me because I love you, and I want you to be my wife."

"I love you too, Donald," I cooed. "I'm embarrassed about us living off your folks. We're not paying for any of the food."

"My folks don't mind. They wouldn't take any money if I offered it to them. I'll work with Dad and get the loan paid off." Patting my hand, he assured, "We'll get married soon. I should get the $150 check from my boss any day now."

Springing to his feet, Don pulled me up and we kissed. "Let's go through the conservatory before we go back," Don suggested. He took my hand and together we ran across the grass.

* * *

I was relieved when the $150 check arrived; that is, until Don tried to cash it. It bounced! His boss apologized and sent another check for $75 which he knew the bank could cover. A few days after receiving the check, we got word that Don's boss was killed in a car wreck. There was no hope of getting the other $75.

It was now July, and we still hadn't set the date for our wedding. It was Mom who forced the issue. Don had taken me to the attic to fly one of his model airplanes out the window. When he didn't come down the back stairway as usual to retrieve the plane, she grew suspicious and came to the attic. She graciously gave her son time to adjust his pants, then she sat down in the rocker and made it clear she wasn't getting up until we set a date. This was not going to continue in her house. I was secretly relieved when we got caught. I'll never know if Mom ever told Dad.

* * *

Saturday, August 5th, became our wedding day! I woke at six and heard Mom already in the kitchen. With my hair still in over one hundred pin curls, each held by two bobby pins, I hurried downstairs. The aroma of cocoa greeted me, as Mom finished making a fresh pot—there were no quick mixes in those days. I came from the dining room through the swinging door held open by a heavy old-fashioned iron setting on the black and white floor, and sang, "Good morning, Mom." Spying the turkey in the sink, I asked, "What can I do to help you?"

"No, no, dear," Mom protested. "It's your wedding day, and you're not doing a thing in the kitchen today. I'll have everything ready so we can eat right after the ceremony at noon. Now you go on, have some breakfast, and get ready to have your pictures taken. What time are you supposed to be downtown at the studio?"

I yawned. "Ten o'clock. We'll leave here at 9:30. That will give us enough time to walk. If the photographer takes too long, we may have to catch the bus back." I sat down at the kitchen table that just fit between the two large, sun-filled windows dressed in ruffled sheer yellow curtains, all hand-washed, dyed, starched, and ironed by Mom twice each year. Altogether, there were forty-two sets of these curtains in the house. I inquired, "Have you seen Don yet?"

"Yes, honey. He left with Daddy about 5:00 this morning to finish up a gardening job. He said he'd be back at 9:00. He'll have just enough time to change before you have to leave."

Mom slid the turkey into the oven as I finished my cocoa and toast. Drying her hands, she smiled. "I know just how I'm going to do the flowers in the entry." She bent over to get the cutters out of the bottom drawer in the pantry where the copper sink was, along with Dad's collection of moustache cups displayed on the opposite wall. As Mom headed out the back door to the garden, I called, "I need to iron something, okay?"

"Sure, honey. You can plug the iron in on the stove."

I rushed upstairs, took off my only nightie, washed it out in the bathroom sink, and hurried back downstairs to iron it dry before Mom returned with armloads of freshly picked flowers. *I don't want anyone to know this is my only nightie,* I thought as I ironed. *It was new when I got here two and a half months ago. I'm glad I have a chance to iron it, so it will look almost new for tonight.*

I needed all the time I had left until 9:30 to comb all the little curls and frame them around my face before I put on my light gray felt hat with a pink ribbon and veil. It just matched the suit I'd had on layaway for almost a year in Boise, along with a frilly pink blouse. When I found the suit, my plan had been to wear it for my high school graduation. Don paid the last $8 owing on it so it could be my wedding garment.

Nervously I waited to hear Don knock on my door, using the woodpecker he had made in junior high school, which hung on this bedroom door. He wasn't late. I opened the door and gasped. He was so handsome, in his black suit and bow tie, with his wavy black hair that always stayed in place.

We stood there, smiling at each other. "Perfect," he said, leaning toward me. "Perfect."

"Oh no," I said, pushing on his chest. "No kisses until we're Mr. and Mrs."

Don handed me a box. Inside was a real corsage from a florist. "Oh, honey, you're making me cry. How did you get this?"

"This morning," he beamed. "I went to the florist and got it. It's pink carnations and roses to match your blouse. Here, let's pin it on. We've got to hurry to get downtown by 10:00."

"Okay. I just want to say, 'hi,' to Kenneth on our way out."

I popped into Kenneth's room and blew him a kiss before Don grabbed my hand. We ran out the front door, down the steps, and practically ran the entire two miles to town. The rest of the day was like a fairy tale.

At noon, we were married standing in the beautiful entry of the Barnett mansion on the curved oak stairway banked with flowers from Mom's garden. The sun lit up the three stained glass windows, which were valued at more than what the folks had paid for the entire home, arched above us. Dad performed the ceremony as only he could. We felt the sweet presence of Jesus fill the room. Joe was best man, and Mom stood beside me. Kenneth heard from upstairs, then was brought down in his wheelchair to help eat the scrumptious dinner Mom had prepared.

Afterwards, Joe chauffeured us in his Model T to the depot where we boarded the train to Seattle. Stepping out on the street from the depot in the big city of Seattle was too much for me; I froze in fright. I couldn't move. Above the noise I heard Don shouting, "Come on, we gotta catch the bus across the street."

"Wait," I shouted back, setting down my suitcase. "I can't. I gotta get my bearings."

Returning to me, Don set down the two heaviest suitcases he was carrying and asked, "What's wrong?"

"I can't handle it," I cried. "It's too much—all the traffic and noise and tall buildings—I can't think," I whined, pressing my hands against my head.

Don took time to hug and comfort me, "It's okay, you'll get used to it. Now come on, just follow me. Here comes our bus!" He grabbed his two suitcases and dashed into the traffic. I gritted my teeth, picked up my suitcase, and ran after him, keeping my eyes to the ground.

When the bellboy opened the door to our room, which we had reserved for $4.50 a night, I was sure he made a mistake. As soon as the door closed behind him, I covered my mouth with my hand and exclaimed, "It's too beautiful! Honey, I'm afraid to touch anything. This can't be the right room; they must have made a mistake."

"It's gorgeous." Don laughed as he hugged me. "If they made a mistake, it's their problem."

"Yeah, but what if they want more money when we check out? We can't pay; we don't have the money."

"Okay, I'll run down and check with the desk clerk just to be sure."

"Oh, good," I said. Wrapping my arms around myself, I added, "I'll stand right here until you come back."

Moments later I heard a rap on the door that's the "private" signal of everyone. Don burst through the door. "It's not a mistake!"

Overjoyed with thankfulness and ecstatically happy, I bounced up on the bed and laughed with delight. It felt so good not to have to hold my emotions in any longer. I giggled, "I'm so happy to be Mrs. Donald Barnett!"

Anxious to show me Seattle's waterfront before it got dark, we left our suitcases and nearly ran all the way down to the old curio shops. We sacrificed the fifty cents required to go up in the highest building west of the Mississippi, the Smith Tower. It was an awesome sight for me as the lights of Seattle came on. Arm in arm, we walked back to the Roosevelt Hotel with hearts full of love. It felt so right to be married.

The next morning was rushed as we had to be down on the pier at 7:30 a.m. to take the Princess ship to Victoria. This time we did run all the way, carrying our heavy suitcases, laden canned goods to keep from having to eat in restaurants while at the cabin we rented for four days on Crescent Lake. Even with the $50 the folks loaned us for our honeymoon, we couldn't afford a taxi.

After spending one night in Victoria, we took the Ball Line Ferry to Port Angeles, where the owner of the cabin picked us up. We drove clear to the end of the dirt road on the other side of the lake to the cabin that was more like what I was used to. It rained the four days we were there, but to me it was like heaven—a wood stove for me to cook on, deer in the woods, a bed on the porch, the rain on the roof, and even a shower on the back porch. Too soon it was time to catch the bus back to Tacoma, and from there leave on the train for Boise and another Bible college year for Don.

Chapter Four

Beginning Our Journey Together in God's School

"Trust in the Lord with all thine heart and lean not on thine own understanding. In all thy ways acknowledge Him and He will direct thy path."
(Proverbs 3:5,6)

"Honey," Don confided as the train neared Boise, "I wish I knew what the Lord wanted us to do. I can either stay at the health club as a partner with the masseuse, or I can try to find a job in Boise. If I found work in Boise, we could get an apartment close to school. Otherwise, we'll have to live in Nampa."

I interjected, "It doesn't matter to me, honey, just as long as I'm with you."

Don squeezed my hand and continued, "The biggest problem is money. Even if I did find a job in Boise, it would be a while before I'd get paid. We'd have to live with your folks for at least two months before we could rent our own place. If I stay at the club, we'll have some

THE TRUTH SHALL SET YOU FREE

income immediately, and if I teach the Nampa Police Department and referee the professional wrestling matches again this fall, we'll be able to make it."

"You can schedule all the classes so you can go to Bible college every morning, " I added.

"Yeah, it will be hectic. I'll have to get up in time to hitchhike to Boise for college, then hitchhike back to the club. I'll work all afternoon and evening, find a ride home, and get up the next day and do the same all over again." He looked at me, "It'll be pretty lonesome for you, honey."

"I could get a job," I suggested.

"No, I don't want my wife working."

"I'll be fine," I smiled. "I just want my own little place. I don't want to stay in Ola's room any longer than we have to."

"Neither do I," Don agreed, as the train pulled into the depot overlooking Boise. "Will you pray about it?"

"Sure, honey."

"I'll work at the club until we know what we should do," Don said, as the train came to a stop.

* * *

It was late after the church service and no one was left in the prayer room but me when the Lord spoke the answer clearly in my mind. "Stay in the health club until spring." With the statement came the understanding that God wasn't always going to direct our lives so specifically; He expected us to walk by faith and trust Him, taking a step at a time knowing our steps would be ordered of the Lord (Psalm 37:23). I walked out of the prayer room thankful and sobered by what the Lord had shared with me. When I told Don, he was relieved and agreed, "It's a good plan."

> *I found that when the Lord chose to tell me something, or He wanted me to see something, He didn't use my physical eyes and ears. They are only instruments—and limited at best—to relay information to my mind. God's Spirit could put the information directly into my mind, and it was as clear as if my ears heard an audible voice. At other times, God's Spirit impressed my spirit, leaving my mind free to make the judgment as to exactly what was meant. The apostle Paul in 1 Corinthians 2 explains how God reveals truths by His Spirit (verse 10) and they are spiritually discerned (verse 14). In cases where God impressed my spirit only, as opposed to putting specific information in my mind (1 Corinthians 2:16), I couldn't be dogmatic as to the interpretation so I said, "I felt impressed by the Spirit..." rather than "The Lord told me."*

With no car, no furniture, and $25 rent money, we set out to find a place to live in Nampa. The days were long, but we were happy. Don left at 6:30 every morning and got home around 10:30 at night, at which time he opened his Bible and studied. Every spare minute found him in the Bible. I joyfully gave him his first Bible commentary by Adam Clarke for Christmas. Don treasured these books, which he put to constant use. He has since worn out three sets and now possesses every commentary and Bible translation on the market. His desire to know the Word of God was unquenchable.

THE TRUTH SHALL SET YOU FREE

Full of questions, he cornered every evangelist and teacher that came to the Latter Rain revival. Over and over again, however, he was disappointed because they either didn't have the answers or didn't seem as interested as he in knowing. One day, while praying about this frustration, the Lord spoke to Don's heart, "You don't need to look for a man to give you answers—I will show you the answers in My Word." Don wept with thankfulness, and his hunger to study grew even stronger.

He never laid the Bible down except to sleep and work. He studied while he ate breakfast, when he came home for lunch, and at dinner. I could feed him anything, because he never knew what he was eating anyway. Sometimes I'd ask him, "What did we have for dinner, Honey?" He had no idea what he had just eaten. The Lord had indeed answered a fourteen-year-old boy's prayer—the Word had become more important to him than food.

Early in our marriage, God dealt with me concerning Don's desire to study the Bible. I found myself losing all interest in reading the Word. Don invited me to join him in Bible study, but before long, I didn't want to participate. Even though I attended all the classes he taught, I didn't know the Bible had become my enemy until God showed me. I was praying for my husband, which I had done ever since I was a little girl. I wept repentance to the Lord as He showed me I rejected Him when I resented His Word. He had put the desire in Don's heart to know His Word. From then on, I had a different attitude about Don studying, but it didn't take away my loneliness.

We were back from our honeymoon less than two weeks when Don got filled with the Holy Spirit. The revival in Boise continued, and we rushed to every service

BEGINNING OUR JOURNEY TOGETHER
IN GOD'S SCHOOL

possible. At this particular service, the visiting minister interrupted the meeting and proclaimed, "Those who want to be baptized in the Holy Spirit, come down to the altar. I feel anointed to pray for you."

Don ran to the altar. Mamma followed, crying. She didn't want to miss it! Immediately the power of God fell on Don and, thinking he was going to land on his face, he bent over backwards. Mamma held him up. It wasn't until after the service the following morning that Don quietly spoke in tongues.

Don testified, "As I walked down the country road with my thumb out, I started speaking in my new language, and the joy of the Lord filled me so that I wished no one would give me a ride. When I got in the shower at the club, preparing for my first judo class of the day, I kept the students waiting. I didn't want to stop speaking in tongues; I didn't want to lose the glory of God that I felt."

* * *

"Jesus," I prayed one morning after we attended our first service at our new church home in Nampa, "I make a commitment to You that I will say, 'yes,' whenever any pastor asks me to do something, and I'll trust You to enable me."

That night after the service, the pastor came to me and asked, "Barbara, I need someone to lead the young people's service that's held an hour before the Sunday evening meetings. Will you do it?"

I gave a silent scream to God, *I didn't expect You to test my commitment this soon. Help!*

The Lord honored my commitment. In just a few weeks, He poured His Spirit out on us. Young people started getting filled with the Holy Spirit, the youngest of whom was the pastor's daughter. I'll never forget hearing that little three-year-old praying in tongues while lying between the pews with her arms raised and eyes closed. The young people's service had no end for her as the adults' service started: throughout the entire evening, she praised her Jesus.

From then on, the services didn't take any leading from me. All I did was begin by praying, and it was as if Jesus took over, as one after another asked for and received assurance from God.

* * *

The Lord knew the health club would be dissolved by spring, even though we didn't. Its demise wasn't because Don didn't work hard enough. He taught a self-defense course to the Nampa Police Department, worked out with the professional wrestlers who were booked for shows on Saturday nights, and refereed their matches. He offered a class teaching sport judo to women.

I came to the club once to accompany Don to an exhibition he was giving at the high school. Carmen, my former high-school classmate entered the reception room, dressed in her judo outfit. "Hi, Carmen," I said, astonished to see her.

"Hi, Barbara," she responded, looking puzzled.

We both spoke at once, "Are you one of Don's students?"

BEGINNING OUR JOURNEY TOGETHER IN GOD'S SCHOOL

She laughed, "Yeah, I'm going to the high school to do the exhibition with him." Adjusting her judo jacket, she inquired, "How do you know Don?"

"Oh, I'm his wife," I responded. "I came in today to go with him, just to watch."

"What? Don is married? Are you sure? He never told me he was married."

"I'm sure," I said, as she turned in disbelief and walked back into the classroom.

Somehow she made it through the exhibition and soon dropped out of the class. Somehow I made it through the fact that after only a few months of marriage my husband's heart had been affected for someone else. I became more afraid that I wasn't pretty or good enough for him.

* * *

When the health club closed in the spring. Don took a job as a supplier for grocery stores and we moved to Boise. We again involved ourselves in the ongoing revival.

In an afternoon service during one of Brother Erikson's visits to our church, he called Don out of the congregation, "Come to the altar and kneel before God; He has something to say to you." Everyone marvelled at what God was doing in the outpouring of His Spirit. The prophetic ministry the Bible explains in 1 Corinthians 12 was a new experience. The ministry gifts had not been operating in any present-day church. Other ministers present came and laid hands on Don. Someone remembered he had a wife, so they motioned for me to come from my seat by the wall in the crowded sanctuary and join my husband.

Everyone felt the holy presence of the Lord; the congregation became silent. Kneeling in reverence, we heard through the mouths of these apostolic ministers what our ministries would be and learned of God's desire to use us in His great plan. The words came with power and authority. A lady took down in shorthand some of what was said: "Don would no longer wrestle with men but with the devil, and he would teach the newborn so they would not be turned aside, for the devil wanted to devour them." None of these ministers knew anything about Don.

God said that I would stand in the congregation and prophesy, and would be a forerunner in the ministry, because the Lord would give me spiritual experiences and visions of things that would come to pass. None of us knew it would be about twenty years before God's Word for us would start happening.

* * *

Don and I were overjoyed when we learned I was pregnant. Carolyn, our first child, arrived on Christmas Eve, after thirty-six hours of labor. Along with our darling daughter came new expenses, and we slipped further into debt. Don's take-home pay of $198 a month was little help in paying off the $400 doctor bill. I wasn't used to much and didn't mind if we didn't always have enough for food, but now we had a baby to feed and clothe, plus bills to pay.

BEGINNING OUR JOURNEY TOGETHER IN GOD'S SCHOOL

Discussing our plight one evening, Don suggested, "I can hitchhike to Tacoma and look for a job there." It's different these days, but back during the Korean War—as with World War II— people were happy to help young men by giving them a ride. On this trip, Don was even picked up by a State Patrol officer and taken three hundred miles, a big boost.

Fearful to be alone, I asked, "How long will it take you to get to Tacoma?"

"Oh, I'd say less than 24 hours, if I'm lucky." Don put his arm around me and drew me in close. "If I find a job right away, I shouldn't be gone more than two weeks. Maybe your sister, Ola, could come and stay with you."

"Okay," I stammered. "This will be the first time we've been apart."

"I know," Don said, "but as soon as I find a job, I'll drive back with the folks in their little coupe. It will be tight, but we can make it, and they can see Carolyn." Excited now, he added, "They can see my brother, Bob, and his wife, Louise, too. Let's have them all over for one of your super dinners!" Don squeezed my hand with delight.

Don prepared to leave the house before dawn with the cardboard sign he'd drawn of a hobo with a knapsack over his shoulder and the word "Seattle" written on it. He stood it beside himself on the road and hoped for a ride.

"Be careful," I called after him. "Don't take any chances. I'll be praying for you."

Closing the door, I wondered, *How can I fix a fancy dinner for eight, including Ola and Louise's mother, without any money?* In desperation, I bundled up my baby, walked to the bank, and asked to speak to the manager. I tried to sit tall in the chair opposite his desk as I explained my plight. I told him, "I am willing to leave you my ring if you will loan me $20, because I'm sure we can pay it back within a few short weeks." He must have taken pity on me. I still remember the look on his face when he handed me the $20 bill after I signed an agreement with my name and address and Don's place of employment on it. I don't know if the $20 came from his pocket or the bank's. He even let me keep my ring.

> *Oh, yes, you can see how early on in my marriage I tried hard to protect Don's image and give his folks a good impression of us.*

Don found a job working the graveyard shift on the green chain at the lumber mill in Tacoma, and he could start as soon as we could get moved.

Leaving Boise and the church where I grew up was a big step, but already man had put his hand to the move of God. The pure stream from His throne was becoming muddy from man's ideas and sins. Don made the statement, "If God ever moves again, I know what my job will be—to keep people in the middle of the road." It seemed we were both learning as much about what not to do as what to do.

BEGINNING OUR JOURNEY TOGETHER
IN GOD'S SCHOOL

> *If only I could have seen my own blind side as easily as we saw the pride, competition, jealousy, and fanaticism that quickly ruined the Latter Rain revival, but I couldn't.*

* * *

Don's folks graciously allowed us to live in the little two-room apartment above the garage, which was the coach house when the old home was built. After many months, we rented a home of our own, and Don started a judo class at the Y. He taught in the mornings after work. He reasoned, "I can make use of the time, since I'm unable to sleep anyway, and we need the money."

Late one morning, Don staggered into the house and threw himself on the couch. I thought, *Oh, no! Somebody drugged him.* His eyes were wild with pain. Before I could say anything, Don shouted, "Don't say a word, or I'll divorce you!" I crumpled into a chair, afraid to move. Then the story came out.

One of his students had done an incorrect maneuver as Don was teaching him a particular judo throw and had severely injured Don's knee, tearing the cartilage in the kneecap. Somehow Don had managed to ride the bus home and walk on the swollen leg all the way from the bus stop. Don feared my reaction to his injury would be what he'd expect from his father, who never supported Don's wrestling and judo.

After kneeling beside him and praying, I coaxed, "Honey, please go to a doctor."

"I've never been to a doctor," Don said through clenched teeth. By now his knee was as big around as my waist. The pain was unbearable.

"I can go next door and call Joe to come and take you in his car," I suggested.

"No," Don responded, "I don't want the folks to know."

He waited a few hours for the pain to subside. I stood in the doorway and cried for him as he made his way back to the bus stop to find a doctor. I was relieved when a taxi returned him a few hours later, on crutches. He had learned that the company's insurance would cover the medical expenses, including transportation to and from therapy.

It was a major decision for Don to step out of the belief system imbedded in him, going to a physician for the first time in his life. It was also the first time he took prescription drugs for pain.

> *Looking back, I suppose Don's decision did wound his father, although such feeling was unjustified. Certainly Don was responsible for his own life. However, defying his Dad's authority, leaving Dad helpless to do anything about it—since he learned of Don's decision after the fact—could be one reason why, in the years that followed, heated arguments between the two over minor issues of doctrine seemed to be a contest for control and respect rather than to resolve doctrinal differences.*

* * *

BEGINNING OUR JOURNEY TOGETHER IN GOD'S SCHOOL

After Don's knee healed, he took a position with Boeing, and we moved to Seattle. He started training at $1.25 an hour and received promotions rapidly on his first assignment working on the B52 bomber.

We found a church in north Seattle with a congregation of 150. After our first service, the pastor asked Don to take over the junior high boys' class. He said, "The boys are so unruly that no teacher lasts for long. I'm desperate." Don entered the classroom and ignored the spitwads flying through the air. He sat down, took the quarterly that was the standard lesson material and threw it over his shoulder, saying, "Who needs these? Does anyone here like quarterlies?" The boys were shocked into silence.

Then Don opened the lesson by asking, "Does anyone know what the four horses of the Apocalypse in the last book of the Bible mean? You should, because it's going to happen in your lifetime." The boys were so eager to learn what this new teacher, who held a black belt in judo, had to teach them, they crowded around him the next Sunday. A few months later, when we moved and had to find a new church, the boys begged him to stay. Don had a special gift from God to make the Word of God plain, even to the newborn Christian.

Don taught a Bible class in every church we attended, but that wasn't the reason he studied the Bible at every spare moment: God had put that in his heart. God also kept His promise to my husband—His Holy Spirit became Don's teacher. As he continued spending hours every day in the Bible, his detailed knowledge of the Word of God deepened. Don knew his calling was to teach. He took every opportunity that presented itself.

THE TRUTH SHALL SET YOU FREE

When we were in Tacoma, we were invited to join a Bible study group of Presbyterians who wanted to debate their theological stand of "eternal security" and "predestination." Don took the opportunity to present carefully-planned studies on the subjects. He added his own testimony, thanking the Lord that we knew our children would go to heaven because they could choose to accept Jesus as their Savior. The group leader's theology left him not knowing if his children would go to heaven, because he didn't know if God had accepted them or rejected them.

After six weeks, each couple dropped their misguided understanding of those doctrines and embraced the truths from the Bible that "whosoever will" to the Lord may come (John 3:16). We left humbled and thankful that the Scripture in Luke 21:15 was real in our lives: *"For I will give you a mouth and wisdom which all your adversaries shall not be able to gainsay nor resist."*

Another opportunity which presented itself in those early days was held at a church in Tacoma. The leading minister of their district challenged Don's father to a debate on who Jesus is. Dad Barnett accepted the offer desiring only to show them that Jesus Christ wasn't just a man but He was, and therefore is, God (John 10:30). Mom, Dad, Don and I prayed that many would embrace the truth and come into a personal relationship with Jesus.

The church was packed with people full of excitement on the warm June evening. The ministers and laymen alike loved a debate; in fact, they seemed to thrive on it. This time they met their match with Dad Barnett and Don as his assistant. Very strict rules were established and followed. Each man could have one assistant. The debate would begin by allowing each minister to speak for exactly twenty minutes. That time could be shared with their assistants. The rest of the first evening would be spent with one minister taking the offensive and the other the defensive. Each man could speak only in the time allotted, with no interruptions from the opposing side or the audience. Equal opportunity was given to each side to take the offensive position.

An easel was set up with a flip chart that had been carefully laid out by the minister—we'll call him Brother D. Brother D, a very large man dressed in a black suit, led a short prayer and began with his introduction. It included his credentials of having won debates in high school and college along with a list of the debates he had successfully concluded as a minister. His colleague then took the platform and verified Brother D's statements.

When it was Dad's turn, who was barely 5'7" and weighed around 140 pounds, he chose not to stand back behind the pulpit, but took his well-worn Bible and walked up in front of the people. Tears filled his eyes as he clasped his Bible to his chest, he began sharing with the crowded assembly, including rows of ministers, how precious the Word of God was to him, because he had a personal relationship with the Author.

He went on to relate the story of how he accepted Jesus as his own personal Savior and how God had recently raised him from the dead and called him to preach His Word. He expressed his gratitude to the Lord for showing him in His Word who He is so he never had to wonder if Jesus heard his prayers. He explained his purpose for coming to them was that they might know Jesus as he did. When he sat down, the room was silent with a holy reverence. Tears filled many eyes.

Knowing how Dad tended to get engrossed in his subject, Don hadn't expected any time left for him to address the congregation, and he was right. But Brother D had not gained his composure after Dad's testimony, so he allowed Don five minutes, which was enough time for Don to relate the prayer he had prayed at age fourteen and how God answered that prayer, because he wanted to study the Bible all the time and couldn't set it down for long. I could have attested to that!

Don's testimony didn't seem to help Brother D gain his composure. As he took his place, this time standing by his chart, he made the statement that he had never heard introductions like these before. With that he began his presentation pointing to the objects on his chart. Dad began his defense by remarking softly, "I haven't yet found in the Bible where God uses such objects to define Himself."

The next night, people were standing against the walls, as there wasn't room for everyone to sit, nor did the crowds diminish as the debate continued for seven weeks. At first, many were motivated to come to witness a heated debate, but as the Spirit of the Lord worked in their hearts, they continued coming because they wanted to know the God they were learning about.

Dad and Don waited until near the end of the debate to bring out the large scroll Don had made, giving an overview of God's revelation of Himself in the Scriptures. They had already answered all the questions Brother D's theology couldn't. More importantly, the people began to receive this unfolding revelation of God in His Word.

BEGINNING OUR JOURNEY TOGETHER
IN GOD'S SCHOOL

Their appetites for a fiesty debate gave way to a desire to really know and understand Jesus.

They began to comprehend the difference in the humanity of Jesus and His deity. They saw Jesus, a man like themselves, who thirsted, hungered, felt pain, and who could have chosen to sin but never did even though He was tempted (God cannot be tempted, James 1:13). He chose only to do what the Father told Him to do, and said, "The Father in Me, He doeth the works" (John 14:10). "In Him dwells all the fulness of the Godhead bodily," (Colossians 2:9) so He could honestly say, "I and my Father are one" (John 10:30); thus showing He was more than just a man. He was Emmanuel "God with us" (Isaiah 9:6).

"And the glory of it all is that we can have Christ in us, in whom dwells all the fulness of God, and therefore we, too, can have all the fulness of God dwelling in us as we are in Christ" (Ephesians 3:19).

Many of the listeners accepted Jesus, and their lives began changing. Some of the ministers attending forsook their former theology and began a new relationship with Jesus. They saw the Scriptures clearly visualized as Don unrolled the scroll which began with Genesis 1:26 where God said, "Let us make man in our own image and after our likeness," and ended with Revelation 22:17, "The Spirit and the Bride say 'Come.'"

When Dad read Revelation 22:17, showing how we as the Bride of Christ have the blessed opportunity to invite people to "Come," something happened in my own spirit. My personal relationship with Jesus, my Bridegroom, became stronger and more intimate helping prepare me for the ministry prophesied over me in the Latter Rain revival.

* * *

Don's teaching ministry flourished when he received permission to conduct Bible studies at the Boeing Company. For most of the eighteen years Don worked for Boeing, he taught Bible classes on his lunch hour. He produced written lessons on subjects such as *Creation versus Evolution, The Authenticity of the Bible, Refutation of the Errors in Predestination and Eternal Security, Water Baptism, Bible Prophecy and End-time Events, The Fulfillment of the Sabbath, The Lord's Day, Fasting*, and more. For over a year he also did an extensive study on *Bible Manuscripts and Translations*. Don put his artistic talent to use, and drew graphics, charts, and pictures which made the material appealing and easily understood.

One study group, mostly Baptists had chosen the subject: *The Baptism in the Holy Spirit*. They researched the Scriptures, determining if the evidence of being filled with the Holy Spirit was indeed speaking in other tongues.

As the studies continued, one man in particular became very hungry for more of God. He was so transformed after receiving the Holy Spirit and speaking in tongues that even the most skeptical were amazed. I first met Izzy after Don invited him home for dinner. He couldn't look me in the eye. He kept his head down the whole evening. Don confided, "That's the way he is all the time. He was so depressed, he once tried to kill himself."

Finally Don convinced him by saying, "If you're going to throw your life away, you can afford to take chances. Become a 'fanatic' like us and let God fill you with His Spirit." Desperate, he cried out for God to baptize him. His hands shot up as he started praising God in his new language. After that moment, he was a new man, full of the joy of the Lord. He went everywhere, testifying and witnessing for Jesus. The last time I saw Izzy, he had quit Boeing and was on his way to Israel to witness to his own people.

* * *

Our lives settled into a routine. Don left for work in the morning with his Bible. He came in the door after work with his mind already full of the Word, having studied on the bus ride home.

Two nights a week he taught judo at the YMCA, and two nights he went to a private tutor to learn Greek to help him in his studies. Wednesday evenings, I went to the mid-week church service while Don stayed home with Carolyn. He seemed to get more out of personal study than what was taught in the Wednesday night study at church. Saturday mornings were reserved for preparing his Sunday morning Bible class.

For pleasure, we'd say to one another, "What would you do with one million dollars?" We'd dream of having a Bible college where students could be accepted on their desire to know God's Word rather than on scholastic ability. We'd sit and draw out whole college campuses, with dorms and a cafeteria that I would supervise. We'd live on campus, too, so we'd really be in touch with the students. At that time, we were not much older than the students would be.

Of course, we would provide free tuition to all who didn't have the funds, as we didn't want anyone to suffer the hardships we were enduring, sometimes wishing we had a nickel to share an ice cream cone. We never once thought the college would ever be a reality. Instead we took every opportunity to minister for Jesus.

We learned lessons in the Lord's school when we took a team once a month to minister in the missions on skid row in Seattle. It didn't matter to those humble people that I didn't have much musical talent as I led the worship service; we all sang together the old hymns they had known as children. For some, it was the only church they had. The experience Don got in preaching instead of teaching was all part of God's plan. We had no problem loving those smelly drunks when they staggered forward to accept Jesus as their Savior. Our naivete caused us to get conned a few times.

One snowy winter night, a young mother came in off the cold street cradling her baby in her arms and sat in the back. She kept her eyes closed after the service and didn't seem to be in a hurry to leave. When I went back to greet her, she stood and with a pitiful look said, "I guess I better start walking home."

I asked, "Where do you live?"

She responded, "Oh, just about five miles from here."

"Oh, honey," I protested, "you should take the bus. It is too cold to walk."

She said, "Oh, no. I don't have any money, and if I did, I would use it for milk for the baby. I don't mind walking."

I thought, *We should do something for her.* I went to get Don. When we returned, the baby was crying and she seemed anxious to go. It's not wise to give money to people on skid row, so we offered to take her home and, on the way, buy some groceries for her. She sighed, "I just couldn't accept such a thing from you. I'll get along somehow." We discussed the matter further, and decided it was better to err on the side of mercy. We gave her $5. We locked up the mission, and stepped out on the sidewalk in time to see her turn into the tavern in the middle of the block. She had fooled us. She acted as if she just couldn't take anything from us, all the while playing into our sympathy so she could get what she really wanted, which wasn't food or a ride home, but alcohol to support the addiction to which she was chained. Even though $5 was a big sacrifice for us, we knew we had given it to her "as unto the Lord."

It didn't dampen my yearning to see people brought into the kingdom of God. I sent for a course on soul winning from Moody Bible Institute, and developed a system to mark a modern translation of the New Testament so the uninitiated could find the passages easily without knowing the books of the Bible. I made a simple chart showing God's plan for mankind, enabling me to give the whole scope in as little as forty-five minutes.

I also simplified one of Don's more comprehensive charts on end-time events and used it to teach grade-school and junior-high students. I made many Bible lessons using visual aids. Don painted background scenes on large squares of flannel, and I prepared pictures from magazines for the flannelgraph by using canned milk to glue flannel material to the backs. From the beginning of our marriage, I worked in Sunday School, set up children's Bible clubs, and worked with youth groups, all part of God's plan to equip me for what lay ahead.

* * *

I learned so much from the pastor and his wife of our new church home in West Seattle. They became very dear to me and a few years later I sobbed openly in the service when he announced he was leaving. We lost a wonderful pastor because the deacon board disagreed with a decision he wanted to make concerning the music. I considered them to be my pastors, even after I became a pastor's wife myself. The Lord did two very significant works in me while we attended church there. One was when I grieved the pastor, and the other was when I grieved the Lord.

The pastor came to me, concerned for the young married couples. "I want to provide fellowship for them," he said. Being anxious to please my pastor, I planned a wonderful dinner with a tropical theme. I personally roasted all the chickens and made ten gallons of homemade ice cream. Just as we were finishing with the elaborate decorations in the downstairs fellowship hall, the pastor came down to see how we were doing. Without saying a negative word, he looked at me for a moment with grief and disappointment in his eyes.

Instantly I knew why. I had created something that could compete with the party atmosphere of an Hawaiian luau, but it wouldn't cause couples to have fellowship with one another. To go to a dinner show was exciting, but to have an atmosphere where men and women could open their hearts and really get to know one another—it just wasn't there. With one look into my pastor's eyes, I understood one aspect of the church's role for it's members.

> *The spiritual work done in my heart through this experience caused me grief when the Chapel's own college banquets were turned into gala events. My weak attempts to do something about it didn't help, until it was too late. In that sense, I was part of the problem.*

The second lesson was between me and the Spirit of the Lord, when He dealt with me about operating the gift of tongues, interpretation of tongues, and prophecy that He had said would be a part of my ministry.

Time and again the Spirit of the Lord came upon me to give a message in tongues, and each time I argued with God, saying, "I can't—who would interpret? The people won't believe me."

My biggest fear, however, stemmed from a past experience. During the Latter Rain revival, someone had "prophesied" that Mamma would see my brother, Jim, who was missing in action in Korea, alive and home again. When it didn't happen, Mamma blamed God and turned her back on Him for fifteen years. I was deathly afraid of speaking a word supposedly from the Lord and it not being accurate.

Finally, the Lord spoke to me, "This is the last time I'm going to anoint you to give a message from Me. If you won't yield, I won't anoint you again." It just so happened I had brought a visitor to the service that night, so

THE TRUTH SHALL SET YOU FREE

I used that as my excuse. When I said "No," the anointing lifted from me, not to be felt again for seven years.

> *Why didn't I realize we were in the school of the Lord? He was preparing us for something bigger, and this was my chance to learn under the watchful eye of a pastor. If I wouldn't take the test, then I'd just have to learn later, but learn I would! God never violates our will—the choice is always ours.*

Chapter Five

Tests of Our Faith in God's Healing and Forgiveness

"He was bruised for our iniquities and by His stripes we were healed."
(Isaiah 53:5)
"According to your faith be it unto you."
(Matthew 9:29)

"Your baby has whooping cough." The doctor said, "It can be fatal for a baby so young." This test, one of many, came when our son Daniel, born when Carolyn was three-and-a-half years old, was just three months old. My mother sent a plane ticket for me to fly home. She wasn't going to let her grandson get any older before she saw him. I'm sure everyone on that plane was glad when it landed, as Danny screamed the whole flight. I learned why when in desperation I took him to a doctor.

I was shocked! The doctor recommended a certain serum that was the only known cure at that time. It was terribly expensive and there was none available in Boise. He advised me, "Take the next possible plane back to Seattle. I'm sure you can get the medication there." He handed me a bottle of penicillin, "In the meantime, give this to Danny."

Danny was too weak to cry on the way home. Carolyn, only three, sensed the seriousness of the situation and consoled me as I prayed all the way. When we stepped off the plane in Seattle, I knew what I had to do. As Don and his brother Joe met us, I said to Don, "I've made a decision to trust God for Danny's healing." When we passed through the door to Joe's car, I dropped the penicillin in the garbage can. By the time we reached home, Danny was peacefully asleep. He awoke ten hours later, with no fever and no cough. God had honored my decision, and our baby was healed!

To our dismay, a week later Carolyn came down with the whooping cough. The poor little thing doubled over coughing. We prayed, of course, and God saw her through. Five weeks later when I took Danny to the doctor for his check-up, the doctor heard Carolyn cough and he exclaimed, "Oh my dear, your girl has the whooping cough! If the baby catches it, it could be fatal!"

He rushed the baby into the next room away from Carolyn. I followed him, telling the story of what happened and how she had actually caught it from Danny. Bewildered, he examined Danny and found him to be completely well. Then he checked Carolyn and concluded she had survived it, too. The cough that lingers after the disease had almost run its course in Carolyn and wouldn't last much longer.

TESTS OF OUR FAITH IN GOD'S HEALING AND FORGIVENESS

> *I was thankful that we knew Jesus, and that Mamma had taught me to trust in Him by her example. Even though we didn't know it, each test helped prepare us for the ministry.*

By the time Daniel was ten months old, we had enough saved for the down payment on a house. We were in our first very own home before Carolyn started school, and nine months later, David, our third and last child was born.

David was barely four months old when he and Daniel came down with chicken pox. David was one mass of pox. I carried him on a pillow and for four days never took my clothes off to sleep. I couldn't leave him for even a minute or he would paw at his face and make lasting scars. Even with mittens on his hands there could be damage done. None of the lotions the doctor recommended seemed to ease the pain. He cried constantly. Poor little Danny didn't get much attention, because I was so busy with David. Then God intervened.

Jesus knows when we are at the end of our endurance. At 6:30 p.m. on the fourth day, when I was changing David, I sobbed to the Lord, " I can't take any more. Please help me." It was as if Jesus told the devil, "Enough! Take your hand off my child!" At that moment, David stopped crying and fell into a peaceful sleep. His little body looked the same, covered with pus, but all the "meanness" went out of the sores. David acted like they didn't even exist. He was never bothered by them again, and his skin healed rapidly.

The Lord is so good, gracious, and kind, and there is as much variety in the way He moves in our lives as there is in the world He created for us to enjoy. Jesus knew something about David that we didn't. To prepare us for what was ahead, He allowed our faith to be tested one more time.

When David was two, we took our first family vacation. The night before our scheduled departure, Carolyn became very ill. When Don left her room after praying for her, he announced, "God has touched her. We will leave as planned, because she will be fine by morning." When Carolyn awoke, she was perfectly normal.

We praised Jesus and were happy as our car left the driveway, but on our second day, David became deathly sick. Within a few hours, he was burning up with a fever and gasping for breath. Desperate by the time we reached Lincoln City on the Oregon coast, we took him to a doctor who was unable to determine the cause, but gave us some penicillin and said, "you should turn around and go home." Deciding to wait until morning, we checked into a motel.

As soon as everyone was in bed, I slipped into the bathroom, knelt down at the toilet, and began beseeching God to heal my child. After an hour of telling God what to do by reminding Him of all his promises, I felt as if He tapped me on the shoulder and asked, "What are you doing? Are you telling Me what is best for My child?"

I wept, "Lord, I am sorry for telling You what is best for David. I don't know the future; only You know what is best for our son. I will not presume upon Your great wisdom. If You want to take David to heaven, You can have him." Still crying softly, I went back into the bedroom, certain David was going to die. His lips and hands had turned blue as he continued his struggle to breathe.

TESTS OF OUR FAITH IN GOD'S HEALING AND FORGIVENESS

My crying woke Don, and he learned what the Lord told me. Gripped with compassion for his son, he headed for the bathroom to plead with God. When he closed the door behind him, God's presence was there. He lifted his hands and said, "The Lord giveth and the Lord taketh away. Blessed be the name of the Lord." With that, it was settled. He too expected David to be dead by morning. Within minutes after Don returned to bed, David's breathing became normal and color returned to his lips. He sank into a peaceful slumber. When we awoke in the morning, David was very weak, but he was healed. Don carried him as we explored the beach, and by the next day he was normal.

Months later, I noticed David wasn't running properly as he crossed the back yards to his friend's house. I thought, *He has outgrown his shoes.* I got him new shoes, but they didn't solve the problem. *Could it be that he has progressive muscular dystrophy like his uncle before him,* I wondered. *It couldn't be true,* I mused. *Kenneth's disease was first detected by him running on his toes and David is clumsy when he runs. When he walks, he looks normal. I'm not going to mention anything to Don until I am sure there is a problem.*

Don had gone through so much embarrassment and shame with his little brother, having carried him on his back to school, that I didn't want to alarm him without cause. When God chose not to heal Kenneth, Don's faith had been weakened. He no longer kept the same stand as his parents. After his knee injury, when he chose to get medical help and reaped the benefits of their knowledge and prescribed drugs, he argued with his father, "There is no difference in removing a sliver yourself or

THE TRUTH SHALL SET YOU FREE

having someone with more experience wearing a white coat remove it. In either case, it wouldn't prevent God from healing." Dad's point always came back to, "If you're trusting man, then you're not trusting God." I agreed, even if they couldn't, that both men had a point.

By the time David entered kindergarten, we knew something was wrong. At his teacher's suggestion, we took him to a specialist. Dr. Martin was unable to diagnose the disease, but took a blood test that determined it was not progressive muscular dystrophy. Although we were relieved, Don did extensive research on the subject and learned that it was hereditary. Feeling a responsibility to his brothers, he informed them of his findings so they could decide if or when to pass the information on to their children. We determined to tell ours when the time came, so they could decide whether to take the chance and have children of their own.

Dr. Martin wanted to perform a biopsy on David, removing a piece of muscle to study. He said, "Perhaps we can determine what the problem is, but it will not lead to a solution." Not wanting to add to the trauma already in our five-year-old son's life, we decided against the operation and chose to trust God. David was a good sport through the whole thing. As his condition worsened, the kids made fun of him when he stumbled and fell. He'd just laugh right along with them. We were a close-knit neighborhood, however, and it wasn't long before the children understood and became very supportive.

Once when David was eight years old, he became discouraged. We were riding in the car, just he and I. He had tried to climb a tree that day and found he no longer could.

TESTS OF OUR FAITH IN GOD'S
HEALING AND FORGIVENESS

Looking up at me, he asked, "Mamma, will I be in a wheelchair someday?"

I answered him honestly, "David, I don't know, but one thing I do know; you belong to God. [I had learned that lesson in the motel bathroom.] Whatever you have to go through, He will be there to help you and go through it with you."

I took his hand and squeezed it. "And I'll be right there with Him, too. We'll go through it together."

That settled it for both of us. There was an unspoken covenant made that day with God that kept both of us from discouragement.

David had as much patience with others as he had with himself. When he stumbled and fell, he never got angry or frustrated, nor did he pout or scream. He'd simply keep trying until he managed to get up and try again. When he did require help and we couldn't make it right away, he'd patiently wait. One time he lay on the floor for eight hours, having fallen out of his chair, before we came home and discovered his plight. The person scheduled to check on him every two hours had neglected to do so. When I rushed to him to see if he was hurt and learned how long he had lain there, his reply was, "It's okay, Mom. It gave me all this time to pray."

Eventually, we learned from a neurologist who tested David when he was fifteen that the disease was called Fredrik's Atactica, which attacks the nerves, causing loss of all motor skills, even speech, sight, and hearing. At that time, there was very little known about what caused it, except for speculation that it was a cousin to progressive muscular dystrophy. Nothing had been discovered that would cure or even slow down the disease. So sure was David that God would heal him, he submitted himself to the University of Washington Medical Hospital, going through hours and hours of tests, so his condition would be documented. He reasoned, "After my healing there will be no mistake about what my condition was, and God will get all the glory."

* * *

By the late 1950's, we built the home we designed ourselves, on a lot south of Seattle. It was ten years before we understood why the Lord wanted us to stay in that neighborhood instead of building out in Federal Way on property we preferred. During this time, we miserably failed God.

Don did well at the Boeing company, working his way up until eventually he was in charge of designing the sealing for the aircraft which included the Boeing 707, 727, 737, and 747 airplanes during his eighteen years of service.

With the promotions at Boeing, however, came new temptations. At work Don upheld his Christian testimony. He was known as "the preacher" because he had his Bible on his desk ready to study on every break. When he was ridiculed for bowing his head and giving thanks to the Lord for his food, too testy, perhaps, he boldly retorted, "What? You live in America where you claim 'In God We Trust,' yet you don't even thank Him for your daily food?" His co-workers soon respected his stand. He wouldn't participate in their dirty jokes, nor get involved with the girlie pictures some had on their desks, even though they were the hardest for him to resist, given his inordinate

TESTS OF OUR FAITH IN GOD'S HEALING AND FORGIVENESS

infatuation with the female form. The devil thought of another trap for him.

As a result of a promotion, Don was scheduled to visit two of Boeing's subcontractors, one in California and one in Texas. He came home bursting with excitement, "I got permission to add a few vacation days to the trip and take you!"

I yelped with joy, "It will be our first vacation alone since our honeymoon."

When the plane touched down on a stop-over in San Francisco, we left the aircraft to stretch our legs before continuing our flight forty-five minutes later to Los Angeles. Perhaps it was because Don felt safe being in a strange city so no one would recognize him, that he went to the newsstand and glanced through a Playboy magazine.

That was just the first step into the devil's web. The next time, he coaxed me into looking at the pictures with him. I felt awful and even more inadequate physically. It caused me to feel he was justified in criticizing my body. *I can never measure up to compete with those girls,* I thought. I started feeling bad that he didn't have one like those to make love to instead of me. Don told me that it made him love me more when I looked at the pictures with him, so when he wanted to go see a topless show in Texas, I consented. I desperately wanted him to love me. My misguided thinking said he deserved to see someone prettier than I. However, I wasn't prepared for my own reaction.

The room was dark, crowded, reeking with cigarette smoke and alcohol. We found a spot at the back, close to the door. I'm sure I wasn't aware of all that was going on between the call girls and patrons under the long tablecloths on the little tables, but I do know what happened to me. In spite of how beautiful and appealing the show girls were, the moment we stepped outside I had an emotional breakdown. I burst into tears even before we reached the car. I cried uncontrollably for hours. In one dreadful moment, I felt as if my spirit had been raped and my soul violated. It took a while before I let Don hold me, because I felt ugly and unlovable.

> *Oh, if only at this point we could have recognized we were playing right into the hands of the devil. But we did not, so little by little we got more entrenched. The perverted behavior took different forms, and I became enslaved, thinking all the while I was being a dutiful, submissive wife by keeping the sin hidden.*

Afterward, Don felt terrible, repented to God, and confessed to feeling like his glands were stronger than the average man's, as was his infatuation with a woman's body. Sometimes he wondered if perhaps this was his "thorn in the flesh" (1 Corinthians 12:7). At times he told me, "I hate the way I feel. I know if I wasn't a born-again Christian, I would be an adulterer."

Don didn't have much tolerance for imperfection. The one part of my body he never criticized was my nose; he loved the shape of my nose. I wanted desperately to have his love and favor even though I felt unworthy, so I did everything I could to please him. I thought my job was to make him happy. I never withheld myself from him. I dressed, acted, talked, and tried to even think like he wanted me to.

Each time we confessed our sins to God and repented, God in His matchless grace forgave us, not because we deserved it, but because He is committed to His Word. "Where sin abounds, grace much more abounds" (Romans 5:20). While God's grace forgives, it doesn't eliminate the effect sin has in our lives. The seeds of destruction were already sown in us.

> *Yet, where had it all started? Back when my brother molested me, or when I didn't receive love from my father? Back when Don had an infatuation for a cute fourth grader or questioned his own birthright? Or when we disobeyed God's Word and went too far before marriage?*

Many times Don identified with the Apostle Paul's words in Romans 7:15-20,22,25: *"For that which I do, I allow not: for what I would, that do I not; but what I hate, that do I. If then I do that which I would not, I consent unto the law that it is good. Now then it is no more I that do it, but sin that dwelleth in me. For I know that in me (that is, in my flesh,) dwelleth no good thing:for to will is present with me; but how to perform that which is good I find not. For the good that I would I do not: but the evil which I would not, that I do. Now if I do that I would not, it is no more I that do it, but sin that dwelleth in me . . . For I delight in the law of God after the inward man . . . I thank God through Jesus Christ our Lord. So then with the mind*

I myself serve the law of God; but with the flesh the law of sin."

"Lord," I prayed, after repenting, "Surely you have a plan to get us out of this. Please help me to find it."

Chapter Six

Discerning God's Leading

"But the Lord was not in the wind: and after the wind an earthquake; but the Lord was not in the earthquake; and after the earthquake a fire; but the Lord was not in the fire: and after the fire, a still small voice—and it was so." (1 Kings 19:11,12)

"Jesus," Don and I prayed one evening, "We yearn for our children to experience a visitation from heaven like we did in the late 1940's and early 50's." Hoping it would help, we changed churches to one closer to home, so our kids could participate in more activities.

The pastor, a humble man, admitted he wasn't a Bible scholar and happily turned the adult Sunday School class to Don. Don's unique wisdom in the Word caused attendance to double and then triple. The pastor was happy, but the board was not. Without our knowledge, the pastor vetoed many of their attempts to remove Don. The church continued to grow, making it necessary to add a larger sanctuary.

In the meantime, my desire to see a revival in the young people intensified until I set aside an hour every morning after our children left for school and prayed.

Every day I prayed, mentioning each young person by name. After several months, the Spirit of the Lord spoke in my mind, "I want you to work with the young people." *Whoa!* I panicked, *I'm not ready for this!* I had a million excuses why I couldn't and shouldn't.

Finally, at 2:00 in the afternoon, I picked up the phone and called the pastor. I spilled out the story of how I had prayed for the teenagers every day for months and what the Lord had just told me. He responded, "Well, Barbara, that's interesting. You know the young people already have a leader—Mrs. M is in charge. Hmmmm. Ah, what would you like to do for the young people?"

My voice quivered, "I'd like to start by teaching a series on end-time events."

He closed the conversation by saying, "I'll talk to Mrs. M to see what she has planned, and I'll let you know."

I hung up the phone and thought, *Maybe I won't have to do it. Maybe the Lord just wanted to see if I am willing, like Abraham had to be willing to offer Isaac.* But the longing to have God move in the teenagers' lives didn't go away. Still, I was surprised when the pastor called the very next day saying, "It's all set." He had spoken with Mrs. M, and I could start next Sunday evening. I could take as many meetings as I needed to finish the subject. He concluded by saying, "Well, Barbara, it's a start, and we'll see what happens from here."

The response from the young people was wonderful. I felt like God gave me an ability to share His Word with them in ways that opened them up to His love like never before. We had so much fun together, too! They became my second family. I taught them how to witness, and we went out door-to-door. We got fellowships started in their high schools, where kids got filled with the Holy Spirit. We played baseball and volleyball with other churches. We won the awards at the regional CA (Christ Ambassador) rallies. Most importantly, these young adults' personal relationships with Jesus were being established.

I didn't know that, after just a few years, it was going to get stopped as suddenly as it had started

Shortly after the new sanctuary was finished, we knew we were going to lose our pastor. His wife, Ruth, and I had become close friends, and together we had started working as Welcome Wagon hostesses, welcoming newcomers to the community. We were also prayer partners, so she felt free to confide in me, although she was very guarded in what she shared. I learned the pastor was discouraged with the board who wouldn't allow him the freedom he needed to help the church.

The pastor came to me once saying, "Barbara, I'm concerned about the children in Sunday School. My own little daughter hates to go to her Sunday School class. She cries every Sunday morning. Yet, as the pastor, I feel I have to make her go. I'll admit she's not learning anything. I don't want my child growing up hating Sunday School. I'm concerned for the rest of the children, too."

I commented, "Pastor, I feel the Lord gave me a wonderful plan that children love. It teaches them systematic theology, but requires team teaching."

After further discussion, he decided it was the answer. He met with the Sunday School superintendent and teachers and explained what he was going to do. Some who were head teachers now would be part of the team teaching system. After the first month, the pastor and students were thrilled. His daughter could hardly wait to get to Sunday School. When I was at their home assembling my Welcome Wagon materials, his daughter ran up to me, coaxing me to tell her what was going to happen next Sunday.

The teachers and superintendent didn't share the same enthusiasm, however. The pastor came to me in tears, "Barbara, it breaks my heart to do this, but we have to put the Sunday School back as it was. The teachers are just too jealous. Along with the superintendent, they are all going to quit."

"Pastor, it's no problem for me." I responded. "I'm sorry you are in such a bind, but you do what you feel you need to do for the church's sake."

What finally caused this fine man of God to resign shortly after the Sunday School incident was the board's reaction to a matter in the treasury. When the pastor uncovered theft and deceit, they refused to dismiss the one responsible because he was one of the founders. We lost our pastor, but we didn't lose our friends.

Our new pastor was a beloved older man, full of the love of God. Whenever he shook my hand, I felt like God's love was being poured into me. Both Don and I said we learned the love of God from the short time we sat under his ministry.

By this time, the adult class had grown from fifty to over two hundred. Many said they came to that church for Don's teaching alone. The board, however, wanted the pastor to take over the class.

The pastor chose to leave Don as the adult teacher, but with continued pressure from the board, the class was divided and all the young marrieds were given to the pastor's wife to teach. No one wanted to leave Don's teaching, but some went in honor of her. It wasn't long, however, until she didn't want the position, and all the students happily returned to Don's class.

Then another idea was devised. Now the board decided the adults needed to be involved in the Sunday School's opening exercises, which included singing Happy Birthday to all whom it applied. Thus, Don's class was cut down to an half-hour, or sometimes as little as twenty minutes. Don felt he had so much to bring in only one hour a week as it was, and the people needed to be fed from the Word so desperately, it grieved his heart. He came to church and went downstairs to pray, so he wouldn't lose the anointing he left home with until their games upstairs were over.

> *Again, we felt like we were learning what not to do if ever God called Don to be a pastor. That day was closer than we knew!*

Finally, the board persuaded the pastor to take over the adult class. When the pastor came with the news, Don graciously consented. However, in the middle of the week, the pastor suffered a major heart attack. Don continued to teach the class for one more year, in which time two very significant things happened—all part of God's plan.

* * *

THE TRUTH SHALL SET YOU FREE

God put Don and I in a new spiritual place. He used the teachings and ministry of an evangelist who came to our area. The first service was so impacting Don took the rest of the week off from work, and we went to the day studies as well. Our hunger for God overcame our desire for food, so Don and I spent the time between the services in the prayer room. We wanted the deeper life in Jesus that was evident in this man of God. In fact, the series was entitled *The Deeper Life*. The lessons included studies on *Dying to Self, The Spirit Man Versus the Flesh Man*, and *The Crucified Life*. Almost simultaneously, God gave us both an experience in prayer of the theology we were hearing. It happened on the fourth day, between the afternoon and evening services.

We were the only ones in the prayer room, me at one end and Don at the other. Suddenly, it felt as if we were emptied out and there was nothing left of us. Don testified that he felt like nothing could hurt him, because he was empty of self and all he wanted was God and His will. It's hard to describe the experience, but now we knew what the evangelist was trying to explain to us—there was a place, a life in the Spirit, that ended all striving to do and be what God wanted.

When we walked out of that room, we felt as if everywhere we stepped was holy. Don wept for days. We spoke in reverent soft tones when we spoke at all. Sunday morning, Don stood before his class, wept and glorified God. When he did start the lesson, it was through tears. For him, the whole Word of God took on a new dimension. The focus of his teaching changed from making theology understandable to a compelling desire to see the Word of God change the listeners.

DISCERNING GOD'S LEADING

Week after week, tears flowing down his face, he taught the message of the deeper life. Our pastor, not fully recovered from a heart attack, was not strong enough to be in Don's class, but he slipped out of his study and sat behind the platform with the door ajar so he could hear. Many in the class wept as they listened, but the board's feelings toward Don didn't change.

I was compelled by the Spirit of God to pray for the congregation. The spirit of intercession came upon me with such power that many times I couldn't remain in my seat during the song service. I slipped downstairs to the furnace room where I wouldn't bother anyone; there I cried before the Lord for His people, and there the Lord gave me a vision. He placed a scene in my mind of many, many lanterns. They were lit, but the glass was smoky and the wicks were black. He spoke to me and said, "This is why the world isn't saved. My people have light, but their lives are dark, so the light can't be seen."

I pleaded, "Lord, I give You permission to clean my lantern, and please, oh God, use me to clean the lanterns of Your people."

Many in the congregation didn't approve of my praying at the altar after the service. One testified during service, "There is something wrong with a person's life if they have to go to the altar and cry before God every service—it only proves they don't pray at home." It didn't stop me, because they didn't understand. I kept on praying.

After this experience, the spiritual realm opened to me. The gift ministry of discerning of spirits spoken of in 1 Corinthians 12 began operating through me, and with it came knowledge or awareness of demons and angels, plus power and authority to take dominion over the demons and to cast them out.

The first time God used me this way in a service, there was an evangelist conducting meetings at our church. Flossy, a church member, brought a friend she had witnessed to earlier in the week. The friend had cut her wrists in an attempt to take her life, but the Lord had prompted Flossy to knock on her door in time to save her. I knew she might be in the service that night, as Flossy had called me and asked me to pray.

After the evangelist finished his sermon, Flossy's friend went out of control. I spun around to see where they were standing. The Lord allowed me to perceive the demons in her. I literally ran back to her, pointing my finger at the demons, commanding them to leave in Jesus' name.

Just as I reached her, I saw the demons leave her and go to a place in the room close to the ceiling. I whirled around, still pointing to the demons, commanding them to leave the room and not return. I saw them shoot through the wall. They were gone! The woman slumped to the floor, sobbing.

As Flossy and I hugged her, she whispered, "Thank you, thank you! What happened to me? I don't want them to come back!" As we prayed with her, Jesus filled her with the Holy Spirit, and she spoke in tongues. I hadn't had time to worry about what the evangelist or the congregation thought. The power of God just came upon me; and as I yielded to Him, He took over. It was as if I were just a vessel for Him to use.

I wish I could tell you that Don and I stayed in that wonderful place—feeling empty of self-desire, with no temptation for worldly lusts—after the initial experience in the prayer room that afternoon in the *Deeper Life* meetings, but we didn't. We don't know the reason why we weren't able to stay dead to self, but at least we knew there was a place in God where it was a reality. It was a disappointment, too, that after Don preached his heart out week after week, the adult Sunday School class didn't seek God for the experience spoken of in the Word. After a while, the anointing to continue on that subject lifted, and Don went on to other truths. He never ran out of subject material.

* * *

Don longed to be in the full-time ministry. After every service, you could find us in the prayer room seeking God. We longed for God to move again like He had during the Latter Rain. Once, in the prayer room, I heard Don speaking in tongues which didn't sound like prayer.. I told the pastor's wife, "I don't know to whom he's preaching, but he's preaching to somebody."

When Don came out of the prayer room, he related a vision God gave him while he was speaking in tongues. He was standing before a very large crowd of people, preaching a message on the love of God. Later he tried to recall the sermon, as it was profound. He said he had never heard a sermon like it on the love of God. He yearned to preach it, but couldn't remember anything more about it.

Don never considered himself to be a preacher. He knew God had called him to teach, but he didn't think he could preach. The Lord spoke to his heart time and again, saying, "Just keep on doing what you are doing, and something will open up."

Then, without Don applying for it, a new job opportunity presented itself. I wondered, *Is this You, Jesus, or the devil?* Just as we were considering it, in came a second job offer. The first one was in southern California, the second in Atlanta, Georgia.

Wondering what to do, we prayed and prayed. Heaven was silent. It looked like southern California was the best offer, but Don decided to tell his supervisor, and seek his advice. Boeing really didn't have anyone to take Don's place, as he had developed the entire sealing program. He was already at the top of his category. Not having an engineering degree, he wasn't qualified to move up any higher. The other companies were not making that a barrier; they wanted his experience and were offering him more than double the wages he was presently making.

When Don told his boss, he said, "There's no way Boeing will break out of their tradition and give you the classification or the increase in pay. There is no record of them ever doubling an employee's salary all at once. But, just in case, let me take it up to 'mahogany row' to see what they say." He came back with a negative report.

Don called me saying, "we are going to California!" I said, "Fine. I'll call the movers." We had to be there in two weeks. I just hung up the phone, when it rang with a call from Atlanta. He had a new offer. I said, "You better call Don quickly, because he is calling California right now."

The call from Atlanta with a better offer cut into Don's call to California. A few minutes later, Don called, "We're going to Atlanta." While we were talking, Don's boss came up to him, so we hung up. I called the movers back and told them to change the destination to Atlanta.

Don's boss requested, "Please wait. Mahogany row is reconsidering. Give us an half-hour before you make your decision."

Forty-five minutes later, Don called me back, "We are going to stay where we are. Cancel the movers. I just got back from being called up to mahogany row where the top officials shook my hand and said they were placing me into the engineering category and nearly doubling my salary from $3.75 to $6.50 an hour. They congratulated me on doing such a fine job for the company."

Whew! It was over. We should have realized the Lord is not the author of confusion, and it was the devil trying to get us out of the area just six months before God opened the door . We were going to need the extra money.

Besides getting financially caught up, the raise in pay permitted us to put Don's latest theological work in print. When a lady in our church learned of the study Don was completing on the baptism in the Holy Spirit called *Glossolalia,* she volunteered to type it. There wasn't any comprehensive study in print on the subject, and her goal was to see it published. Later, the book was revised and expanded, given a new title—*Speaking in Tongues*—and is now in many of the nation's Bible college libraries.

God continued giving me opportunities to witness for Him through my Welcome Wagon job. I had so many people wanting Don and me to come back in the evening to talk to them about the Lord, we couldn't get to all of them. I asked the pastor, "Perhaps other members of the church would like to help?" No one was interested.

THE TRUTH SHALL SET YOU FREE

There was one old couple, the Shamps, who like us sat up front in the church. They sat on one side of the aisle and we on the other. Everyone else sat at least four pews behind us. Old brother Shamp told us, "You fill up your side, and we'll fill up ours." We agreed. The Lord must have agreed, too, because it started happening!

Chapter Seven

Charismatic Explosion

*"And God added to the church daily
those being saved."
(Acts 2:47)*

It was another one of those rainy days in Seattle, and I had no idea my life was about to change. The chill of fall in the wind didn't dampen my faith, as I ran up the street without taking time to put on my coat. Bursting with excitement and the glory of the Lord on my face, I knocked on the door of my friend's home who attended the same church as I. Dorothy knew I was a "Welcome Wagon" hostess along with our pastor's wife, Ruth. Besides acquainting newcomers to businesses in our area, we also had opportunity to introduce them to Jesus. Dorothy flung open the door. "Hi!" she exclaimed, catching my excitement.

"Dorothy, quick," I panted, "I need to borrow your copy of *They Speak with Other Tongues* by John Sherrill."

"Sure, Barbara. Is it for my new neighbor?" she asked.

"Yes. I'm so excited," I said, bouncing up and down. "They're wonderful Lutherans, Keith and Joanne are their names. They have five children, but two of them are her brother's. Anyway, Joanne is so hungry for the Lord, I know they're going to get filled with the Holy Spirit."

Dorothy handed me the book, "My name is in it, so tell her I'll come and get it when she's done reading it."

"Oh, good. Keith will read it, too, as he rides the bus to work. Let's pray," I said, taking her hand. "Jesus, we're so thankful we can be workers together with You in these days when You are pouring out Your Spirit on all flesh. Open the hearts of those who read this book to receive all You have for them. Amen."

"I've gotta rush back," I said, as I opened the door. "Joanne thinks I just went to my car to get this book, but I must have loaned out my last copy. I'm so glad you had one."

"No problem," Dorothy called after me as I ran down the street. "God bless you!"

God answered my prayer, and it was the beginning of something that was going to change not only our lives, but thousands of others.

* * *

Just two weeks after I met Joanne and loaned her John Sherrill's book, *They Speak with Other Tongues,* our church hosted the district Young People's Christ's Ambassadors Rally. I called Joanne and invited her and her husband, Keith. On that Saturday night, our church was packed, including the balcony, which our congregation never had to use.

I prayed that Keith and Joanne could make it, as I sat on the front pew where the pastor had asked me to open the service in prayer. When I finished, thankfulness welled up inside me when I saw my friend, who lived on Joanne's street, sitting with her. This was Joanne's first Pentecostal service. *I'm glad it's a young people's service, where the people sing with all their hearts,* I thought. At the altar call, Joanne knelt and opened her heart to Jesus.

Keith said, "As soon as Joanne stepped through our front door, I knew she was different." Jesus had touched her, and even though He didn't baptize her in His Holy Spirit that night, it caused Keith to desire the experience. Fortunately, the Full Gospel Businessmen's monthly meeting was the following Saturday evening at a downtown hotel, and Keith received the Holy Spirit.

He could hardly wait for other couples in his Lutheran church to learn about the baptism in the Holy Spirit. He asked Don, "Would you give them a Bible study on the subject, if I invite them to my home?" Thrilled, Don said, "Yes." It started a chain reaction, which, like a snowball rolling downhill, gained size and momentum as it went.

In the meantime, old Brother Shamp met a Baptist family with six children. Bob, the father, was starved for more of God. He came to church with Brother Shamp and met Keith, sitting across the aisle. Keith invited Bob, the Baptist, to join the Lutherans at his home for the Bible study on Tuesday evening. But they weren't the only ones who came. Don faithfully witnessed to the group of men who worked for him at Boeing, and God began moving in the hearts of a Catholic family, whose father's name was also Bob.

To open Bob's heart, the Spirit of the Lord used testimonies of healing in Don's family. Bob was intrigued with the supernatural and had looked into various religions. When he heard how God had raised Dad Barnett back to life, and other healings from Don's childhood, Bob said, "I really want to give my heart to the Lord, but I want to wait until my wife is ready. She is a devout Catholic and I want her to be willing, too."

Don advised Bob, "Don't pressure Kathy." Handing Bob some *Voice* magazines, Don suggested, "Just lay these on the coffee table, then wait and see what happens."

Every morning, as Don waited at the bus stop to ride to work, he prayed for Kathy. Kathy, a bubbly little Italian lady in her late twenties, related this story: "I hated Don Barnett. Even though I had never met him, I hated him. I felt like he was taking my husband away from me. Bob never did like the Catholic church, and now he wanted to talk about Jesus all the time. I blamed Don for the change in my husband. I got angry when I saw the *Voice* magazines laying there, but after Bob left for work, I'd pick them up and read them, and I'd start crying. I wanted what these people had, but I didn't want to admit it."

When we invited Bob and Kathy to our home for dinner, she accepted; but she didn't want to be pressured into anything. She said, "I know God. When I go to church, I say, 'Hello, God,' and when I leave, I say, 'Goodbye, God.'"

At the end of the evening, Don said, "I would just like to pray before you leave, if you wouldn't mind." Kathy turned and knelt at the couch. Before Don ended his prayer, he said, "And now, Lord, if Kathy would like to accept You as her own personal Savior, help her to pray this prayer..." (he repeated the sinner's prayer). When he finished, Kathy stood—eyes brimming with tears and her face glowing, she hugged the man she had hated. She thanked him for leading her to Jesus. Now Bob and Kathy both wanted to attend the Bible study at Keith's home.

At the first study, there were three Lutheran couples, one Baptist, and one Catholic couple. They seemed to devour the Word of God, and they didn't want to wait a whole week before meeting again, so we set the next meeting for Friday evening. On Sunday mornings, they went to their respective churches, but on Sunday evenings they came to our church's service. We now had two of our four rows filled, and old Brother Shamp across the aisle had filled one.

On Sunday morning, Don stood during testimony time and told the congregation what was happening and who the people were who would be attending the service that evening. He discouraged any members from coming to the Bible study in our home, explaining that he was teaching the basic foundational truths with which they were already familiar. We certainly did not want the pastor or board to think we were trying to take people away from the church.

That Monday, Don called me from work, "Larry [another one of his draftsmen] is ready to receive Jesus as his Savior." His voice didn't conceal his excitement. "I want to invite him home to dinner." I rushed to the store, picked up a roast, and slid it in the oven before leaving to make my Welcome Wagon calls. *I'm going to have to quit this job; my life is getting too filled up feeding the new converts,* I thought.

By the end of the meal that very evening, Larry wanted to ask Jesus to come into his heart. In his fifty-two years, he had tried everything to find peace. He'd even taken drugs with his twenty-three-year-old son, one of the leaders of the hippie movement in Seattle. When Larry arose from his knees after accepting Jesus as his Savior, his arms shot up in the air as he literally jumped up and down shouting, "Hallelujah! I'm free! This is wonderful! Jesus is real! I'm free!" It was a sight I'll never forget. There was no holding him back from expressing the new joy he felt. He hugged both Don and me at the same time, and continued shouting, "Hallelujah!"

The following Tuesday, after just three lessons on the baptism in the Holy Spirit, those attending the studies wanted it. We decided that the next Friday evening meeting at our home would include a time to pray. They were ready, or so they thought. When Keith was filled at the Full Gospel Businessmen's meeting, it wasn't a very emotional event. They had taken him into a back room, sat him on a chair, prayed a simple prayer, and told him to begin to speak with tongues, which he did. When he returned to us to ride home, he was trembling and he knew God had touched him. This group had never actually seen anyone get filled with the Holy Spirit, so I was hoping the Lord would do it nice and proper so no one would be startled. God had other plans.

When Friday night arrived, Bonnie, Scott's wife, was excited. Scott and Bonnie were in their early twenties, a delightful couple full of energy. Scott worked for Boeing, and with his broad shoulders and strong arms—not realizing his own strength—would crush a lady's hand in a simple handshake. His personality was a lot like the apostle Peter's must have been. However, his blunt, dogmatic statements, expressed with the ferocity of a bulldog, could be quickly changed the instant he saw he was wrong. Bonnie was a petite, stylish blond, capable of saying more words in thirty seconds than most people say in five minutes. She had a demanding job with a computer company which took her out of town on frequent business trips. In fact, she had to leave early the next morning for Boston. We fell in love with Scott and Bonnie the first time we met them at Keith and Joanne's.

Bonnie confided in me during the break for refreshments before we started praying. "I've been getting up in the middle of the night and praying to be filled, but something must be wrong, because I always get distracted by the furnace clicking on."

I asked her, "Bonnie, are you praying out loud?"

"Oh, no!" she replied, "I never pray out loud."

Smiling, I said, "Well, tonight try praying audibly, just loud enough so you can hear. You have to be speaking in order for the Lord to give you a new language, so start by thanking and praising Jesus."

Once back in the living room, everyone knelt at their seats. Both Don and I began praying out loud, asking Jesus to baptize them in the Holy Spirit, then we started praising Jesus, first in English, then in tongues. I realized just hearing us was a new experience for some of them. Then, sensing the Holy Spirit was coming upon Bonnie, I slipped over beside her to hear if she was praying out loud.

I laid my hands on Bonnie's shoulders, and the power of the Lord fell. She trembled and cried. I took her arms to lift them up, when, suddenly, her body fell back into my arms, with her face toward heaven. She cried, "Thank you, Jesus! I love You, Jesus!" No one in the room had trouble hearing her. She laid on the floor just like a Pentecostal. Her words in English gave way to her heavenly language.

To my dismay, everyone else in the room except Scott fled down the hall to our bedroom and Don had to rescue them. Cautiously they came by, one by one, to watch Bonnie and hear her new language before they slipped out the door. Bonnie was unaware of any of this, however, as she was lost in Jesus and didn't sit up until 2:30 in the morning. Full of joy, she laughed, "I wanted to pray for everyone and everything I could think of, just in case this was a one-time experience and I'd never get another opportunity like this again."

Impetuous Scott was now more anxious than ever to receive the Holy Spirit. He implored us to let him come back the next night to pray again, and although they didn't leave until 4:00 a.m., we said yes. Bonnie made her 7:00 a.m. flight to Boston with a glowing report on her return that she had spent every spare minute in the glory of God, reading her Bible. Along with the experience of speaking in tongues came an intense desire to know everything the Lord had for her in His Word.

The following evening, the power of God came on Scott with such force, he felt as if he were being pressed into the floor. Instead of yielding to the Holy Spirit, he unintentionally resisted. Although he said his jaw was sore the next day, he wasn't discouraged. After the Sunday morning service, Jesus gave him a sweet baptism, and Scott softly spoke in tongues.

The Lord filled Kathy, the Catholic mother of three boys, while she was standing at her kitchen sink. Kathy, who always laughed a lot, remarked, "It only makes sense that that's where God would fill me, because that's where I spend most of my time. I had pictured myself kneeling at the altar in my Catholic church, looking up at Jesus hanging on the cross. Instead, I had my hands in a sink full of dirty dishes, just thanking the Lord for all His blessings, when the Spirit of God came upon me. I knew what to do because of the Bible studies, so I just knelt right there on my kitchen floor and started speaking in tongues."

Kathy and Bob's two-year-old boy, Brucie, had a club foot. His foot turned in so badly he stumbled and fell when he tried to run after his two older brothers. When Kathy learned from the Word of God that God provided healing for His children, Bob and she brought Brucie to our Sunday service after they attended their Catholic church. At the conclusion of our service, she brought Bruce up to Don and showed him the twisted foot.

"No wonder he can't run" Don exclaimed, as he motioned for Brother Shamp. With Don's hand on Brucie's head and Brother Shamp holding Brucie's knee, they prayed. Suddenly, the leg began shaking under Brother Shamp's hands. When the shaking stopped, Brucie's foot and leg were perfectly straight! Kathy stood him on the floor and he took off running.

That night, Kathy, her eyes gleaming with gratitude, reported, "Brucie ran all afternoon, only stopping long enough to shout, 'See, Mamma!' Then he would take off running again." Bob, Brucie's father, didn't speak, but the smile on his tear-soaked face told us how he felt. God had performed a miracle right in front of our eyes.

By now we had all the rows on our side of the church filled and all but one on old Brother Shamp's side, but he was one of the few in the congregation who was happy about it. The church board was even more troubled. Keith and Joanne's Lutheran pastor was troubled as well.

Being thankful and thrilled with the rewarding changes taking place in their lives, Keith and Joanne went to their pastor with the good news. They invited him to attend the Bible study on the Holy Spirit at their home. After they presented him with a *Voice* magazine entitled, *Lutherans and the Baptism in the Holy Spirit,* he said he would try to come to the next meeting.

Bonnie literally jumped up and down with the delightful thought that her pastor could get baptized in the Holy Spirit and the whole church have a mighty revival. It was a pleasant evening when their pastor came to the Bible study. We felt honored. He even made some favorable comments; however, within a few weeks he rejected the Biblical truth of speaking in tongues as the evidence of the baptism in the Holy Spirit.

Soon afterward, their pastor asked them not to teach what they believed in their Sunday School classes. He had a problem with creation being taught as a fact instead of a theory and that the Bible was the infallible Word of God. After his teachers got filled with the Holy Spirit, they couldn't teach the way the pastor believed. It wasn't long until, with sad hearts, they resigned their teaching positions. It didn't dampen their enthusiasm, however, as they wondered, "What will God do next?"

* * *

I was surprised to hear Joyce's voice on the phone when it rang at 9:30 one morning. Everyone knew not to call me before 9:30 a.m., because I wouldn't answer. I had established my prayer time from 8:00 to 9:30 every morning, when I first started praying for the young people several years ago, and I knew if I let phone calls interrupt me, my time with the Lord would disappear. Joyce was a young mother with beautiful red hair, whom I had met a few months earlier on a Welcome Wagon call. She had turned away from God and showed little interest in Him—that is, until she witnessed a horrifying death.

Now she called me with news of a teenager whom the Lord had laid on my heart the day before he came to her home. I had met the young man when he came to watch a baseball game played by my church's young people, and I had taken him home. As I was on my way to make a Welcome Wagon call, the Lord spoke to my heart and said, "Go visit that boy and tell him how to be saved." It was late in the afternoon before I finally got to his house, and no one was there. So sure was I that the Lord had impressed me to visit him, I left a booklet explaining salvation on his doorknob, with a personal note telling him what I felt the Lord had told me.

At Joyce's home the next day, he showed her the tract; they talked about it before he got on his motorcycle for a quick spin. He didn't wear his helmet because he planned to come right back. He ended up in eternity. He hadn't seen the chain stretched across a private dirt road, and he was instantly killed.

When Joyce called me, she begged me to come and take her to church, so she could come back to God. I rushed to her. Upon entering the empty sanctuary, she ran to the altar and wept her way back to a very loving and merciful heavenly Father. We'll have to wait until we get to heaven to know if the boy accepted Jesus before it was too late.

The next call I got from Joyce was at 2:30 in the afternoon several weeks later. She was weeping this time, too, but for a different reason. "Barbara," she stammered, "I've been praying and the Spirit of God is all over me. I'm shaking so hard, I can hardly hold the phone. What shall I do?"

Bursting with joy, I said, "Joyce, that's Jesus. He wants to baptize you. Just channel all that energy you feel into speaking in tongues. You start speaking, and He will give you the utterance." I started speaking in tongues right over the phone, and Joyce did, too. She was still speaking in tongues when we hung up an half-hour later.

I wondered, *What news will this call bring?* when a week later I answered the phone and again heard Joyce's excited voice. "Barbara, guess what?" Before I could guess, she answered, "I just met a doctor's wife—she's the cutest little thing—I know you'll love her. She and her husband are Lutherans, but they are filled with the Holy Spirit. She got so excited when I told her about the Bible study; I got her phone number so you could call her."

After hanging up the phone, I told the Lord, "Jesus, this is too much! I don't feel qualified to talk to a doctor's wife. I'm just a country girl. I'm scared."

When I finally made contact with Mary, she proved to be a very gracious little lady who wasn't sophisticated at all, but a down-home type of person whose nature is to give, nurture, and bless in every way. She asked if she could bring her son with her to the studies. His hunger for God and His Word was unusual for a boy eight years old. The second time they came, God filled Bradley with His Holy Spirit.

CHARISMATIC EXPLOSION

What I didn't know was the important role Dr. Cal and Mary would play in God's plan, because the whole group was going to change dramatically—and soon. One change resulted from the news we got from Larry, the father of the hippies, Ron and Katie.

* * *

After Larry's conversion in our home, he got filled with the Holy Spirit, and, a short time later, he went to the University of Washington district where the hippies hung out, in search of his son, Ron, to tell him about Jesus and invite Ron's wife, Katie, and him to meet us. After days of inquiring, he learned they were living in a neighborhood mostly occupied by hippies.

The tiny house located back off the alley on a steep hill was little more than a shack, a far cry from where Katie grew up in the prestigious Mercer Island home of her father, a prominent doctor. Ron and Katie supported their drug habits by stealing and dealing drugs. It was clear to see they had rebelled against our plastic society (as they called it), using the American flag as a shower curtain.

Larry finally found them, and with all of our prayers and a free meal from Larry, they came to "show us where love was really at." Hippies felt they had found love the rest of the world knew nothing about.

We opened the door, and greeted two of the funkiest hippies you would ever see. Everything on them was dirty, except for Ron's white cap. I later learned was his pride and joy and the only thing he insisted on being clean. It was pulled over to one side with his dark hair sticking out over his forehead and halfway covering his eyes. The rest of his straggly long hair covered his shoulders and back. Katie's strawberry blond hair was long and straight and never let both of her eyes be seen at once. We fell in love with them immediately! They were completely taken off guard by our total acceptance of them.

Before that first evening ended, Don, using the Bible, showed Ron the difference in the camaraderie of the hippie movement he was experiencing and the love of God that we knew. I also learned that Katie was three months pregnant. They let us pray with them before they left, and promised to come to the Bible study on Friday evening. They were overwhelmed when we gave them a baby shower. It was this kind of tangible love that touched their hearts. Nine months later, when their baby son, Sam, was three months old, Katie was ready to give her heart to Jesus, because He gave her the miracles she asked for.

The very day Katie got her miracles, the Spirit of the Lord spoke to my mind and said, "Go to Katie's house today." I called Don at work to get directions from Larry who worked for him. Don, concerned for my safety, cautioned, "Don't get out of the car if you see anyone in the neighborhood who looks dangerous."

I didn't see a soul as I parked in the alley and peered over the bank onto the rooftops of the tiny houses looking as if they had been planted in a row on the side of the hill. I stepped out of my car and wondered how I was going to tell which house was Katie's, when from nowhere two very hippie-looking men stood by a car in front of me. I hadn't even seen the car parked there. Had the Lord blinded my eyes to them, knowing I wouldn't get out of the car if I had seen them?

It was too late now; I was already standing right in front of them. With chills running up my spine, I tried to act casual, managed a weak smile, and asked, "Could you tell me which house Katie lives in?" Pointing, one answered, "She's in that one right down there."

I tried to hide my shock as I approached the door, held open by a garden hose running from a tub under the kitchen sink full of sour water waiting to be siphoned out to the yard. The house reeked of musty incense. Katie clapped and danced on her toes like a three-year-old when she saw me. She proudly placed their darling three-month-old son, Sam, in my arms, and made no apologies for the filthy house or how dirty Sam's clothes and blankets were. Her face was radiant, and I knew she had met Jesus. She giggled with joy and squealed, "I just knew you would come, because Jesus came to me last night!" The story bubbled from her melodious voice amid tears and laughter, as she relived what happened.

Katie went to bed with the pain in her side, there ever since she gave birth to Sam. After Ron fell asleep, Katie prayed, "God, if You are really real like the Barnetts say You are, then I want You to do three things for me."

Katie stopped and told me some of the horrible hellish experiences she had while on LSD, to the point of almost leaping off the top of a building in the University district. She said the terrible fear she lived under resulting from the drugs caused her to be traumatized at the thought of letting Jesus into her heart. She knew she wanted what we had, but she was afraid that Jesus would give her the same terrifying, yet real, spiritual experience she'd had with the devil when she became trapped, with no way out, once LSD had entered her body. Besides plaguing Katie's mind with fear, the more than three hundred "trips" on LSD had also dulled her senses. She could no longer enjoy all the things that brought her happiness as a girl: the singing of a bird, the sound of rain, the beauty of God's creation. I thought to myself, *Maybe that's why she can live in such filth.*

Katie finished telling me her prayer. She said, "God, if You're real, I want You to, one, take away this pain in my side; two, take this fear away and give me peace; and, three, I want to be able to hear the rain on my windowpane again. And, God, don't do any of these until tomorrow." At 11:00 p.m., Katie fell asleep.

At 2:00 a.m. she was suddenly awakened. She rubbed her eyes and looked at the clock. Her first thought was, *It's tomorrow!* She felt her side. The pain was gone! She listened and burst into tears as her ears picked up the sound of rain on the window. Instantly, she felt a deep peace settle over her that only comes from Jesus.

Tears of joy fell from our eyes while I spoke thanks to Jesus for such a beautiful visitation of His grace to His daughter. There together, while I held Sam, Katie knelt at my knee and asked Jesus to be her Savior.

In the course of the conversation that followed, I asked, "Where's Ron?"

Katie answered, matter-of-factly, "Oh, he's out with his friend robbing a house."

Having learned of a family that had gone on vacation, they pulled a truck up to the front door, and planned to break in and take anything they knew they could sell at pawn shops or used furniture stores.

As Katie was telling me the story, a light went on in her mind. Suddenly she realized what a horrible thing they were doing. I reasoned with her that she and Sam could be in danger if this kind of lifestyle continued. When Ron walked in a few minutes later, he seemed upset. Katie, her fingers crossed behind her back, sheepishly asked, "Did everything go as planned?" Both Katie and I breathed a silent prayer of relief when he said, "No, there was a problem," and walked into the bedroom.

Before I left, I sensed that while Katie's heart was opening to Jesus, Ron's was closing. I promised Katie I would ask Larry, her father-in-law, to pick her up for our Friday evening meeting, just in case Ron wasn't willing to come. In that meeting Jesus baptized Katie in the Holy Spirit—what a glorious infilling it was!

There were about twenty of us there, and we decided to stand in a circle and join hands to start the meeting with prayer. I had no sooner taken Sam so Katie was free to join in, when tears started streaming down her face. I passed the baby over to Caroline, a mother of six, took both of Katie's hands in mine and lifted her graceful arms heavenward.

Immediately the power of God, like a stream of soft white clouds, flowed through my hands to hers. I spoke to her through my own tears of joy and said, "Katie, it's Jesus. He's come to fill you right now. Just yield to Him by speaking in tongues." Everyone rejoiced as they heard her praising God in her new language. For some, it was the first time they had ever seen the Lord baptize someone in His Holy Spirit. Everyone felt the glory of His presence.

With Katie's baptism came an irrepressible desire to see all her friends saved. She yearned for knowledge in the Word of God to lead them to Jesus. Many times Katie couldn't sit through the Bible study Don was teaching. Instead, she asked me to go with her to the University of Washington district to witness.

One particular night we were searching for a man named Bill. Katie seemed to know just where to find him, and, sure enough, there he was, slumped down in a heap on a darkened sidewalk at the corner of a building. Although there were hundreds of hippies milling around, no one seemed to notice his pitiful state. We stooped down over him, Katie took his face in her hands and told him she had found Jesus and that He loved him, too. I prayed for Bill, and we saw a spark of life return to his eyes before Katie let his face fall back onto his chest. I hated to leave him there, but Katie assured me he was used to being there. She was sure he would give his heart to Jesus as soon as he wasn't stoned on drugs. We hurried back to the Bible study in time to tell the group about Bill and have them pray for him.

As Ron's heart towards the Lord closed, Katie made a hard decision. She took Sam and moved out. Before she did, we persuaded Ron to talk to Don one last time. The conversation ended with Don's prediction: "Within six weeks Ron will be addicted to heroin." When I closed the door behind Ron that night, I received a spirit of intercession for him like I had years ago for my own brother. It lasted for the next nine months. Incidentally, Ron was injecting himself with heroin in less than six weeks.

Katie wrote Ron a note explaining why she was moving out, and I picked her up one afternoon and delivered her to Keith and Joanne's. Everyone in the group had opened their home to Katie.

The next nine months were full of spiritual trials for Ron. The experiences I had in prayer, interceding on his behalf, let me know the Lord was still dealing with him, and there was a spiritual warfare going on. One day, Katie called me and asked, "Will you go with me to see Ron? I think he is in trouble."

It was dark when we arrived at their house. We decided I should wait in the car while Katie checked to see if Ron would talk to me. Katie returned to the car almost immediately, her shoulders slumped and on the verge of tears. I couldn't imagine what caused her optimistic attitude to change so quickly. She plopped down on the seat beside me and sighed, "There's another woman in my bed." She looked at me with helpless eyes.

I patted her shoulder and asked, "What did you do?"

She responded, "Nothing. I didn't think I should do anything now that I'm a Christian."

We sat silent for a moment as I struggled with my thoughts: *I know how to advise this new Christian, but in my heart I know I've failed to "practice what I preach."* The words I spoke seemed to be for me as much as for Katie, "The Lord doesn't expect you to tolerate this kind of behavior from Ron without letting him know how you feel. If you don't, he'll think you don't care. Your love for him is proven by the fact that you are hurt and upset by his action. Even God says about us that He 'jealously desires the whole of us' (Deuteronomy 5:9). He doesn't want us to have any other gods before Him. Now, do you feel strong enough to go back in there and tell Ron how you feel?"

After we prayed, Katie marched back into the house, jumped up on the table, and screamed above the din of music that rocked the neighborhood, that she was hurt. I got out of the car and started towards the house when

Ron ran out with a club in his hand. Hate filled his eyes and I knew it wasn't Ron, but demons that wanted to kill me. I stood helpless, as Ron rushed at me.

Suddenly he stopped, three feet in front of me, as if he had hit a wall. His hands dropped to his sides, and he spoke in his gentle soft voice that I knew was the real Ron. He told me he really didn't want any woman but Katie. He said he wanted Jesus, but he wasn't ready. He wanted to make it on his own; he was going to put together a band, and then Katie would come back. He accepted my hugs and prayers before he turned with slumped shoulders and walked away.

The next day I had an unusual spiritual experience while praying for Ron. It was as if Jesus let me stand in Ron's behalf and feel the weight of his sins. It was awful! I'll never forget the horror of his sins and how they were destroying him. I pleaded for mercy and began repenting in Ron's behalf and by faith accepted the blood of Jesus to wash them away. I knew Ron still had to pray himself, but something very significant happened in the spirit that day which bonded me to this man who God would someday use to intercede for others.

You can imagine Katie's and my excitement when, after much pleading and coaxing, Ron promised to attend a David Wilkerson meeting with us. We felt David Wilkerson was coming to Seattle just for us. We had given his tracts and books to scores of hippies, and knew they would come to one of his services when they wouldn't come to our fellowship held in a "straight home." Katie knew where to find Ron, when he wasn't at their house where we were supposed to pick him up.

CHARISMATIC EXPLOSION

We found him, wearing much the same outfit he'd worn the first day I met him, except this time he was loaded on heroin—he was barely conscious. He slumped into the back seat and I wondered how we would ever get him out and up the steps to the side balcony where Katie wanted to sit. As the service started, it looked like Ron didn't even know where he was. Katie kept repeating, "It'll be all right," reassuring herself as much as me. Then a miracle happened!

As soon as David Wilkerson stood at the pulpit, Ron was delivered of the effects of the heroin he had injected prior to our picking him up. His eyes popped opened, and they were clear. He heard every word of the sermon. He went forward at the altar call. When we took him home, he invited us in while he flushed his remaining heroin supply—which I later learned was worth $2,000—down the toilet. He said he wanted to move in with Katie at Keith and Joanne's. Don and I were skeptical, but Joanne was willing to try it. So, Ron had a new home, but not for long.

Don had the ugly task of telling Ron he had to leave, when he refused not to have beer and drugs in the house. Shortly afterwards, Katie realized it might be a while before Ron would really be willing to walk with God. With her parents' support, she found a little apartment and got a job delivering mail. It was nine months before we heard again from Ron.

In the meantime, the entire Bible study changed—because of a phone call.

Chapter Eight

One Door Closed, Another Opened

"...He that openeth and no man shutteth; and shutteth and no man openeth."
(Revelation 3:7)

    A little after 11:00 p.m., late one Saturday night, the phone rang. Don was putting the finishing touches on his Sunday School lesson, a complex study on the Seventy Weeks of Daniel, which he'd worked on for many weeks.

    Drying my hands from washing potatoes, I picked up the phone and heard the chairman of our church's deacon board ask to speak to Don. I thought, *Perhaps the pastor has had another heart attack.* He had been fully recovered for some time now, but said he appreciated Don's ministry so much he asked him to continue with the adult class. The pastor had, quite often from the pulpit, told the congregation how much he loved us and was thankful for all the souls we were getting saved and filled and adding to the church. He even said how much he appreciated my work with the young people. He was such a loving man, and had our love and respect. I soon knew the pastor was okay by what I heard Don say into the phone.

"Brother B, when is this in effect?"

(*pause*) "...Well, I've studied for many weeks for this lesson. Do you think calling at close to midnight before I'm scheduled to teach in the morning is proper notice?"

(*pause*) "...Brother B, could you tell me why this action has been taken? What did I do wrong?"

(*pause*) "...Well, Brother B, even in the world when they fire someone who has worked for them for seven years, they give him an explanation."

(*pause*) "...If the pastor wanted to teach the class, why didn't he come to me and tell me? I would have been happy to step down. However, the last time I spoke with him he said he was thankful that I was teaching the class."

(p*ause*) "...Brother B, what are you going to tell my class? Many of our new converts will be there in the morning. What will they think? Can I at least come and tell the class goodbye? After all, I've been their teacher for seven years, and I love them and they love me."

(*pause*) "...Well, Brother B, I want you to know I'll always love you. Goodbye."

Don hung up the phone and went back to his lesson before he realized he didn't have to finish it. I finished preparing the roast for Sunday dinner. We sat at the dining table, stared at one another in disbelief, dazed by the suddenness of it all. What would the class think? Should we try to call the new ones and tell them ahead of time? No, it was too late. They would find out in the morning. Should we go and just sit there? They won't let us say anything. They wouldn't give a reason; they said they didn't need a reason—they didn't owe us an explanation.

It would be easier for the pastor if we weren't there. We didn't want to cause a church split. What would we tell our kids in the morning? We always went to Sunday School. They had never missed. What would they think? How shall we tell them? What about the young people? Could I go tell them goodbye? At least the Youth for Christ meetings we had helped start in the high school would give our fifteen-year-old daughter Christian fellowship, now that we wouldn't be involved with the church. The sorrow inside me turned to tears and streamed down my face.

No sooner had the Sunday School class been dismissed, when Scott came bursting through our door. He said, "No explanation was given to the class. The pastor was shaking so badly he could hardly teach. I was concerned he might have another heart attack right there."

I wondered why Scott was so excited. Maybe it was because of what he had recently experienced with his own pastor, or maybe it was because of the little potluck fellowship he was going to that afternoon. Soon we were besieged with calls and visits from the members of the class, wanting to know what happened. Don told them he couldn't give them an explanation, because he wasn't given one. He encouraged them to support their pastor.

(Three weeks later we received an invitation to the pastor's home for dinner. He apologized to Don for the way things were handled. He admitted it was his responsibility as pastor, not a board member's, to come to Don. He was grieved in his spirit with the board's decision and actions. Before we left, the two men embraced and expressed a mutual love and respect for one another. Just a few days later, that beloved pastor died of a heart attack.)

Scott, hurrying to the potluck fellowship, announced the news of Don's dismissal. They called and invited us to join them at Lyle and Caroline's home. Lyle and Caroline lived in a rambler just a few miles from us with their six children. They were Lutherans. Lyle, a lawyer, had received the Holy Spirit through contact with the Full Gospel Businessmen's Fellowship. He had been offered a position with the State and was soon moving to Olympia, the state capital.

Until now we had only been with these people in our Bible studies and worship meetings. The excited voices Don heard behind Scott's on the phone seemed to pour healing oil over Don's devastated soul. Yet, neither of us knew, when Don said "yes" to Scott's invitation, we were about to step into what God had prepared us for all our lives.

* * *

We arrived at 2:30 with what was left of my Sunday dinner after feeding our children. The room was full of talk about how none of us had a church home: Bob and Kathy had dropped out of the Catholic church; Keith and Joanne, Scott and Bonnie, Lyle and Caroline were all out of their Lutheran church; Bob and Mary, the Baptists, and Larry, Ron's father, had attended our church just for the adult class Don taught. By the time we finished the meal, we were all one-hundred-percent agreed—we would start a church!

Simultaneously, their voices rang out with the question, "Don, will you be our pastor?" Bonnie bounced up and down, Scott beamed, while Mary's gleeful laugh filled

ONE DOOR CLOSED, ANOTHER OPENED

the room. Scott and Bonnie said we could use their home for Sunday services. Even though their house was still under construction, the living and dining room would work fine for a sanctuary. At this time, the walls had just been sheet rocked. We could use all the other rooms for Sunday School classes for the children, twenty-nine in all. Joy swelled in our hearts as we discussed how wonderful it would be to give the children opportunity early in their lives to know God and His Word.

It was getting dark as we gathered in Lyle and Caroline's living room and stood in a circle, all twenty-seven of us joining hands to praise and worship Jesus. That's when it happened. I was caught totally off guard. Suddenly, the Spirit of the Lord came upon me and said, "Now is the time, and this is the people I wish to speak to."

It had been seven years since I had said no, and now God was giving me a second chance to be His mouthpiece. I remembered how I had recently wrestled with this issue in prayer, until I'd promised God, "The next time You anoint me with a message in tongues and interpretation or prophecy, I will yield to You."

I trembled under the power of God, and uncontrollable tears flowed down my cheeks. I could hardly stand. The anointing came upon Keith; he started interceding, praying in tongues. A conversation between God and me began in my mind, so loud and clear I was afraid everyone in the room could hear. I told the Lord, "Okay, I'll give the tongues, but use Keith to give the interpretation."

The answer came from God, "No! You are going to give both. Keith is interceding for you."

"Okay, Lord...."

I began speaking out in tongues. *It definitely sounds like a message, instead of a prayer,* I thought, *That's a relief.* Everyone in the room became silent with reverence at the thought that God Himself was speaking to us. The message continued in tongues, but my mind went completely blank. I prayed, "Lord give me the English words. I won't have anything to say when the tongues stop." The tongues stopped and my mind was still completely blank. I had nothing to say! What should I do? The Lord said, "Speak!"

I said, "Lord, I have nothing to say!"

Again, He said, "Speak!"

So I opened my mouth, and with a deep breath said, "Behold...."

After that first word, the whole message from God tumbled out of my mouth as if it were being spoken by someone else. When the message ended, someone handed me a tissue while everyone else praised the Lord.

I wish I could remember what the Lord told us that day, but when God uses me to give a message, often I can't remember what is said, as I'm busy yielding to the Holy Spirit. And since the words don't originate in my mind, I can remember only the parts I manage to hear. The essence of the message to this newly begotten church was that God Himself had moved in our lives to bring us together, and He had worked in Don's and my lives to prepare us for this day, as it was the beginning of something He desired to do in His people in these last days.

Each of us found a place to sit, and Don spoke with an anointing from the Holy Spirit. By the spirit of revelation, he laid out God's plan for our church. All the aspects of the church began unfolding, and with each one, praises escaped from all our hearts.

We would have Sunday School classes where the children would learn the Bible in a systematic way. Their worship times would give them opportunity to get filled with the Holy Spirit and also minister to one another. We would plan outreaches for children so they could win their own neighborhoods to the Lord.

A Christian School with Spirit-led chapel services and Spirit-filled teachers was part of the plan. We'd have a teen center and a halfway house where drug addicts could be rehabilitated, plus a Bible school that would offer only Bible and Bible-related subjects.

Our desire was services full of body ministry where every member would be involved in ministry, including music, praying for the sick, and operating the gifts of the Spirit. It would be a church where people could come to get filled with the Holy Spirit and learn about *The Unfolding Revelation of God*.

As soon as Don spoke these words, the Lord gave me a revelation about this very important truth in God's Word. He didn't want us to just teach people the truth about the nature of God and who Jesus is from the Bible, but He wanted to bring us into experiences in Christ that would cause our relationship with Him to be an unfolding revelation of who God is (Colossians 1:26-27). I shared this with the group, but I had no idea what the depth of the revelation was or what we would go through for it to become a reality in our lives.

Keith picked up the guitar and to our delighted surprise, led in songs of praise to the Lord. We hadn't known Keith played the guitar and sang in an easy country style. He blessed all of us. It was after midnight before the children, who had fallen asleep on the floor, were gathered up and the last goodbye was said.

That night, just after Don fell asleep, I asked the Lord, "What do You want us to call Your new church?" He spoke the name in my mind, and with each word came an explanation of why He wanted that word included. I nudged Don and said, "Honey, remind me in the morning to tell you what the Lord just told me the name of our church should be."

He said, "Well, I'm awake now. You might as well tell me." I knew he couldn't wait until morning.

"Community Chapel and Bible Training Center. Community, because He wants it to have the closeness of a family. Chapel, because He wants it to be a warm place of worship. And Bible Training Center, because He wants His people to be trained—not just learning the Word, but experiencing and becoming the Word."

Don responded, "Perfect! I hope all the people will agree." With that, we both fell asleep.

* * *

Before we had our first worship service as a church, the new Saturday Bible studies on *The Book of Revelation* and *End-time Events* began attracting college students. One Saturday, shortly after the study began, I was surprised and pleased to see a nice-looking blond young man walk around the side of the house to join us in the back yard. He was alone, but must have known that we had moved the event to our back yard patio after outgrowing our living room. Tom disappeared at the close of the study, but I couldn't forget the grin that never left his face. I wondered if we would ever see him again.

Sure enough, the following Friday Tom was back, with his former high school buddy, Mike. That night we learned that Tom and Mike had both recently been filled with the Holy Spirit. Tom was in his junior year at Pacific Lutheran University in Tacoma, and Mike was a senior at the University of Washington in Seattle.

In just a few short weeks, when the fall term opened at PLU, God used Tom to start a fresh wave of His Spirit on that campus. The Friday following the semester's opening day, Tom burst through our door, interrupting the meeting that was already underway, with exciting news. Jesus was filling students with the Holy Spirit, and Tom brought Dave with him to prove it. Dave was even taller than Tom, with a smile that reached from ear to ear and a clear baritone voice. God's Spirit was spreading across the campus like wildfire, drawing others besides Dave to Tom's off-campus apartment where he lived with his wife, Mary. "We'll have at least one carload to bring over to the Sunday service," they laughed, their faces aglow with the glory of God.

A shout of praise went up from everyone in the room, and I said, "Oh, good! All of you can have dinner at our house and stay over for the evening service, too." The campus was thirty miles away. "It's no problem for me to slide a turkey in the oven before we leave for church in the morning, and it will be done and waiting for us when we arrive home. I've had plenty of practice feeding large groups of people." The college students, hungry for a home-cooked meal, happily accepted.

* * *

There was enough of the presence of God to fill the largest cathedral as we began the service Sunday morning in Scott and Bonnie's unfinished home. Nobody minded that the pulpit was a cardboard box that had delivered the folding chairs we had purchased with the first offering—we were in the sanctuary of the Lord! Every chair was filled, as two carloads of college students found seats among the hippies and families, with children seated on the floor.

Thankful for the experience I'd had at the Mission, I led the song service, as no one else knew any choruses. Keith played his guitar to keep me in tune as everyone learned the songs. Right away we decided to take up another offering for songbooks. Little Bradley, the doctor's son, practiced the organ tirelessly so he could be good enough to play.

How can I describe the excitement and thrill everyone felt as we experienced God's Spirit in our brand new church? Joyful praise accompanied each song. No one wanted to stop singing one song long enough to learn another. We sang "There's Power in the Blood" over and over at every service for months. In fact, one man came to us and asked, "Do we have to learn any more songs? We know three now, and they are wonderful! We don't need any more."

Excitement mounted each time the Lord used me to give a message in tongues and interpretation. The newly

ONE DOOR CLOSED, ANOTHER OPENED

spirit-filled Christians would exclaim how the words and inflections in the message in tongues matched the words in English. They began analyzing their own prayer language so much that I became concerned they were getting their eyes off the Giver and onto the gift. However, their wise new pastor decided to wait and see if the problem wouldn't correct itself before he said anything to bring a balance. Sure enough, before long praying in tongues was just as normal to them as praying in English.

Very quickly we outgrew Scott and Bonnie's home. I was now feeding as many as thirty students on Sunday afternoons. Actually, they started coming on Friday evenings with their sleeping bags and would stay over until after the Sunday evening service, waiting until the last minute to tear themselves away from the prayer time after the sermon, and rush back to their dorms by curfew. Thankfully, the Lord had added a number of new families to the group, so almost all of us had college students sleeping on our living room floors every weekend. The only exception was Cal, the doctor, and his wife, Mary; their home was full of hippies, not just on the weekends, but during the week, too, because God started saving the hippies.

Time and again, God instantly delivered the hippies from their drug habits when we laid hands on them and prayed. Many times they came to the meetings so under the influence of drugs they had to be helped out of the car. Often, God's power flowed through us, and He allowed me to perceive the demons in them. With the authority of Jesus we rebuked the demons and watched them come out of their victims and flee, fearing the presence of Jesus that filled the room.

THE TRUTH SHALL SET YOU FREE

Once sobered and in their right minds, these misguided and disillusioned men and women accepted Jesus as their Savior. Often, the Lord filled the hippies with the Holy Spirit immediately, giving them His power to live their new lives. How could we take these baby Christians back down to the University district and drop them off on the street corner to slump down on the sidewalk and try to sleep leaning against a building? That's why Cal and Mary took in many of the men. Their home became as full as their hearts, helping these men adjust to a new life in Jesus.

As soon as Cal and Mary came to a Sunday service at Scott and Bonnie's and saw how crowded our "church" was, they offered to complete their unfinished daylight basement so the whole recreation room could be used for the church services. It had its own entry, plus a bathroom, extra bedroom, and laundry area; we wouldn't have to go upstairs to their living quarters, except for Sunday School classes for the children. We were reluctant to accept their generous offer, realizing the added strain it would put on their family. Besides their son Bradley and two younger daughters, they had four ex-hippies living with them. But Cal insisted that the project would be a good experience for the new converts, and he wanted to finish the basement anyway, so the plans got underway.

In the meantime, with the arrival of our new songbooks, Bradley learned to play a new song on his organ at home and teach it to Cal. On Sunday, Cal was prepared to teach it to the congregation. To my great relief, it wasn't too long until I no longer had to lead the song service.

ONE DOOR CLOSED, ANOTHER OPENED

On our first Christmas, as a gift to the congregation, Don and I presented them with a communion service set. We had our first communion service on New Year's Eve. The ladies were happy to make the bread from the recipe given in the Word of God, which we continued to do even after our congregation grew to over two thousand members. That particular service was such a blessing that the students from PLU decided to partake of communion several times a week over on the campus.

Already Don found himself fulfilling the prophecy spoken over him in the Latter Rain revival, to teach the newborn so they wouldn't be "turned aside." I can't remember all the different ditches these zealous, newly Spirit-filled students wandered into, but for a while it seemed every weekend when they came for the services we learned of something new they were sure was "God's leading."

But it was better to have to put out wildfire than have no fire at all. It was an awesome experience beholding the fire of the Holy Spirit sweep through the Northwest, gathering people from all walks of life—families, hippies, and college students—and placing them in His body, the church. It was as if the book of Acts happened all over again.

On the PLU campus, God used Tom to reach one type of student and a man named Kristian to reach another. Kristian had been Spirit-filled for seven years and was in his senior year when he heard about what God was doing in our newly formed church. His floor of the men's dormitory housed some of the more radical and liberal students at PLU who, by their own testimony, would have never opened to the Gospel from Tom, who represented the legalistic side of the campus.

By spring of that year, Kristian had persuaded Lanny and Rick to accompany him to a Friday evening service, now being held at Cal and Mary's almost completed "Chapel." The room was already packed. Lanny, a blond man who looked too young to be even out of high school, also brought a girl friend. When I spoke with Lanny after the service, I thought he was a junior high school student. I had no idea that in a few years he would be my son-in-law.

After that service, Kristian's room in the dorm became a prayer room where many students accepted Jesus as their Savior and were filled with the Holy Spirit. It was estimated in that year alone that well over fifty students on the PLU campus received the Holy Spirit with the evidence of speaking in tongues, and of those fifty, twenty-five made Community Chapel their church home.

Besides our services and Bible studies, God used the Full Gospel Businessmen's publications and Dr. Dorenfield's testimony and book, *Have You Received the Holy Spirit?* to influence the students. Somehow Dorenfield's book found its way to the campus of the University of Puget Sound, where God reaped a harvest of souls, including a man gifted in music. George eventually became our anointed music ministry director.

Also, I must tell you about a very special little person I saw in the meeting one Sunday morning. I turned around in my seat to see a chubby, freckle-faced, darling redhead boy about eight-years-old, bouncing up and down in the narrow aisle with his arms raised and the glory of God radiating from his face. Joey had reason to be happy.

ONE DOOR CLOSED, ANOTHER OPENED

The Lord saved him and filled him with the Holy Spirit, and also just healed his father, who had been dying in the hospital. Here's what happened:

Keith learned that Joey's father, Jerome, whom he had known from Wisconsin, was in the hospital dying from kidney failure. The doctors had discovered that both his kidneys were diseased and beyond medical help. Jerome wasn't expected to live beyond a few more days when Keith learned of Jerome's plight. He went to the hospital, laid his hand on Jerome, and prayed for God to heal him. In utter amazement, the doctors said Jerome had new kidneys. He was made completely well., and at the same time delivered from alcoholism.

Little Joey was so thrilled that Jesus had healed his daddy, he gave his heart to Jesus and came to church with Keith and Joanne, even without his parents. But that didn't dampen Joey's faith. When I saw him, he was asking Jesus to save his family. Neither was he discouraged when it took a few weeks before Jerome and Joanne both had mighty conversions and the Lord baptized them in the Holy Spirit.

Jerome's countenance was as radiant as his son's. He put all his energies into serving his Savior and Healer. Because of his own suffering, Jerome had an insatiable desire to see other pain-filled lives healed. God entrusted him with a powerful gift of healing. As his ministry progressed, the Lord added the gift of the word of knowledge, which enabled Jerome to know, by the Spirit and without being told, what ailments people suffered from. The healing ministry, however, didn't come without testings and trials.

THE TRUTH SHALL SET YOU FREE

One day we received a call informing us that a car Jerome was repairing had fallen on top of him and crushed his chest. With supernatural strength, his wife lifted the car up and got Jerome out and into the house. Jerome was determined not to seek medical help, but trust God for his complete healing, even though the intense pain made breathing unbearable. After days of pain, his faith gave him a miraculous healing from the Lord. Later he developed a cancer on his face that the doctors said would cost him his nose if they could save him at all. Again Jerome put the matter before the Lord. With much prayer, after many months, Jerome was healed by Jesus.[2]

Eventually, Jerome traveled as far as Europe and Africa where the Lord healed hundreds through his ministry.

* * *

One Sunday night service just a few weeks after Jerome and Joanne came to the Lord, I noticed out of the corner of my eye a girl, with straight dark hair covering part of her face and falling over her shoulders, sitting about two-thirds of the way back and across the aisle from where I sat on the front row. I guessed her to be in her early twenties. She pressed against the wall as though she were hoping to hide in it. It was evident that she didn't want to be there, hearing what she was hearing about the love of God. Her anger manifest in the handful of kleenex she was wadding up and throwing on the floor piece by piece. At the close of the sermon, the Lord spoke very clearly in my mind and said, "Walk back to that girl, take her by the hand and bring her up to the front row; kneel down with her and pray. Don't say a single word to her. Just do it."

ONE DOOR CLOSED, ANOTHER OPENED

Immediately I turned, walked back to Judy, took her by the hand and walked her without resistance to the front row of chairs. As I knelt, she knelt. No sooner had her knees touched the floor when the power of God shot down through both of us and we began shaking. I started praying in tongues, and within minutes Judy was praying in her new language, too, for the first time. God just baptized her in the Holy Spirit!

I don't know how long we stayed there praying and crying, but I knew Judy would never be the same again, because the Lord had allowed me to see the horrible cloud of demons that surrounded her life. I knew it wasn't me, but a heavenly warrior angel—to which I had grown accustomed—that spoke through me in a language those demons of hate and anger understood, and commanded them back to their chief who had given them their assignment.

> *Pondering this later, I reasoned the Lord must have given me the understanding of what the angel spoke through me to teach me how to deal with demons. If the angel would have spoken through me in English, perhaps Judy would have been frightened, being a brand new Christian.*

When Judy and I finally got up off our knees and sat next to each other, I saw that her countenance was wonderfully different. Although her face was wet with tears, her eyes had been washed clear of all those ugly demons, and the fresh glow about her caused me to feel as if we were sitting in a beautiful flower garden after the rain.

THE TRUTH SHALL SET YOU FREE

The fragrance of Jesus lingered as I learned that Judy was a friend of Katie's, having grown up together on Mercer Island.

After taking drugs which resulted in getting hepatitis, Judy had tried to give her heart to Jesus in her Lutheran church, but no one there told her the plan of salvation. Jesus had reached down anyway and healed Judy of hepatitis. When she came to our service that night, it was after she had spent many months in bed with the illness.

From that night on, Judy had such a compassion for souls that everywhere she went she told people about Jesus. She had a fearlessness, too, that allowed her to press right past all demonic walls and get into a person's heart. She went with Katie and me to the University district to witness, as well as on her own and with others. Only heaven will reveal how many souls are there because of Judy.

* * *

In the middle of the next week we heard the alarming news that Ron, Katie's husband, had been arrested and was in jail. Ron had become a heroin addict. Ron and a friend had been stopped for reckless driving by the State Patrol, who in turn found a kilo of marijuana in the vehicle.

Two weeks later, Mary called, speaking in hushed tones and overcome with emotion. "You're not going to believe this," she whispered, "but Ron is sitting at my kitchen table."

ONE DOOR CLOSED, ANOTHER OPENED

The miserable life he had been living came crashing in on him while Ron was in jail. He realized he had reaped the wages of his sins, having lost everything—his health, his wife, his son, his freedom. He hit bottom. Ron said he felt the presence of Jesus come into his cell. When Ron spoke the name of Jesus, he surrendered his life to Him. Instantly his mind was clear, his body was healed, and he was a new creature in Christ Jesus! All the hatred, anger, bitterness, and desire for drugs were gone.

His whole appearance and countenance were so changed that Mary did not know who he was, even though she had seen him many times before. His hair was short and he was well-groomed, with kind eyes full of peace. His voice was soft and tender. Mary invited Ron to stay for dinner and attend the evening service. He cried all through the sermon, and afterward received the Holy Spirit. It was glorious for everyone.

Soon after Ron's conversion, Katie and he tirelessly told their story in schools, clubs, and churches. At a retreat for teenage girls, Katie and I felt the presence of Jesus as we entered the crowded room with many girls sitting on the floor. It was as if Jesus was there like a blanket, wrapped around each one. We knew God was going to meet the spiritual hunger evident on many faces.

Katie's voice was soft and warm as she explained the difference between the two spiritual worlds she had experienced—the horrible darkness the devil led her into with over three hundred LSD trips causing fears, nightmares, filth, sleepless nights, and a tormented mind; and the wonderful joy and peace that living in the light of Jesus brings. She relived her conversion and her baptism in

THE TRUTH SHALL SET YOU FREE

the Holy Spirit with the great advantage of now being able to pray in tongues.

As Katie finished speaking, one girl stood and said, "I want to receive the Holy Spirit. Will you pray with me?" I had to respond. The girl trembled as she felt the presence of Jesus. I explained to her what was happening and encouraged her to praise Jesus out loud. She opened her mouth and began speaking in tongues. Tears streamed down the cheeks of her friend. I slipped my other arm around her and said, "That's Jesus; just praise Him in your new language; He is giving it to you right now."

Just as I finished that sentence, I felt a strong tap on my shoulder. It was the assistant director. He ordered me to meet him in the hall. The director, in turn, took me by the shoulders and ushered me out of the room and down the stairs. He commanded us to leave at once.

As we approached the door, a young lady ran up to me and threw her arms around me. She said, "I am Pastor —'s daughter. Daddy said to tell you he's so thankful you came! He is Spirit-filled, but he can't say much because of his position, but he has been praying for something like this to happen. You were able to do what he has wanted to do. He wouldn't dare come and thank you himself, so he asked me to. I'm Spirit-filled, too!" Katie and I left skipping for joy because we knew the Holy Spirit hadn't departed just because we were forced to. We got to reap in joy what that pastor had sown in tears (Psalm 126:5).

Ron and Katie accepted an invitation from a group of parents and educators who had formed a committee to see what could be done to keep their children and other young people off drugs. Ron's answer to the problem wasn't well-received, because it required the adults to do something about their own lives instead of building more playfields and forming more clubs.

After finishing their testimonies, Ron's solution made me give thanks to the Lord for what He had done in Ron's heart in such a short period of time. He told that group of adults that they couldn't expect their children not to smoke when they did themselves. He said, "You can't expect your children not to party all night, get drunk, and have illicit sex when you do. The only difference between you and them is they have access to drugs as well as alcohol."

He spoke with kindness, and in a soft voice pleaded with them to let Jesus change them as He had changed him—then their desire would be gone for the lifestyle they were living in front of their children. One lady stood, and as a spokesperson for the group responded, "We are adults and have earned the right to drink, smoke, and party if we choose." And with that, she thanked us for coming and dismissed us from the meeting. After that experience, Ron and Katie decided their time was better spent talking to those who knew they needed a Savior, even if it was one-on-one instead of groups.

* * *

Our little chapel in the doctor's basement was bursting with activity. Our services were so packed, crowds remained outside. On more than one occasion, demon-possessed souls stood outside and prayed to the devil, asking him to confuse the speaker and the minds of the listeners, but the power of God set the pray-ers free instead, and they wept their way to Jesus.

One tall young man with dark brown hair, a high school drop-out, lived in a patch of woods that adjoined a beachfront park not far from our meetings. Al wasn't part of the hard-core hippie community of the University district, but he was a leader among young, local drug users. When Al came to us, his eyes were wild from the effects of speed. He couldn't sit still for a minute, so he paced back and forth and in and out of the doorway, chewing frantically on a big wad of gum.

Mary, full of Jesus' love, stuck right with Al, who, after the service, gave his heart to Jesus and was filled with the Holy Spirit. Now sitting peacefully with a glow from Jesus and shining eyes, Al told me why he and his twelve-year-old sister were living in the woods.

Al's father and mother moved to Japan right after the war, starting an export-import business. Some time after Al's little sister, April, was born, their mother's mental health failed, rendering her incapable of caring for her own children. After Al and April came to Seattle to live with their aunt, Al got messed up on drugs, took his little sister, and camped out in the nearby woods.

Almost panicky, I asked, "Al, where is your little sister right now? Does your father know where you are living?" Up until now he hadn't considered that they couldn't live that way forever. When I spoke with their father, Ben, in Japan, he asked if I would try to find a home for April and he would fly to Seattle to take care of all the financial arrangements.

When Al brought April to meet me, I wasn't prepared for what I saw. This twelve-year-old was already a stunning 5'6" tall girl with beautiful thick dark brown hair halfway down her back. Underneath the sloppy jeans and oversized shirt was a shy and apprehensive little girl who didn't want to change her lifestyle, but felt pressured into it. She was indifferent as to where she wanted to live, so it was up to me. I had only three days before her father would arrive.

That afternoon, when I discussed the matter with our daughter Carolyn, she said, " Mom, I'm willing to share my room with April." I turned so she couldn't see the tears well up in my eyes. I hadn't even thought about the possibility of April living with us. Our family unanimously agreed to invite April to live with us if she could accept certain house rules, one of which was "no drugs." We realized that only the Spirit of the Lord could change April's heart and give her a desire for Him. We couldn't insist that she live as if she were born-again.

Three days later, it was a delighted father who knocked on our door with April in a darling red plaid dress and black slippers her father had bought her that day. I felt so sorry for her as she sat on our sofa so straight and proper. She was a beautiful girl, but much more comfortable—in her present state of mind—in the sloppy jeans and sandals she wore in the woods. I later learned April's willingness to live with us was only because of her father's ultimatum, "If you don't accept the Barnett's offer, I'll put you in a home for girls."

Two weeks after April joined our family we took a much-needed vacation to Disneyland. En route, in Don's brother's church in Boise, April responded to an altar call and accepted Jesus as her Savior. We were ecstatic.

THE TRUTH SHALL SET YOU FREE

April, full of energy, with influence over her peers, soon brought her girlfriends to church. One was the daughter of a Nazarene pastor who occasionally visited our services after he witnessed the difference the baptism in the Holy Spirit made in his daughter Cathy's life. After being in our praise-filled services, this pastor concluded the reason for all the joy radiating from every face was because Acts 1:8 was experienced daily—"You shall have power after the Holy Spirit comes upon you and you shall be My witnesses." It was true; our church was full of excited new Christians who carried their Bibles everywhere they went, winning souls to Jesus.

In an attempt to get Al's life stabilized, we persuaded his father to fund Al's admittance into a Teen Challenge center in Los Angeles. Al agreed. When he returned to Seattle six months later, he began dating Cathy, the Nazarene pastor's daughter and April's best friend. They were married by her father and attended his church on Sundays and ours on Friday evenings.

On the 4th of July, fourteen months after they were married, Al and Cathy, who was five months pregnant, were hit by a drunk driver. Cathy was killed instantly, and Al was in critical condition with head and back injuries. Judy, full of compassion because of her bout with hepatitis, was like a big sister to Al and lovingly devoted many months to Al's recovery.

Judy wasn't the only one who gave unselfishly of her time and resources. I remember one college student in particular, whose constant loving compassion for children compelled him to the grade school playgrounds early every morning. Before school started, Mike stood by the fence and told Bible stories to the children who

ONE DOOR CLOSED, ANOTHER OPENED

crowded around him. His faithful witness was rewarded each time a child asked Jesus into his heart.

Another brother in the Lord gave his car to someone who didn't have transportation to work. He said, "I don't need a car, because I can ride my bike to work."

But we were about to witness sacrificial giving unparalleled to anything Don and I had ever seen, as God moved our budding church along at a fast pace.

Chapter Nine

"Pastor, Please Let Me Give"

"Except the Lord build the house, they labour in vain that build it."
(Psalm 127:1)

Cal and Mary's home was bursting at the seams with crowds at every worship service. We needed our own building—but how?

"Jesus," I prayed, "We have no money for a building, no property, no credit. No bank anywhere will loan us any money. What should we do?" We needed a miracle, and that's what we got.

I drove up Eighth Avenue South on my way home from the grocery store, something I'd done hundreds of times in the past twelve years since we had lived in that neighborhood. For some reason I had never really noticed the small farmhouse sitting off to the right on almost five acres of fenced pasture land with a few fruit trees towards the street.

This time, my head spun around as I drove past the driveway and in my mind I heard the words, "Go, ask them if they want to sell their farm." I drove on a few more blocks before I pulled into a driveway and turned around. I thought, *If that was the Lord, I better do what He said; and if it wasn't, then it won't hurt to have them say no.*

I got out of the car, walked boldly up to the front door, and knocked. *What should I say,* I wondered. Before I had a chance to worry about it, the door cracked open and a medium-sized lady in her fifties looked at me with questioning eyes. I said, "Hello. I'm Barbara, and I live up the street on 194th. This might sound a little strange, but I was wondering if you have considered selling your property here."

The troubled look faded from her face, she opened the door a little wider, and said, "As a matter of fact, my husband and I just decided three days ago to put it on the market." I was beside myself with excitement at the possibility of building our church on a piece of property large enough to allow for expansion and within walking distance of our home.

We purchased the whole parcel, they carried the contract at 5 1/4% interest, and gave us the deed to the property one section at a time, as it was paid for, allowing us to purchase the first section next to the road with our down payment and receive the deed to it so we could start building on that portion. If for some reason we couldn't pay off the rest of the loan, we wouldn't lose the church building, because we would own that much land free and clear. Not only that, we could rent out the house, too, and the rent money would make our $278 a month payment. You can imagine how we rejoiced in the Lord, because we knew it was He who put in their hearts to sell us their farm in the perfect location for our church.

"PASTOR, PLEASE LET ME GIVE"

Now, I thought, *With the deed to a piece of property and two thousand dollars left over for construction, surely a bank will loan us the money to build our church.* I was wrong. With no promise of a loan, Don started drawing up the plans. In our past daydreams of having a Bible college, we had researched the cheapest and easiest structures to build, so now even that knowledge came in handy.

With Don's already pressed schedule, driving a hundred miles round-trip to work every day, preparing and preaching three sermons a week, plus two Bible studies, he somehow managed to complete the blueprints for our little church that would cost $74,000, if everyone pitched in and volunteered to do most of the work. But where would we get that much cash?

The Lord knew there were no rich people in our congregation mostly made up of college students, ex-hippies and drug addicts, and families most of which had at least three children. Don and I were about the oldest members, at ages 38 and 36. We had no savings. We had been giving every extra cent, besides our tithe. The only thing we had was our home, which could clear $15-20,000. We decided to sell and rent an apartment. We reasoned, *"It will at least get us started on the building and maybe when that money is gone, God will cause more cash to come in. If not, we'll just build as we can."* Don called a special meeting for Saturday night to inform the people.

As we walked through the door, the ones who had arrived before us were already praying. Early on we had taught and set the example of praying before the service, so now, even though this was a business meeting, the people were on their knees seeking God and His will. The presence of the Lord was so sweet it was with hesitation Don finally started the meeting. There were exactly 47 adults present.

Don began by recapping what had happened so far, and conveyed our plan to the people. Immediately after he asked everyone to pray that the Lord would cause our home to sell quickly, so we could get the foundation poured before the weather turned cold and rainy, a single girl stood to her feet. "Pastor Don, please let me give," she proclaimed through tears. "I don't have much except a few dishes and pots and pans that I had when I was a hippie. I will sell them and give the money to the building fund."

We all wiped tears from our eyes. Next a young wife stood and said, "Everyone knows I'm married, so I don't need my engagement ring. I'll sell it and give the money for the building."

A man stood and said, "I have an insurance policy I can cash. It's worth $4,000; I'll give that."

All at once there were two or three people standing at a time, each anxious to give. The room filled with the sounds of laughter and cries of joy. Don and I sat in awe.

Someone had a boat to sell. One family agreed to sell their second car. Others gave their entire savings. One couple gave the $700 saved for college. A businessman raised his hand and said, "I'm working on a business deal that will close soon and should net $10,000; I'll give it."

These people were actually sad when they couldn't find anything else to give. Even the children volunteered to give their toys and allowances. Don hadn't asked for anything from anyone! Don and I had never witnessed anything like this.

To our absolute amazement, before the evening ended, those forty-seven adults had given enough to complete the building! We would soon have a chapel to hold 150 people to start, but could be easily expanded to twice the length, plus a balcony. We would have a foyer with restrooms and a small office, as well as a row of classrooms for Sunday School. There were no frills.

The most difficult part of the building project was placing the large arched beams. They had to be fastened together at their peaks, which was forty-two feet in the air. Fearless Al rode the crane up and bolted each plate on the huge glu-lams. All the experience I had in building our own home was now needed to get the best buys on materials, and help assist the volunteers who worked on the building at all hours of the day.

Don and I were disappointed when all attempts to sell our home failed, even after listing it with the realtors. Finally, we took it off the market, resigning ourselves to the possibility that the Lord, for His own reasons, didn't want us to sell it. Perhaps it would have been too much of a strain on David at that time in his life, having been forced to quit attending classes at school and be tutored at home. He no longer could get from class to class or manage on his own. More than ever, he needed the friendship in the neighborhood, and God had provided the finances for the building in other ways.

* * *

Before the architectural blueprints for the church were drawn, Don's attention had turned to establishing a church government and drawing up by-laws to meet the state's requirements to be a recognized church, receiving tax-exempt status. Don wouldn't compromise what he believed was the biblical outline for proper church government with the state's requirements, so the wording of the by-laws was critical.

In Don's mind, the first problem he faced was the appointing of elders. He knew the New Testament clearly supports the offices of both elders and deacons, defining their qualifications and duties, with the elders overseeing the spiritual aspects of the church, and the deacons tending to the mundane matters. Realizing our congregation consisted of all newly born-again people, there were no men who met the Scriptural requirements of an elder, simply because their knowledge and experience with God was limited.

Don's solution was to form a special board he called a "Steering Committee," with himself acting as president. Their function would not include the spiritual direction of the church, which would remain in the hands of the pastor, but they would be responsible for all other matters pertaining to church government. This committee would continue to operate until such a time that a church building was built and occupied. Then the congregation would nominate and vote on deacons forming a board to take charge of the church's mundane affairs.

Don would choose elders as the need arose, to oversee the spiritual ministry. Thankfully, God had already sent us Lyle, the lawyer, who helped get all the paperwork processed in Olympia as soon as Don had it completed. By the time we made the offer on the little farm, the steering committee was in place and handled all the details.

* * *

Right before we occupied our new church building, Keith came to Don with startling news. After a Sunday evening service. Sitting on the front row, Don learned that God wanted to send out our first missionary. Keith confided, "For several weeks now God has been dealing with Joanne and me about going back to our home state of Wisconsin to witness to our relatives and friends. The Lord wants them to see the difference the baptism in the Holy Spirit has made in our lives. I don't especially want to leave my new job here or whatever the Lord is going to do with this little group, but both Joanne and I know God is telling us to move back." It was hard to lose them, because Keith played the guitar and sang beautifully, plus they were anchors in the church and their neighborhood.

Don's first concern was how effective Keith could be without more knowledge in God's Word, so we agreed to tape all the services and send them copies each week. It was with heavy hearts that we all bid them goodbye just a few weeks before the completion of our new building. None of us knew Keith and Joanne weren't going to be welcomed with open arms in the church back there, so God used Keith to start his own church. Community Chapel in Wisconsin became our first satellite church.

* * *

The day was fast approaching when we would move into our new building. Everyone was both excited and nervous. Excited because all of us had taken part in paying for and building it. Nervous because we didn't want to lose the closeness we experienced in the crowded room with most of the children sitting on the floor. We encouraged one another by proclaiming that we wouldn't let a more formal setting keep us from spontaneously responding to the Holy Spirit with praise and sharing what God was doing in us.

The college students had happily worked on the church between jobs all summer . Already the chapel had been filled with songs of praise as these joyful young people climbed up on the scaffolding singing as they stained the walls and beams. Before their classes were over for summer break, on Sundays around the table at our house they expressed a desire to enroll in a Bible college instead of going back to secular school in the fall.

As we were finishing up the dishes, one girl confided, "I sent for catalogs from different colleges across the country, but I can't find one that satisfies what I long for. I don't want to leave what God was doing here, either." She sighed and said, "I wish we had a Bible college." I dismissed the thought. We were barely able to build the chapel and a few small classrooms for the children. Plus, Don was close to total exhaustion. He was working full-time, doing all the teaching and preaching (with the exception of his father's occasional visits from Tacoma) because as yet no one else could, plus being the architect for the building project.

Just a month before moving into the chapel, the steering committee made a decision that changed our lives. They announced, "We want to put you on a salary, Don, so you can quit your job at Boeing! We will match your present wage. We suggest you give two weeks' notice, and use the vacation time you have coming to take a much-needed break."

"PASTOR, PLEASE LET ME GIVE"

Don held me in his arms as he told me the news. I cried, "I know how you feel." He said, "It's humbling to accept a salary from God's people. I don't feel worthy. Remember how many times I've told the Lord I'd work for half the wages if I could be in the full-time ministry?"

I nodded and looked into his teary eyes. He continued, "Now the Lord saw to it that my salary was doubled just six months before we met Keith and Joanne."

"Instead of working for half, He's giving us double," I whispered, conscious of the holy presence of God surrounding us. "I'm so thankful you didn't take one of those other job offers. We would have missed God's will."

Suddenly we realized Don would have only one more week to work before wrapping up eighteen years at Boeing. It seemed too good to be true. We went into the living room, sat on the couch, stared out at our neglected garden, and contemplated the awesome ways of God.

Chapter Ten

A Dream Comes True

*"Study to show thyself approved, a workman
that needeth not to be ashamed,
rightly dividing the Word of Truth."
(2 Timothy 2:15)*

As we drove out of town for our vacation, the fact that Don would be a full-time pastor didn't stop the torment in his mind. He was plagued with thoughts that he wasn't really a pastor because he hadn't been ordained by a denomination. However, three men of God with recognized apostolic ministries had laid their hands on him and, anointing him for the ministry, had prophesied of the very ministry in which God had now placed him. Just because it happened nineteen years ago didn't make it invalid. King David was anointed by the prophet Samuel many years before he became king. God must have known our own church would dismiss us before we had the opportunity to ask them to lay hands on us and pray God's blessing on the ministry.

Although he tried not to be, Don was affected by the rejection of most of the other charismatic ministers and leaders in the area. One minister even called Don and confessed he believed the same way Don did on a particular doctrine. His advice to Don was, "Do like I'm doing. Don't teach it and don't bring it up, because if you do, Brother— won't accept you. And if you're rejected by him, all the other ministers will reject you, too. You don't want to get on the bad side of Brother—."

Don's response was, "Has the Gospel come to this? Where we can't teach or preach what we believe to be the truth because we fear one man who happens to be popular? How can we ever hope to come to the unity of the faith if we won't keep the unity of the spirit by loving and accepting one another in spite of doctrinal differences? I would like an opportunity to speak with Brother— about the doctrinal issues we don't agree on, but he said he'll speak with anyone except me." Saddened, Don hung up the phone. Later, Brother— published a tract called *The Potato Bug*, referring to the Chapel.

Rumors spread, too, that Community Chapel didn't believe in the deity of Jesus, teaching that Jesus was just a man. Other rumors proclaimed we believed in "Jesus Only," and therefore didn't believe in God the Father or the Holy Spirit. Still other rumors were circulated that Don stayed in a church only long enough to get a following of his own.

In spite of warnings not to have anything to do with us, one Lutheran pastor who had received the Holy Spirit invited Don to come to his office to discuss what Don did believe. At the conclusion of the two-hour discussion, when the pastor understood that Don believed Jesus to be both God and man, he said, "I don't see anything you shared to be concerned about. There's nothing here that shakes me up."

Don also battled feeling inferior and insecure before ministering because of a slight speech impediment he had struggled with all his life. He's unable to properly pronounce certain letters, the most noticeable one being the letter "R." It never bothered any of us like it bothered him.

Don was never at a loss for words. With his vast knowledge of the Bible, his natural teaching talent, and unique gift of wisdom from God, he always had a Biblical answer.

* * *

After a few wonderful days' rest on the beautiful Oregon coast, we started home. While driving, our conversation shifted to our people and the need so many had expressed to go to Bible college. Suddenly, I heard a voice in my mind, "You could have a Bible college." Wow! It took me a minute to process the thought.

I turned and quizzically looked at Don driving, wondering if he'd heard it, too. Thinking aloud, I said, "Let's see. What does it take to have a Bible college? Well, it takes students; it takes Bible subjects and teachers; it takes classrooms. We've got the students; we've got the subjects; and if we didn't divide that one Sunday School classroom which isn't yet completed, we would have one room big enough!"

The light went on—we would start a Bible college! We began listing the subjects. We already had a booklet he had written on the baptism of the Holy Spirit, called *Glossolalia*. Then there was one called *Evolution Refutation*, and one on water baptism and . . . the list grew. Don glanced at me. "Would you mind driving? I need to start writing."

THE TRUTH SHALL SET YOU FREE

We stopped the car and changed places. Nervous with excitement, he said, "Now don't talk to me. I've got to get all this down on paper. You know, we could have our first class this fall. That room will be big enough to hold thirty desks. We can do it!" Almost giddy now—realizing his lifelong dream was within reach—Don trembled as his thoughts spilled out like water rushing over a falls. "We gotta get home in time to tell them to leave out that one wall. It's not a support wall, so it won't weaken the structure any. If we get home in time, we can make a college bulletin showing the first semester classes and give it out Friday night after the service."

The only sound the rest of the way home was that of Don's pencil. My mouth was still, but my mind went racing ahead to how this change might affect our lives. Suddenly, I was overwhelmed with gratitude for every bit of training and experience Don and I had throughout our lives, because I could see there was nothing that God couldn't use for his glory.

All the Bible classes we had attended, all the sermons and services of different pastors we had heard and sat under, all the Latter Rain ministers we had heard teach. The healing ministries we had witnessed. All the working with children and teenagers I had done. All the Bible classes Don had taught. All his study in the Bible that averaged at least six hours a day. And even the private Greek lessons he had taken when I hated to have him leave me alone in that creepy neighborhood two nights a week to go to his class. All of it. Every bit of it was going to be put to use now. Even the soul-winning experience; the door-to-door witnessing; the setting up of Bible Clubs in the high schools and in neighborhoods.

If only I had been faithful to practice the piano, I thought. Mama had worked so hard to get a piano for me and pay for lessons. We wouldn't have had such a gap in that area. But little Bradley was getting really smooth on the organ, and a couple with grown children gave their organ to the new chapel, so Bradley could keep his to practice at home.

In my mind I talked to the Lord: *"Jesus, I'm so thankful for all the knowledge we have about You and all that Your Spirit has taught us all these years when we didn't always realize what You were trying to make us into. Lord, I'm excited for the people who will have their own church, and for the students who want to learn your Word so they can become your ministers, and for Don because he no longer has to build airplanes, but can teach your Word full-time.*

"But, Jesus, I'm scared. I'm scared for my kids. I'm scared for Carolyn, Jesus. She's heading off to ORU, and I can't even go with her to be sure she gets settled in okay. She's never been away from home. Keep her, Jesus. I'm thankful ORU is letting her take just the classes she wants, so she can be used by You in her chosen fields of English and writing, but I want You to protect her and bring her back to us so she won't be left out of what You are doing here.

"Jesus, I'm scared for Daniel. His father hasn't been involved in his life lately, except to disapprove of his hair and dress. Lord I don't want the church to be a threat to Danny so he feels like You are taking us away from him. Help me to keep sensitive to his heart and support him in whatever interests he pursues. But most of all, Lord, whatever happens, keep his heart from blaming you.

"Jesus, I'm not that worried about David. Maybe it's because I've already given him over to You so completely

that I know You can take care of his heart; or maybe it's because David has surrendered his life totally and is trusting You with his future. Just bless him, Jesus, and heal him in Your own time.

"Jesus, I'm really scared for me. I don't feel capable of teaching a college class, but I remember how a few years ago You helped me teach a group of doctor's wives. You gave me answers to their questions and directed me each step of the way, so I'll trust You to do it for me again. Lord, I ask You to grant me this one request: I want the subjects that I teach to be more than theology. I want to experience your Word and teach in such a way that the students experience You. I want You to use Your Word to perfect us as your Word promises. Jesus, I'm willing for You to use me in anyway You can to make Your people into Your Bride without spot or wrinkle or any such thing" (Ephesians 5:27).

I continued talking to the Lord, saving my greatest fear until last. *"Jesus, I'm so scared for my marriage. I wish the perversion was gone, but it's not. Can't You just make it go away? I'm thankful Don hasn't had that instant attraction and magnetic pull to other women when we've passed an attractive girl on the street lately. Jesus, please don't let it happen with the girls in the church."*

My thoughts turned to the Word of God, and I remembered that the Lord had anointed David king, even though He knew David would sin. And God's Spirit remained on Samson all the while he was with Delilah, the harlot. Samson, with God's strength, carried the city gate to the top of the hill. I thought of Peter who was just a fisherman when Jesus called him; one time, Jesus had looked at Peter and said, "Get behind me, Satan," showing Peter's mouth had been used by the devil to tempt Jesus. I reasoned that if God waited until He had a perfect person before he called anyone into the ministry, He'd have no one but Jesus. I marvelled at the grace of God, and continued my prayer.

"Lord, help me not to get in the way of the love you put in a pastor's heart for the flock. I don't want to be a hindrance that would prevent You from loving Your people. Help me and deliver me from jealousy and insecurity. I promise You, Lord, that I will not interfere with Your love being expressed through my husband. And Jesus, if something wrong does happen, help me to get through it. Jesus, please don't let our marriage problems affect these precious people. Help us, Jesus. Help me. Help me always to run to You for strength and help. Thank you for always being there for me, Jesus. I love You."

We were getting close to Seattle when Don broke the silence, "I have worked up a Bible college curriculum that will easily fill up four years of classes." He beamed and added, "I want to get Dad's input on the Old Testament books especially. I wonder if I'll have time to run over to Tacoma this evening? We're almost home."

Turning toward me, he said, "If Dad will teach a few hours a week, and if you will teach, I'll just need one more teacher besides myself, and we will have all we need for the first semester. I think we could use Gil, the Baptist minister who has taught a college class before, to teach a class on Bible lands and customs. I want this college to be a Bible college where students can come and get a degree by taking all Bible and Bible-related subjects."

He interrupted his own train of thought, "You know Sue, that student from the Philippines? I was talking to her last week. She is here in America getting her degree so she can go back and minister to her people. They are desperate for her to hurry and get trained in the Bible. It was a big financial sacrifice for everyone, including her family, to send her here. And do you know what subjects she is having the hardest time with? Geometry and American History! Now, why does she have to take classes like that in order to get a degree in theology so she can go back to her own people to teach them?"

There was righteous indignation in his voice, "I felt ashamed of our Bible colleges in America for requiring students to take non-Biblical courses when they are here for the sole purpose of learning the Bible. Our college isn't going to be like that!"

As I turned the car off the highway and into our neighborhood he said, "I want to write to my Uncle Tom to see if he would be willing to move here from east of the mountains and teach, starting next semester." Tom had been in the ministry for years, but at this time didn't have his own church.

As we were turning into the driveway, Don said, "I know you can teach the subject of *Gift Ministries*. You have both the theological knowledge and experience. And you'll have three weeks to prepare. I'll help you with assignments." He didn't try to hold down his excitement.

Before I could answer, he added, "Now, don't mention this to anyone. I want to tell them myself Friday night. And, oh, I think it's better if we don't say that God gave the idea to start a Bible college to you."

> *It really didn't matter to me, but I didn't realize how subtly I was supporting Don's insecurity and fears. It gave me a pretense of humility and made me the hero in my own mind. As time went on and other incidents similar to this one arose, I continued in the same pattern—always giving my husband credit while building a hidden pride in me.*

After stepping into the house, Don hardly left his desk until the Friday evening service. Come to think of it, he hardly left his desk for the next three weeks.

* * *

How Don could keep the announcement of the Bible college until the end of the service on Friday, I don't know, except he has the ability to be very solemn and matter-of-fact when he is serious about something and doesn't want it left open to conjecture or questioning. I could hardly sit through the service.

Of course, we had an altar call at the close of the service; there wasn't a meeting that someone didn't get saved or healed or filled with the Holy Spirit. When the praying had subsided Don asked the congregation to return to their seats and, without any explanation, he passed out our first Bible college catalog. It consisted of one 8 1/2 x 11 sheet folded in the middle. On the front were the words, *Community Chapel Bible College.* Inside was a list of the courses for the first semester along with a brief explanation of each class and the number of credits. Included on the back page was a form to fill out to enroll.

For a minute—that seemed like forever to me—the room was strangely quiet. Then joyous laughter flooded the room as if a light had suddenly been turned on. Comments could be heard all over the assembly: "Is this really true?" "Oh, praise the Lord!" "Oh, goodie. I'm signing up right now!" "I can't believe it." It's wonderful!" "How much does it cost?"

We kept the tuition as low as possible. Don's wages as pastor took care of his salary. I wouldn't receive a salary, but Gil had to be paid. Don insisted on paying his father something to cover his driving expenses, so Dad took the money, then gave it all back in the offering.

It was after 2:00 a.m. before we left for our car to go home. Poor David had been waiting for us to leave all this time, but he didn't mind as he was making his own plans to become a Bible college student.

The next day at the work party to clean the chapel for the installation of the pews on Monday, everyone discussed where the students would live. Ron and Katie volunteered an attic room to house a couple of male students, and that was the beginning of student housing. Mrs. Snyder, a widow, opened her heart and home; she continued to be a "dorm mom" for many years.

Someone shouted, "Budget Rent-A-Car is hiring men part-time to work on their lot near the airport." I guess the Lord knew we needed to be close to these kinds of jobs, since the property was located within minutes of the airport. It just so happened, too, the county was completing a freeway with an exit just a few blocks from our church, so downtown Seattle was only twenty minutes away.

A DREAM COMES TRUE

Having learned that the Seattle school district was getting rid of some out-dated desks, tables, and chairs, I asked one of the young men to go with me. Praising the Lord for this unexpected blessing, we laughed together as we searched for all the very biggest ones—which were for sixth graders—realizing they would challenge some of our college men who were well over six feet tall and played football. Imagine how delighted everyone was when they learned we got all the classroom furniture we needed for a total of $150!

Some students were already planning to call their parents that night and tell them of their decision to go to Bible college before continuing their education at a university. It wasn't going to be easy to make their parents understand, when they couldn't feel the drawing of the Holy Spirit their child was experiencing. Being a parent myself, I certainly could not blame any parent who had difficulty with their child's decision and tried desperately to talk them out of going to Bible college.

My heart went out to one father, especially, who came to our home and, while sitting in our living room with his son, asked Don, "Please persuade my son not to attend Bible college." Of course, Don could not. Upon graduation, this son became one of our beloved college teachers and eventually our son-in-law.

Another father, a huge man, showed more emotion. He stormed into our home, ready to tear Don apart with his bare hands. Don, having been an instructor in self-defense, wasn't worried. As it turned out, Don didn't have to use any of those skills. Instead, he empathized with the father, and before the conversation ended, Don had made a friend. As he left, this father thanked us for rescuing his daughter from drugs, and made Don promise to contact him if his daughter got into any more trouble.

One new Bible college student-to-be, Maureen, expressed a desire to drive home to her parents' farm in eastern Washington and talk to them face to face. She seemed hesitant to go alone, and I didn't like the idea of her driving all that way by herself. I suggested, "Perhaps Mike could go with you; the drive will take less than a day." It started a romance that grew to marriage, and Mike and Maureen were the first couple to be married in the chapel.

* * *

We went to church Sunday evening, realizing this would be our last service in Cal and Mary's basement. Neither Cal nor Mary ever complained of all the extra work and wear and tear having the church in their home had caused them. It had been one and a half years since our first service there. I'm sure they were greatly relieved to have that period of their lives over, and a little sad, too.

After the service, one of the three members of the steering committee confided in me, "We were puzzled that the pastor didn't trust us enough to tell us ahead of time of his plans for a Bible college."

Without stopping to consider the long-range effect my answer would have on the steering committee's relationship with their pastor, I took the role I'd been taught to take. I made excuses for my husband, stating, "The pastor probably won't tell you when he's sure he has a direction from the Lord; he doesn't want to be talked out of it."

> *These men weren't asking to know ahead of time so they could persuade their pastor not to follow God's leading, but rather so they would be prepared to support him in it. Nevertheless, a position was being established that would keep them, and all future elders, in the place where the pastor felt safe—at arm's length—and they got their cue from me.*

* * *

At last, it was Friday evening—our first service in our new church! Everyone had helped build it, both with their pocketbooks and their hands. Even the children had worked with their parents every Saturday.

Long before the usual hour of prayer before the service, the two small prayer rooms were full of the sounds of eager Christians praying in English and other tongues. They wanted God to move in His own marvelous way upon each one who came to the meeting. We'd decided to use these two rooms behind the platform—which doubled as dressing rooms when we had a baptismal service—to pray before the services, because some felt visitors could be frightened if they saw us praying at the altar and around the front of the sanctuary.

Services were never planned ahead of time, to allow the Holy Spirit to control them. We waited on the Lord until He directed us, rather than try to make something happen. It didn't really matter whom He moved upon to minister, just so it was He. Don prepared a sermon, not knowing when he would preach it or if he would preach at all.

Occasionally, he tried to get a sermon, and although he had tons of Bible data, the Holy Spirit didn't anoint any of it. Then, as the service progressed, lo and behold, God had given the sermon to someone else, and all who heard it knew it was God's Word for the hour, with perfect timing.

We never had a problem getting people to come on time, because they didn't want to miss anything God did.

The lights in the prayer room blinked, signaling it was time for the service to begin, and we filed out, hurrying to sit as close to the front as possible. Just as we were finding our seats, the anointing of the Holy Spirit came upon me to speak a message from the Lord.

> *I recognized this anointing, because it only happens when He wants to use me for a message either by tongues and interpretation or prophecy.*

I walked directly to the microphone that was placed on the floor in front of the platform.

I opened my mouth, and words in an unknown tongue came rushing out with power and volume that was far greater than my own soft voice. I felt as if I was just an instrument the Spirit of the Lord blew through, making the words pour out of me. When the message was completed, the tongues stopped, and after a brief pause, words in English began, with the same unction and tenor as the tongues. When the last word left my mouth, the anointing left with it. I walked to my seat, feeling drained and empty, but thankful that Jesus had chosen to speak to us words of confirmation and encouragement. It was He who had formed us into one body and He would continue to make us like Himself. He asked for our obedience to His Word so our purpose in this life, as well as in eternity, could be fulfilled.

No one sat down. Every hand raised in praise and voices blended into a volume of thanksgiving. Hearing a sudden explosion of joy behind me, I turned and saw the Lord fill someone with His Holy Spirit. Tears of joy streamed down her face and those around her held up her arms, as the power of the Lord was upon her so strongly she could hardly stand. You could see her mouth trembling. I thought, *This is certainly one example of the Scripture in Isaiah being fulfilled where the Lord said, "with stammering lips and other tongues will I speak through this people..."* (Isaiah 28:11). With a little encouragement to speak and let Jesus give the words, she burst forth in her new heavenly language.

Well, I thought, *Being in our new chapel isn't hindering these people at all. Neither is the Holy Spirit intimidated.* The worship took the form of singing, as someone went to the piano and Cal walked to the microphone to lead. One song led into another. If ever there was a break, someone shouted out a number from the songbook and we sang that one. It wasn't long before a little group formed around Cal, and that was the beginning of our Music Ministry.

When Don went to the pulpit to address the congregation, he was overwhelmed—the chapel had no empty seats! "We must have been cramming more people into

Cal and Mary's basement than we realized," he said. What were we to do? We certainly couldn't tell the people to stop witnessing and getting souls saved. Everywhere they went, these delightful new Christians, radiant with the joy and glory of the Lord, shared their faith. The service was full of testimonies of how souls had been won to the Lord.

After the service was formally dismissed, it was like phase two began. People headed to the prayer rooms or the altar to pray. There was prayer and sharing the Word in the pews as well, with the older ones in the Lord answering Bible questions as best they could. Jerome was somewhere praying for the sick. (He made himself available day or night to pray for anyone who needed him. The list of those who were healed by God's power was getting longer each week.)

After about an hour of prayer, someone went to the piano and by the inspiration of the Holy Spirit began singing—first in tongues, then in English. A new song was born, and others quickly joined in. The sweet presence of Jesus seemed to fill the room like falling rain, and nobody wanted to leave.

Soon it was after midnight. We didn't have a problem getting people to come to church. Our problem was getting them to leave. The ushers turned the lights down and nudged the people out the door. Most of us had been there since 6:00 p.m. If our bodies could have held out and earthly obligations didn't exist, there would have been no stopping. *Later, I learned that many college students piled into their cars and continued worshipping the Lord until 3:00 or 4:00 in the morning.*

Our ride home was only eight blocks long now, so we talked over a cup of hot chocolate for Don, a cup of coffee for me. Don said, " I hate the thought of starting another building project when this one isn't quite completed, but with the sanctuary already full, what will it be like a year from now?" We didn't know we would be in a building project every year except two for the next eighteen years.

The first service in our new building was only the beginning of our journey into an unfolding revelation of Jesus and His plan for us.

Chapter Eleven

A Vision From God

"Where there is no vision, the people perish."
(Proverbs 29:18)

I awoke on Monday morning with an unusual sense of the Holy Spirit's presence. It was as if He were tugging at my heart, impelling me to come. All throughout that day and the next the tugging continued, bringing a rush of emotion. I sensed my Heavenly Father yearned to show me something. By the time I had finished preparing dinner on Tuesday, I could wait no longer. After putting dinner on the table, I told my family, "I'm not hungry. I'm going down to the church to pray for a little while; I'll be back shortly."

I'm so thankful for this new little prayer room where I can be alone, I thought, as I slipped to my knees and began worshipping Jesus. I put all my own cares and thoughts aside, so they wouldn't hinder me from receiving whatever Jesus wanted to show me. Immediately, I found myself on my face, with sobs coming from deep within me and escaping through my mouth, forming the words, "Oh, Jesus!" I don't know how many times I repeated those two words through the sobs until I began feeling in my spirit like I was being lifted up beyond this realm of time.

I turned on my back and raised my hands into the air. I knew my spirit wasn't leaving my body, but what I was about to experience was taking place in my spirit which seemed to be immersed in God's Spirit. It became so all-consuming that soon I was unaware of anything else—the time, the room I was in, the position of my body, anything. Enclosed in God, I experienced a vision. I say "experienced a vision" because it was more than just seeing a picture. I experienced it. I became a part of it and it became a part of me.

Because it was a revelation of our church, I experienced it for the whole church as a body, not just as one person experiencing it, but as many members. The impact was so great it went far beyond my human emotion. Once the experience started, all weeping and verbal expression ceased. If you were to walk into that room, you could have thought that nothing was happening at all, because all you would have seen was me lying on the floor with my hands raised, motionless, for hours.

As the vision ended, I knew there was one part that I wasn't allowed to see. The Lord spoke to me, "Later, I will take you into that part, but for now this is all you need to know." When I became aware of my surroundings, I was shocked to realize it was 11:30 p.m. Five and a half hours had gone by and I thought I had only been praying for about a half-hour and I could hurry home in time to help April with the dishes.

It was well after midnight when I quietly opened our bedroom door and went to bed, as it took me a while to come back down from the holy presence of God and get re-acquainted with the reality of this world. Throughout the rest of the week, there remained in my spirit an awesome reverence for the Lord and what He had shown me. I prayed, "Lord, when the time comes for me to share this with the congregation, anoint me and them so they will be as affected as I am." That time came in the very next worship service.

When I stepped out of the prayer room as the service began, it was as if the Lord opened my spiritual eyes and I saw angels fill the chapel like a halo above the people. I hardly ever told the congregation when Jesus let me see angels, because I didn't feel the Lord wanted me to. Perhaps they would have gotten all tied up in the sensationalism of the supernatural and let that become their focus, rather than their relationship with Jesus. At any rate, I was confident the people's hearts would grasp the significance of the vision with the help of the angels, otherwise it could sound like nothing more than a picture that I saw and was trying to describe.

After the worship service had gone on uninterrupted for about 45 minutes, the Lord spoke to my mind, "Now is the time." I felt the holy presence of the Lord envelope me like a cloud, and all nervousness vanished. I walked up on the platform and stood behind the pulpit. I felt reverence flow over the congregation as I invited everyone to be seated. My voice carried the same authority as when the Lord gave a message in tongues and interpretation through me. . . .

"Then as I was placed in the awesome, holy presence of the Lord, we were standing at the entrance to a huge—larger than a football field—indescribably beautiful expanse of lush, living, green carpet. The color was more vivid than any I have ever seen on earth, and the texture was more exquisite than the best manicured lawn or the most luxurious carpet. To view it was to experience it.

"We all simply stood there with Jesus, experiencing it and knowing that it represented our salvation and our life here on earth with Jesus. The marvel of His unending grace filled us with gratitude and joy impossible to describe. The sensation was far beyond the greatest pleasure of anything on this earth." I paused and closed my eyes for a moment as the sensation again swept over me.

"For quite some time we didn't see anything else but this splendid, unending expanse of green, nor did we seem interested to see anything else. We weren't even too conscious that Jesus was there with us. Instead we were consumed with the reality that *we* were there, *we* had come into salvation. Every time one of us moved or whenever another person came in, all the rest of us would be overcome with the glory and excitement of it all over again.

"I have no idea how much time went by, because it seemed like I was experiencing it forever. I am experiencing it again right now as I speak, and I'm sure it will continue for the rest of my life. On the other hand, it seemed like only a moment before we became aware of another area. There was an archway located across the field and to the right of where we had first entered.

"Bursting with excitement when it came into view, we all began leaping and dancing toward it. When we got close we saw that the archway was actually the opening to an arbor, with all manner of fruit growing everywhere. The archway was covered with fruit, the walls and ceiling were covered, even the floor was loaded with fruit. They were all different varieties and they were all growing. None had been picked and put into containers; everything was waiting to be picked and eaten fresh.

"Again, I can't really describe the incredible colors of the fruit. And some of the most desirable ones were at the very top of the arbor, so you had to be extremely tall to reach them. If you picked any fruit, you had to eat it, and no one could pick for someone else. Although we initially tried to pick fruit for one another, Jesus stopped us. If you wanted some of the delectable fruit up high, you had to grow tall enough to reach it for yourself. We could, however, encourage one another to grow in order to reach the higher fruits—and we did so with great enthusiasm. We all wanted everyone else to experience everything available to us in the arbor.

"Some, after unsuccessfully attempting to reach the higher fruit, gave up and settled for whatever they could reach. When they did, they found just as much joy and contentment as the ones who could pick the higher ones. Let me tell you we were all full of pure jubilation at every new fruit we experienced, and we encouraged everyone to partake for themselves." For a moment, my eyes scanned the congregation, and I saw they were eagerly taking in each word.

"I was made to know that the fruit arbor represented the ministry and the gifts of the Spirit. Every member has gifts and ministries to perform and each person was necessary to make up the complete body. Some would grow tall enough to reach the bigger ministries. Others would not, but all were equally important. The excitement we felt when someone was able to perform a ministry at ground level was just as great as when one could perform a ministry at the top level.

"Fun was what we were having in that arbor! So much fun, in fact, that most of us didn't even notice Jesus beckoning us to come with Him to experience something else. He wanted us to move on, but He saw we were still too caught up in the excitement of the ministry and everything we could do now that we had all this fruit. He decided to wait a little longer before trying again to show us what was more important to Him.

"As I stood with Jesus, waiting, I was aware that He had no anxiety regarding the situation. He wasn't concerned that we kept Him waiting when He had something else to show us. He just patiently waited.

"I was also aware of many other entrances around the edges of the green expanse. The Spirit caused me to know that they represented other churches. They were in a haze throughout the vision, and I didn't experience anything more about them except to know what they stood for.

"Standing there with Jesus, I could just barely see the chamber that He was waiting to take us into, a little ways off to our right. Finally Jesus moved toward it, motioning us to come. A few of us followed immediately. A few more, when they saw us go, left the fruit and followed. Others were more reluctant to leave the fruit; however, after some hesitation, they came along also. And some watched us go but decided to stay where they were in the fruit arbor.

"As we approached the chamber, so dazzling white that it almost blinded us, we bowed down and were pressed back almost off our feet with the pure white holiness. It looked more like the most beautiful snow cave you can imagine—ice crystals sparkling everywhere, reflecting clear brilliance, instead of rainbow colors."

Crying, I explained, "All I can do at this point is pray that the angels can cause you to know the beauty of it, because there is no way I can describe the holiness or the whiteness of this chamber. Even the floor was more spectacular than any carpet of snow imaginable."

As the emotion of it flooded over me again, I could hardly speak. I struggled to continue, "As I stood near the entrance with Jesus, He put the understanding of what this room represented in my mind. Suddenly I knew why this was the most important part of our whole life with Him. His heart longs for us to enter into a wonderful, awesome, holy, intimate, indescribable love relationship with Him and His Father, which far transcends all the spiritual fruit, all the ministry, all the good things we can have and do—it makes the fruit arbor look shabby in comparison. The reverence we felt as we considered the honor of having that kind of a relationship with the Almighty King of Kings and Lord of Lords was overwhelming."

I had to stop a moment, for I was weeping too hard to speak. Tears were coursing down the cheeks of those present whose spirits were affected with what the Lord was telling us. I went on when I was able.

"Jesus turned to me and said, 'You can't go into this room yet, because you are not ready. If you went in now, you would just spoil it.' I was terribly disappointed, so He said, 'Here, I will show you what I mean.' He allowed one person to step into the entry and then back out. When he did, the man left horrible black footprints that looked much like the black scorch marks of a too-hot iron on beautiful, white fabric. We were heartsick to behold it. Jesus spoke as He turned to lead us back to the fruit arbor, 'See, your walk must be cleansed before you can enter into that holy place with Me.'

"As the rest ran ahead to the fruit arbor, Jesus told me there was more He wanted to show us about the chamber of love; however, now was not the time. I watched those who had returned to the fruit arbor, and I noticed they were not at all sad about having to wait to enter the white room. They enjoyed the fruit arbor with the same enthusiasm they had before seeing the chamber of love."

Before I sat down, I thanked the Lord for being so good to us. I also prayed that He would bring each of us to the place in our walk with Him that we could enter into the depth of His love signified by the white room. At the close of my prayer, Don stepped to the microphone and preached a spontaneous sermon on the many-membered body of Christ and how Jesus, the glorified Son of man, was the head, from whence came all the direction for the rest of the body. Proving each point by reading many Scriptures, he explained that every individual in the church is a part of the whole body, each having its function, with no member less important than the other.

He encouraged us to dedicate our talents and abilities to the Lord and to look for ways to serve the Lord. He said, "Don't wait until you are asked to do something. Take the initiative to find a ministry that fits you, then begin to do it. Everyone has a place to fulfill, and together we will have a whole body of Christ."

Because this foundation was laid early in the growth of the Chapel, everyone felt free to get involved in the work of the Lord, helping one another grow, plus working in some capacity to build the church. Likewise, everyone accepted the responsibility for each service—that it would be anointed, that people would find Jesus and have their needs met—they came anointed and praying for God to use them and in some way to contribute to the meeting.

The enthusiasm and faith were so high for each service that people could hardly wait until Friday night service, excited to see what God would do and how He might use them to bless the body. Our former pastor and friend once commented, "Don, you can't help but have a powerful service with enthusiasm like this."

It was wonderful to have a congregation full of people prepared to minister if the Lord should anoint them. We always had so many people ready to minister a song, testimony, a truth from God's Word, or whatever they felt the Lord gave them, that we never had time for them all—even though our services lasted four or five hours.

At the close of Don's sermon, someone went to the piano and began singing. The congregation could wait no longer to seek God for His will for their own lives. Soon the whole sanctuary became a prayer room. People prayed for themselves and one another.

A little over one year later, the Spirit of the Lord renewed my vision of the white room. This time, as the experience began, Jesus and I were alone. The beauty was even more wonderful than I had remembered. I was conscious that I was weeping, yet I felt detached from my body, since the impact on my spirit was far greater than the emotion expressed.

As Jesus and I stepped into that room, I discovered an intimacy with Jesus that surpassed our current personal relationship. Even though I had walked with Jesus all my life and couldn't imagine life without Him, this union with Him in His love was something I hadn't dreamed was possible.

My understanding was opened. I knew the kind of love relationship Jesus as the Christ (the anointed One)—who was born and lived on this earth with all its trials, pleasures, temptations of the devil, and went through death—longed to have with us. A portion of Hebrews 12:2 flashed through my mind: "*...Who for the joy set before Him endured the cross....*"

Instantly I understood His "joy" was not just our redemption, but rather our becoming one—not just with Jesus, but with one another, as well. By receiving His love and giving Him ours—a spiritual melding with Jesus occurs that places us into a holy union with God the Father. I felt I was understanding for the first time why Jesus prayed the prayer He did in John 17:21-23 ("*That they all may be one; as thou, Father, art in me, and I in thee, that they also may be one in us: that the world may believe that thou hast sent me. And the glory which thou gavest me I have given them; that they may be one, even as we are one: I in them, and thou in me, that they may be made perfect in one; and that the world may know that thou hast sent me, and hast loved them, as thou hast loved me.*). Now I knew how God planned to fulfill that prayer."

Then Jesus spoke to me, "First, my people must know Me; who I am as man, and who I am as God."

Scriptures flooded my mind:

"The Word was made flesh and dwelt among us." (John 1:14)

"I and my Father are One." (John 10:30)

"If you have seen me, You have seen the Father." (John 14:9)

"Emmanuel, which is God with us." (Matthew 1:23)
"The Father in Me; He doeth the works." (John 14:10)
"I speak only what the Father tells Me." (John 8:28)
"I will pray the Father and we will come and make our abode in you." (John 14:23)

    I had always been thankful for the personal relationship with Jesus that He and I enjoyed, but now I understood there was a love relationship with Jesus, something *He* longed for, that was far greater than just He being with us as a Friend and Helper. This was an intimate love that had to do with eternity, and it was so much greater than all His wonderful love I had experienced so far in my life. I imagined that my feelings paralleled Ezekiel's when he said he *"saw it* [the glory of God] *and fell on his face"* (Ezekiel 1:28).

    No sooner had my spirit comprehended the love relationship with Jesus, than He beckoned me to look deeper into the chamber. At the very back I saw a cave-like area even more spectacular than where we were standing. Instead of sensing the whiteness all around me, as I did where I was standing, being in that cave would be like going inside the very substance of the whiteness itself. There seemed to be a little urgency in Jesus' voice, as he motioned for me to go deep into the cave.

    Then, for the first time I became aware of others beside me entering the room and experiencing what it symbolized. As the urgency in Jesus' attitude increased, I knew it wasn't enough to just step into the room. We needed to get as far back into it as possible; better yet, we should move into the cave-like area. Suddenly, my understanding was enlightened and I knew the cave represented the intimate love relationship and union that Jesus had with His Father God, and that relationship was ours to experience also as equal heirs with Him. I also understood why there were others there with me: our intimate relationship with Jesus fused us together, and we became one.

The very thought that Jesus was urging us into that intimate place He had with His Father staggered my mind, yet I knew the Word of God substantiated what I was experiencing. Romans 3:23 says we have all fallen short of God's glory, but Christ in us is our hope of glory (Colossians 1:27). In Christ dwells all the fulness of God (Colossians 2:9), and in God's presence is fulness of joy (Psalm 16:11). Not that we will ever be God as Jesus was, but we are His temples (1 Corinthians 3:16), His body, and in Christ we are enjoined to be seated in heavenly places with Him (Ephesians 2:6).

For a moment, my mind went back to the potluck fellowship where we decided to become a church, and how the Lord had revealed to us that He wanted us to experience the Word, as opposed to merely learning the truths about God and who He is. Now I understood what we needed to fulfill His will—an intimate love union with Jesus and His body, His Bride, His church, but I didn't know how or when it would happen.

Now Jesus was saying, "Hurry! Hurry! It will soon be too late if you don't hurry!" I looked out of my place in the cave; I could see people all over. Some had come all the way in. Some were at the entrance to the cave. Others were inside the room. Some were barely in the doorway while others hadn't yet quite entered the room. Still others were on their way to the room, and some were still in the fruit arbor. Jesus was hastening people into the room, because a storm was coming that would sweep them away if they weren't safe inside.

Suddenly it was too late. I saw a fierce, black storm sweep across the field. With howling winds it swept away everything, including the people who were in the doorway of the white room. They were sucked out as the storm swirled around the opening. Nothing was left outside except the expanse of green which now looked damaged and tattered. The fruit arbor was totally destroyed. I can't describe the horror of the storm any more than I can relate the beauty of the white room.

For a brief instant after the storm and before the vision ended, I experienced Jesus' attitude. The only word I can think of to describe it is "blank." He wasn't angry, displeased, upset, heartsick, happy, thankful, anything.

The Lord never told me what the storm was, nor how or when it would come. All I knew was that it would surely come.

Chapter Twelve

Bible College Tests, Not All On Paper

*"...Satan hath desired to have you,
that he may sift you as wheat."
(Luke 22:31)*

 Thirty-seven students filled the first three rows of one side of the chapel. They were so full of faith and anticipation of what the Lord was going to do in their hearts and minds, that you would have thought they were seated in the largest and grandest chapel on any campus in the world. Registration had taken no time at all—everyone took every subject offered.

 All the students that first semester had at least one year of college, and none had a grade point average less than 3.0. The Lord had certainly blessed us with the cream of the crop, with about as many women as men. Under their arms were their new Thompson Chain Reference Bibles (because they contained extensive study guides) and a notebook, the only requirements. Students were anxious to build their own reference libraries with

THE TRUTH SHALL SET YOU FREE

priority given to a concordance for finding passages in the Bible.

The bell rang at 9:00 a.m., signaling the end of chapel, and students filed out, making their way through the foyer and into the classroom they had helped build, singing as they went. There was barely enough space for everyone, as students squeezed into the desks we had purchased from the school district auction. Radiant faces greeted their first teacher of the day.

As soon as the pastor began, all the radiant faces disappeared and only tops of heads were seen, as they filled their notebooks, visualizing how they would make use of each truth they were recording, when God placed them in their own ministry.

Students cheered when Dad Barnett walked into the classroom at 10:00 a.m. to teach *Pauline Epistles,* because no one was sure Dad would be there. Just a week earlier, we had received a call from Mom, "If you want to see your Dad before he dies, you better come right away." Don promised her we would be right over. We rushed to the church and asked all the workers to stop working and pray for Dad.

We hurried through the kitchen door of the big old home and were shocked to see Dad. His face, neck, and shoulder were swollen and as dark red as a beet. He had lost weight and was so weak he could barely stand. The pain was excruciating. He couldn't tolerate clothes touching him, and at the same time was burning up with fever. He shook with chills and burned with pain, crying, "Pray."

It wasn't over three minutes after we laid our hands on him and started praying until Dad cried again, "The pain is leaving my face!" A few seconds later, he said, "The pain is leaving my neck. Now it's leaving my shoulder." He laughed and cried, "I can feel the pain moving out of my body!" Only a faint redness was still visible on Dad's face this first day of Bible college.

Although we set up a bell system that signalled the end of each class hour, Dad Barnett would get so engrossed in his subject he seldom heard the bell. The students were loving what they were learning so much they wouldn't stop him. Too many times his classes went right past noon (when college was over for the day) until 1:00. We always scheduled Dad's classes back to back, so he would have two hours to teach. Some days he would continue *Pauline Epistles* for the full two hours and then make up the difference the next day by teaching *Prophecies of the Last Days* both hours. It was no problem for any of the students, except me.

I was the only part-time student. I managed to squeeze the *Pauline Epistles* class into my already crowded schedule. When I entered the class, I never knew if I was going to get Zechariah or Ephesians. The students dearly loved Russ and most of them called him either Dad or Pop Barnett.

These new babes in Christ were cutting their teeth on beef steak from God's Word. I still remember one day I was in the foyer when Bill, the ex-hippie that Katie and I had taken off the sidewalk in the University district and brought to the meetings where God delivered and saved him, walked out of Dad's class and came straight to me, shaking his head. "Barbara," he said, "I can't stay in that class; it's too deep for me. I can't figure out what he's talking about. It just doesn't make sense."

I took him by the shoulders and said, "Bill, just keep listening. Don't worry about the part you don't understand. If you'll just keep listening, it will all fall into place."

THE TRUTH SHALL SET YOU FREE

Still shaking his head, Bill responded, "Well, okay, if you say so. I will just have to trust you, because it doesn't seem like it to me." With my hands still on his shoulders, we prayed for God's help.

I didn't know it at the time, but Bill had a brilliant mind, which God restored from the effects of all the drugs he had taken. His grade for that class was an A-.

Dad always sat down to teach, and he surprised the students with some of his illustrations. Because Dad got so engrossed in his subject he became unaware of his surroundings, we thought this was the case when he began to slip to the edge of his chair as he was warning the class about the danger of seeing how close to the edge of God's line of morality they could walk and still not be violating Scripture.

All of a sudden, he tumbled off the chair and landed on the floor. He acted completely startled to find himself there. With his feet in the air, he threw up his hands and shouted, "Hey! How did I get down here? That's just what will happen to you if you see how close to the edge you can get. The devil will push you off and you'll be wondering, 'How did I get down here?'" Dad sat up and continued with the lesson, sitting there on the floor. If the students didn't remember anything else he said, we never forgot that.

> *As I sat in that class, I remember thinking, Lord, I'm already "on the floor," and I don't know how to get up and please my husband, too. I didn't know my concept of authority and submission kept me there. Did a story Dad told about Mom Barnett only serve to fortify my beliefs?*

BIBLE COLLEGE TESTS, NOT ALL ON PAPER

He read the 5th chapter of Ephesians, leaned back in his chair and, tipping his head back, said, "My wife, now, she's something else. She always does what she pleases. That's right. She goes out and does whatever she pleases." Shocked looks appeared on the faces of the students. Dad continued with a question, "Do you know why she does what she pleases? Because she wouldn't be pleased if it didn't please me. I can trust my wife to do what she pleases, because it always pleases me."

The acceptance and respect the students gave Dad hastened the Lord's healing all the old wounds Dad suffered from being unjustly judged and rejected by his peers. The harshness of accusation in Dad's preaching melted away, as his true heart of compassion for people was manifest when unashamed tears freely flowed. He was consumed with a desire to help all of God's children, no matter what their state was or station in life.

I witnessed God's plan in action. The students were being used by God to make man into His likeness. Even though they were unaware of it, they were workers together with Christ (2 Corinthians 6:1). The body of Christ was healing itself, as do our physical bodies. Dad was nurturing them with his knowledge of God, and they were nurturing Dad by what they could give—love, support, and acceptance. It was beautiful to watch the transformations taking place.

But the problem between Don and his father couldn't be healed by the student body. In fact, the role Dad found himself in, teaching and preaching under his son's authority, only served to expose the conflict between the two men. As one who knew and loved both men dearly, I witnessed what went on, but was helpless to contribute in any appreciable measure to the solution.

Contentions usually arose over minor doctrinal issues that Dad felt were new revelations in the Word which he wanted the liberty to teach in the college. Don, as pastor of the church and president of the college, set the policy that no doctrine would be taught with which he didn't agree. The angry disputes between these two men who deeply loved each other didn't hinge on proving the validity of the doctrine in question as much as who would relinquish their authority and control. Dad could not lay down his father role, and Don would not relinquish what he felt was his God-given control over the church and college.

Although Dad never taught the divisive doctrines in his classes, it appeared as if he never submitted to his son's authority in his heart. When each man said things he later regretted, I concluded the devil had a role in the confrontations which sometimes lasted for hours. One time I stepped in and suggested we confront the demons of control. To my dismay, out of Dad's mouth came accusations about me that I knew weren't how Dad really felt.

Afterwards, Don would be hurt and feel so badly for hurting his father, he would tell me, "The next time it happens, you get me out of there. Tell me it's time to go and make me leave." I felt guilty for letting it happen.

When I saw Don develop more fear of losing control of his position, I wondered how God was going to deal with it. The end result in Dad's life after he left his teaching ministry to take care of Mom, who lost her eyesight and was bedridden as the result of a fall, was that when Dad was present, she wasn't given the freedom to even express how she felt.

BIBLE COLLEGE TESTS, NOT ALL ON PAPER

When we went to visit Mom, and I asked her how she was feeling, Dad answered, "Don't ask her how she feels. She doesn't know how she feels. I know better than she does. I'll tell you how she feels."

> *Secretly I feared the same control might happen to me. Looking back, I wonder if perhaps this book would have had a different ending if this father/son relationship could have been dealt with and solved. One thing did eventually become clear to me: Don had a need to prove his worth to his father and receive his acceptance, but something was always there to block that from happening.*

Unknown to me, I was about to run into my own little blockage in the second Bible college semester. When I walked in my first class, which was *The Apocalypse,* I noticed that two students were missing. I didn't address their absence, to do so might interrupt the anointing that was on me to teach. I had just come from the prayer room, where I had waited on God. I knew I couldn't be effective without a fresh anointing, even though I told the Lord when I started to study for my classes, "Jesus, I can't teach the Apocalypse without You causing me to experience it. I have the knowledge about the book from being in Don's classes over the years, but this is a revelation of You. I want to experience the revelation of You in every verse of every chapter, because I want the students to leave this class, not just understanding John's visions of the end time, but with a burning desire to know You and be one with You in what You do in their lifetime."

THE TRUTH SHALL SET YOU FREE

The Lord was faithful to do just that. Each time I stepped from prayer into that classroom, I had experienced what I was about to teach. The difference it made was like having someone tell you how to fish when he had only read how, but never actually been fishing himself.

I remember when the lesson was the four horses in the sixth chapter. I left the prayer room with tears streaming down my cheeks, because Jesus gave me a vision of the fulfillment of John's vision. I was so shaken, I could hardly speak as I relayed the horrible terror I saw on people's faces as the burning and destruction took place at the hand of the Antichrist. It wasn't easy to always take notes in the classes I taught, but the spiritual impact remained on the hearts of the students long after their notebooks were closed. Even twenty years later, some of those students testify how the spiritual impact of the knowledge of end-time events is still fresh in their lives.

After class, I learned the two absentees had decided they couldn't sit under the teaching of a woman, because they believed a woman was not allowed to teach or usurp authority over a man. Don tried to convince them that I wasn't teaching any new doctrine, but only being his helper, and I wasn't usurping authority because he had given me permission to teach the class.

Their legalism, however, wouldn't allow them to take the class from a woman. One did listen to the class by tape later, and decided he could take *Gift Ministries* from me. He reasoned that I would be relating my experiences in the Spirit more than teaching doctrine. I was thankful the Lord had done a work in my heart years ago that prepared me to not be hurt or hindered by criticism.

BIBLE COLLEGE TESTS, NOT ALL ON PAPER

Having failed to block me with legalism, the devil knew my weakest area was self-worth, so he was preparing to use it to stop my ministry. God prepared my heart just in time. I wish I could say I passed this test with an A, but it was more like a C or D. At least I didn't fail, even though there were times when I came close.

* * *

God used a pastor's convention in Palm Springs to prepare me for the test I came home to. Don and I saw an advertisement about an international charismatic fellowship of pastors who planned to meet together for three days to share and wait on God. We could benefit from the acceptance and support from others who, like us, found themselves pastoring the new ones God was filling with His Holy Spirit. We shifted the Bible college schedule, and went to the convention in Palm Springs.

On the plane trip down, I noticed Don seemed to be aloof and preoccupied. He didn't open his briefcase to study the Bible, which was not normal. Sitting beside him, I thought, *His behavior has been different for several weeks. Instead of going right to his desk in the mornings, he showers and rushes out the door to the college. Many times he's called me at noon after college was dismissed for the day and informed me he would be staying at the church to take care of things so he wouldn't be home for lunch. When hours later I called to find out when he planned to be home, no one had seen him or could find him.*

One day, he came home and asked if I thought he should approach the board about hiring one of the college girls to come to the house and do some filing for him. He really was way too busy to take care of all the paperwork, too. He seemed relieved when I agreed that it was a splendid idea and thought the girl he had in mind was a good choice. I tried to dismiss my concerns as our plane touched down at the airport, and we stepped out to ninety-degree weather, a welcome change from rainy Seattle.

The hotel van picked us up at the airport and delivered us to our hotel. Even though it was two miles to the hall where the meetings were held, we decided to walk. Don was ahead of me, and I thought to myself, *He's so preoccupied, I could probably stop walking, and he wouldn't even notice until he's all the way there.* It just wasn't like him. Usually he would be talking all the way there and back. As we approached the meeting hall on the first night, Don turned to me and said, "I really need a touch from the Lord, so I hope you'll pray for me."

We weren't surprised to find we were the first ones there, as we were accustomed to coming early to pray. Don switched on some lights and found his favorite place to pray by the piano. I felt the presence of the Lord fill the room even before I knelt at one of the folding chairs that hadn't yet been arranged in rows for the meeting. I didn't even hear the ministers and their wives as they arrived for the service, because God had closed me in with Him. I felt His presence pour over me, beginning at the top of my head and flowing down like oil over my whole body. With that anointing, these words were put into my mind as indelibly as if they were carved in granite: "I, the Lord your God, have anointed you to be a pastor's wife."

BIBLE COLLEGE TESTS, NOT ALL ON PAPER

When I got up from my knees, I was surprised to see most of the chairs in the small room full of men and women with their hands raised, praising God. I made my way to the seat Don had saved for me on the front row, wondering if anyone else was feeling the presence of the Lord as I. I don't remember much about the meetings themselves, except the main speaker preached some powerful sermons that inspired Don to record all kinds of other subjects and Scriptures brought to his mind. He walked away with germ seeds for several sermons forthcoming.

The very next Sunday after our return home, Don excused himself from the dinner table to take care of something at church.

When the urge to pray overcame me, I put on my coat and walked to the church. Opening the back door, I hurried into the small prayer room, hoping no one had seen me. I needed to be alone. I cried out to God; sensing that something was very wrong, I begged God to show me why His Spirit was so grieved.

Almost two hours elapsed before I sensed what I assumed to be an angel at my left side. His presence was so strong that I opened my swollen eyes, thinking I would actually be able to see him, but there was no visible image. I never directed any questions to the angel, only to the Lord. Yet it was the angel who answered me. Completely calm now, I asked, "Lord, what is wrong?" The answer was spoken into my mind, "Your husband has unintentionally fallen in love with another woman."

"Lord, is she C?"

"Yes."

"Lord, are they together right now?"

"Yes."

"Lord, are they in her bed?"

"No."

As I continued to ask the Lord specific questions, the angel answered with either a "yes," "no," or "you don't need to know that." Then I asked, "Lord, does anyone else know about this?"

"No."

"Oh, thank you, Jesus, that no one else knows. Jesus, why are you telling me about this? You know how much this hurts me."

At this point, the angel placed himself about three feet behind me. Now Jesus answered my question. He could have said, "You've been begging me for the last two hours to tell you, so I told you." Instead, he lovingly gave me the answer, "I know it hurts you–and it will continue to hurt–but I need to use you to help get this love back in balance before it ruins my plan for this people. Trust me; I will tell you what to do. Go to the service tonight, and don't tell Don anything about this. I will direct you as to when you should tell him."

I felt honored by the Lord's confidence in me to handle such an assignment. Yet sensing the strength of the angel behind me, I wondered how strong I would feel when he was gone and I was on my own. I felt the angel touch my mind before he left, and remembered the Scripture in 1 Timothy to gird up the loins of my mind to guard against the onslaught of the devil.

I hurriedly walked home, concerned that Don would wonder where I was, only to discover he wasn't back yet himself. Realizing it was almost time for service to begin, I quickly washed my face and made plans to start the

BIBLE COLLEGE TESTS, NOT ALL ON PAPER

meeting without him. Just as I was leaving to walk back to church, his car pulled in the driveway. As he rushed to the bathroom, I noticed the mud on his shoes, but knew I shouldn't ask any questions. Now wasn't the time.

Early the next morning, Don jumped out of bed and was in the shower before I was fully awake. I laid in bed and prayed, "Jesus, I don't think I can go another day without confronting Don. What shall I do? What do You want me to do?"

Jesus seemed to brush aside my fears, as He gave me step one: call Tom (our first paid staff member) at the church office. I was told to ask Tom to deliver a note to Don to come home as soon as possible."

I met the car when Don pulled in the driveway, and we drove down to Puget Sound, only a couple of miles away. Somehow I managed to stay calm. I related exactly what had happened to me in the prayer room. Staring at the water, Don admitted, "Well, you are right in everything you have said.

"In fact," he continued, "C was afraid God might reveal to you what was going on. She said, 'Don, what if God tells Barbara what has happened and what we are doing? She's so close to God and He talks to her, you know. What will we do if He tells her?' I told her God wouldn't tell you because He wouldn't want you to know because it would hurt you too much."

He glanced at me for a second, then turned back to the water. "I didn't come straight home from class when I got your message, because the minute I read it, I knew God had told you. So I went and got C out of her class and took her to the prayer room and told her about the message and said I was afraid God had told you. She cried. She said she would leave Bible college and go to a college out of state to keep from hurting you." He began crying. "She's in the prayer room right now, still crying."

As he reached into his pocket for his handkerchief, I said, "Donald [I always called him Donald], I want to go to her right now before she decides to leave and reassure her God is going to see us through this. Somehow He's going to see all three of us through." By now we were both crying. Fortunately, I had come prepared with a purse full of tissues.

Don said, "No, not yet. She promised me she would wait right there no matter how long it takes. She said for me to take as long as I needed to explain everything to you. I have her permission to tell you everything." He stopped, blew his nose, and continued, "She's so sweet! She'd do anything to keep from hurting you. She'd ruin her own life if she left. She couldn't find the same thing God is doing here anywhere else. Jean [he always called me Jean], I can't bear to have her leave. I couldn't stand the thought of her leaving. I couldn't go on in the ministry if she left. How would we explain it to everyone? I can't live without her. I'm in love with her."

His shoulders shook as he sobbed. It was as if he didn't remember the statement I had just made, that I wanted to keep her from leaving, not tell her she had to leave. The thought of having her leave had never entered my mind.

Throughout the rest of the conversation, which lasted another hour, Don was unable to consider how devastating all the information he was giving would be on his wife. He had put me in the role of a counselor in the past when he needed someone to talk to about his relationship with his father and also his own sexual problems and unfulfilled areas for him in our marriage. Because of this it seemed normal for him to tell me everything he had been going through in the last couple of months. He was relieved that finally he could get it all out.

Staring back at the water, he seemed to forget I was listening. "She's everything I ever wanted. You know, I never did really fall in love with you. Well, you know C I've told you this before C but you just weren't attractive to me. You've fixed yourself up a lot and you're a lot prettier than you used to be. Anyway, I didn't mean to fall in love with C. It just happened. In fact, I fought it for a long time. I'd see her sitting in my class as I taught, and her face would be all smiles and glowing. I could tell she had respect for me. She'd come up after class and tell me how wonderful my teaching was and how she marvelled at how much I knew. I guess I never got that from anybody before. You know, Dad's always trying to tell me something like I don't know anything. Oh, he's careful. He brings it in the right way and I know he wants to help me be a good minister. He does tell me I'm doing a good job sometimes, but it's not the same. Do you know what I mean?"

He glanced at me for a split second, "And you. Well, I know you appreciate my teaching, but now when you teach or give a message from the pulpit, you are always anointed, and sometimes I feel like you do better than I. But C, she would just follow me out of the class, her face beaming, and tell me how handsome I was and how good of a pastor I was until, well, I just wanted to be around her more and more, so we started finding time to be together.

"Then, one night after service, when everyone had gone home, and I was turning off the lights, we were saying goodbye and, well, we kissed. Jean, it was the most wonderful kiss I had ever experienced. I didn't mean to, but I knew at that moment I had fallen in love with her." He put his hand to his mouth. "I said to her, 'C, I'm in love with you!' She said, 'I'm in love with you, too!' We were both so happy and sad at the same time."

He cried again. "Jean, these last several weeks—well, since before Christmas—I have been in hell. We have tried to break it off, but every time we get together to try to break it off, it just gets stronger. I don't know what else to do. I can't live without her, and yet I know I can't divorce you. I don't even want to divorce you. You are my wife. But I want C. I want you both. I told the Lord, just rapture out one of them like You did Enoch. I know I couldn't stand it if she left, and I know I can't just leave and marry her. I wouldn't blame you if you left me. I've been a lousy husband, and now I'm a lousy minister, and I'm in love with someone whom I can't have. I have to go the rest of my life without having what I need."

We were both crying as we reached for each other's arms. He put his head on my shoulder and sobbed and sobbed. I prayed that the Lord would help us and show us the way through this. Then I said I wanted to go talk to C. He looked up with fear in his eyes. "What will you tell her? I don't want her hurt. She has been through hell, too, and she's trying to keep up with her classes staying up late and getting up early. She really loves you, Jean, and I don't want you to hurt her."

Wiping my eyes, I said, "Don't worry. I won't hurt her. I know what to say."

BIBLE COLLEGE TESTS, NOT ALL ON PAPER

He said, "Let's stop by home first so you can fix your face. Your eye make-up is all over your cheek."

As we drove home, he said he wanted to see her first, then I could spend as much time with her as I wanted to. He also made it clear to me that he didn't want me to tell him or her how to handle this. He said, "I have to work through this my own way."

> *Right here is where I let my own insecurities and fear of losing my husband, coupled with my misconception of submission, rule over what Jesus told me in the prayer room, i.e., He wanted to use me to help. Perhaps if I hadn't failed the Lord at this point, He could have done more to solve the deep-seated problem.*

When I walked into the prayer room, she was lying down with her face to the floor. Her eyes were as swollen as mine from crying. We held each other and cried. She cried for me. I cried for her. We cried together for both of us, for Don, for the church, and for Jesus. She said she was glad the Lord had told me what was going on, and we cried again out of thankfulness to Jesus for watching over us. I prayed in English, while C spoke in tongues.

"Jesus, we trust You. We accept You as our Friend and Guide. We don't know what to do, but we want to do the right thing, whatever it is. Jesus, please protect our church from being hurt by this. We don't want anyone else hurt, Lord. Jesus, keep C from making a mistake and leaving the church where You have placed her. You have the best solution, Jesus, and we will wait until we know what You want before we will take action.

Strengthen C, Lord, to be strong when Don is weak, and strengthen Don when C is weak. Jesus, use me in any way You can to help both of them bring their love for one another back into balance. Oh God, most of all, use this trial to make us into Your perfect Bride that we might be all You intended us to become for Your great name's sake. Amen."

Before Don came back into the room, C promised me she would not pack up and leave. I was satisfied that she wouldn't leave when she said she knew in her heart that God did not want her to go. What she and Don did the rest of the afternoon and evening, I don't know, but I knew I would have to wait until tomorrow to worry about it. I needed to see that David had something to eat, take Daniel to track practice, and study for my class scheduled in the morning. So, as usual, I buried my own hurt, and hurried home.

Wouldn't you know it, the next morning's particular lesson would prompt the young legalist to ask me to define what I meant when I spoke of the word "knowledge" as our subject was the gift of the word of knowledge. No matter how much explaining I did, he wasn't satisfied. Finally Frank, a fiery redhead sitting across the room and in the front row, raised his hand. When I recognized him, he turned in his seat and spoke to the young man instead of to me. "Look, T, you already have a degree in the English language. Surely you know what the word means. We didn't take this class to learn word definitions, but to learn what the lady knows about the gifts of the Spirit, so would you let her get on with the lesson?"

It may not have been the most polite way to handle it, and I don't know if Frank could sense I was about ready to burst into tears, but it was what I needed to get me through the rest of the class. (By the way, Frank and I became really close after that. Often he would sit down beside me after a service and slouch down in the pew to make his shoulder even with mine. He'd say, "Hi, Mom, how're you doing?")

As I walked home after class, I began to sink into a dark hole of despair. The devil was right there telling me everything was my fault, and I believed him. Over and over, his accusations played in my mind: *I had no business even trying to teach these college students. I got what I deserved today. They couldn't learn a thing from me. I got what I deserved from my husband, too. I wasn't good enough for him. I was just a country girl. I never would be good enough for him. He had a right to fall in love with somebody who could make him happy, someone he loved to kiss because he didn't hate her upper lip like he did mine. I should be happy for him. The best thing for me to do would be to get out of his life while he was still young enough to enjoy his life and have what he wanted. She could meet all his needs, where I couldn't. I could never be as pretty as she was.*

On and on my mind went. I didn't know the devil had set me up.

When I opened the door and saw them both together in the study, I couldn't handle it. She had fixed her hair almost exactly the way I wore mine, and Don had one of the curls wound around his finger as he sat at his desk telling her how he wanted his file set up. I took my notebook and Bible to the bedroom, got the car keys, and left.

THE TRUTH SHALL SET YOU FREE

I knew the perfect place to drive the car down a hill and off the road into the water. It was isolated, so no one would see it happen, and it would look like an accident. No one would know I did it, so it wouldn't hurt the church any, and Don could have what his heart longed for. It was the best and easiest solution, and I would be in heaven where I wanted to be. As I started down the hill, the car was suddenly still! Motionless! It didn't skid to a stop. I wasn't thrown forward. It just stopped. A voice thundered in my head, *"I THE LORD YOUR GOD HAVE ANOINTED YOU TO BE THE PASTOR'S WIFE!"* The words were shouted over and over. Each time, a different word was emphasized: first, I; then, *THE LORD*; then, *GOD*; then, *HAVE;* then, *ANOINTED*; then, *YOU;* then, *TO BE*; then, *THE PASTOR'S*; then, *WIFE*. I held my head and cried and cried. I asked the Lord to forgive me for taking my life into my own hands.

I didn't see the truck coming, until it was right beside me. The man rolled down his window and asked, "Are you okay?" I nodded. He said, "You must have fallen asleep and driven off the road, huh? Good thing you woke up when you did or you'd be a goner. If you just back up easy, you'll be all right. Be careful, lady." I waved him a thank you as he drove away.

I drove back to the church. Once again, I slipped in the back door to the prayer room and sought the Lord, this time for me. I asked Jesus to take out of me everything that didn't belong. I wanted to be a better wife, a better mother, and the right kind of pastor's wife. I asked Him to help me compliment my husband more and not criticize him. I felt the Lord lifted something out of me that day, and I felt different—empty and clean, but very weak. I felt humbled by what had happened. I didn't know how I would handle whatever happened next.

* * *

Fearful that Don would compare me to her, I never shared with him what happened to me that day, except to tell him that God had met me in the prayer room, and I wanted to be the kind of submissive wife he desired. That night I also asked Don to promise me one thing: that he would never kiss C again. He promised.

The next couple of months were the hardest. We went through the same scenario over and over. Don couldn't stand it if he couldn't see her, so I'd say, "Go ahead, and spend some time with her." I would be fine until he came home. Then I ran to the prayer room and cried my hurts out to Jesus. Don felt so bad that he had hurt me, he'd say he wouldn't see her again except at church, college, and when she came to the house to do filing.

She tried hard to change her bubbly personality and smiling face so Don wouldn't like her so much. I saw her changing, and I got concerned. She and I talked and prayed together. I never shared with her what I was going through, but told her of my concern, "You have to be yourself. Don't change who you really are."

As time went on, she turned more and more inward. She tried so hard that there would be times she acted like she hated Don. That would hurt him even more. When he came home, he blamed me for the way C was acting towards him, stating that if I could handle it better, she wouldn't be so cold towards him. I begged Don to let me go to our former pastor, but he was emphatic in refusing my request, saying he would divorce me if I did.

At one point, I felt I just had to get away, so Don and I went to Harrison Hot Springs for a couple of days. It wasn't good, however, because he told me a lot more about their relationship. I fell apart emotionally, and screamed, "I just want to beat you up!"

He said, "Go ahead, if it will help. I deserve it." I pounded on his chest until I was exhausted. Then he held me and let me cry. A few days later, after the Sunday evening service, marked a turning point for Don.

After inviting C to our home after church, Don promised, "I only need to talk with her for about a half-hour." It was 2:30 a.m. before she left. When he opened the door to our bedroom, I was a bundle of nerves. I went out of control emotionally when he told me he had forgotten that he had promised me he wouldn't kiss her any more. He had been kissing her all these weeks when I thought he had stopped.

My body went into uncontrollable convulsions. For the first time in our marriage, Don took physical action. He got what is called a sleeper hold on me. (That's a judo hold where the Vegas nerve behind the ears is pinched so the person soon passes out and will actually die if the hold is held too long. It only takes a few seconds for a person to become unconscious. As soon as that happens, the hold is released and within a minute the person regains consciousness.) In this case, he placed his arms around my neck as I was lying on the bed, and began applying pressure. He intended to apply only enough pressure to cause my body to relax, but not enough pressure so I would pass out. The problem was, once my body relaxed, he forgot to let up on the pressure on one side of my head.

As I lay there, helpless, he told me over and over again that I had to accept the fact that he was in love with C, and that he wanted her in his life for the rest of his life. If I didn't accept their relationship, he would divorce me, and they weren't violating Scripture, since they weren't having sex. It wasn't until he told me to repeat out loud, "My husband is in love with C" that he realized I couldn't speak. My whole right side was paralyzed, including my face.

Fear gripped him. He released the hold and groaned, "Oh, God! What have I done? Jesus, help her! Jesus, I'm sorry. I only wanted to calm her down. Jesus, help me! Oh, Jesus, please help!" He tried to get me to move my arm and leg. I couldn't. He lifted me onto the floor. I stood on one leg, but the right one wouldn't respond. We tried walking me back and forth a few times with him holding me up to see if the movement would increase the blood flow and cause the feeling to return. I seemed to get a little better, but I was in bed two days before I could walk. He didn't want anyone to see me in that state and, of course, neither did I, so he asked Maureen to come and fix all the meals. It took four days for me to regain enough use of my arm to comb my hair. I noticed if I turned my head a certain way, I would lose control again. After about a week and a half, I was back to normal.

The whole incident scared Don so badly, he made a greater effort to change his behavior, and I resigned myself to the fact that he wanted her in his life. I thought to be a good wife, I would just have to live with it. I determined not to see them together, just in case C could detect anything in me that would cause her to think I wasn't doing well, as Don had said that was the case. I never mentioned to C how I was doing, and after this incident, I also kept my feelings hidden from Don.

Once was I tempted to discuss my plight with a particular man in our church who was a few years older than Don, but I was afraid I'd fall in love with him. I found the spiritual strength to surrender it to Jesus at the prayer room instead. Consequently, no one found out about the problem except the three of us. Many times in the next few months, I felt as if the devil held me in his teeth and shook me like a rag doll. I know in part how Peter felt when he experienced what Jesus had told him, "Peter, Satan desires to have you that he might sift you as wheat; but I have prayed for you that your faith fail not" (Luke 22:31,32).

* * *

By the end of the second semester of Bible college, the relationship between Don and C was back in balance. The three of us put it behind us and went on, although I felt that part of C's personality had disappeared in the process; and I had developed a physical heart condition that didn't go away.

> *However, the intrinsic problem wasn't solved, and at this point, I couldn't see my blind side. There would be more mountains to climb and rivers to cross before I would see the sin of my ways.*

BIBLE COLLEGE TESTS, NOT ALL ON PAPER

As for Don, he was faced with another problem that was looming on the horizon. The question was, could it be dealt with soon enough and with enough wisdom not to hurt anyone and also prevent a church split?

Chapter Thirteen

Blessed by Men of God

"And he gave some apostles, and some prophets, and some evangelists; and some pastors and teachers, for the perfecting of the saints, for the working of the ministry, for the edifying of the body of Christ . . . maketh increase of the body."
(Ephesians 4:11, 12, 16b)

"I'd sure like to go to a camp meeting and hear other ministers to get built up in the Lord," Don said. After our first year of Bible college closed, the building project adding the balcony and another section of classrooms was in full swing for the summer.

As we drove out to a campground located about an hour's drive away, where we had attended camp meetings years ago, Don shared his concern about a growing tendency toward legalism in our church.

"I'm glad we were able to start the college when we did, because it has allowed me, with God's guidance, to establish the doctrines being taught, but Tom concerns me. He is legalistic and some of what he taught the students at PLU reflects that legalism. I really love Tom. I wasn't sure he was going to let loose of the students who went to his studies and let them come to Bible college, but he did. He even encouraged them to come although it meant giving up his little flock. And he was humble enough to come to Bible college himself. I allowed him to teach, even though he's young in the Lord, because he has a degree, and he'd been teaching Bible studies on campus.

"I felt like Tom's heart was right with me as long as I was preaching and bringing lessons on dying to self, letting loose of worldliness, crucifying the desires of the flesh, etc. What concerns me now is, once I started preaching on the grace of God, I feel like Tom's heart is no longer with me. Jean, I know God directed me to bring the other side of the truth. He let me know the people could get off-balance and start being too hard on themselves and one another by trying to cut worldliness and sin out of their lives by themselves. It's not a matter of their getting good enough; they have to understand and accept the grace of God. I know I have to keep preaching on grace until I feel released by God.

"I can't preach rules. I hate 'clothesline' preaching, but I know we have to have some standards for dress. I won't take the hard line stand the UPC takes—no make-up, no elbows showing, no haircuts for ladies. Well, you know, we've heard these rules all our lives. Anyway, I'm worried about Tom. He may be feeling he's losing the allegiance of some of the PLU group, because what I'm preaching now conflicts with what his stand has been. I don't know. If I let him teach *Pauline Epistles* this fall, it could give him a platform to undermine my teaching, even though the apostle Paul certainly has the balance between grace and law. But Tom, because of his own bias, could set the students against my teaching and cause a church split.

"On the other hand, I don't want to take Tom out, because that could hurt him, and I love him very much. He's a help in the church office, as well."

As we pulled into the parking lot at the campground, we were surprised there weren't more cars there. These camp meetings used to be a big event for the Pentecostal churches in Seattle. Don finished the conversation by saying, "I'd appreciate it if you'd pray about it. I know I have to preach what the Lord lays on my heart. I would like the Lord to take care of the matter. Unless He tells me otherwise, I'm going to wait and see what happens in the fall semester."

Disappointment filled our hearts as we sat through the camp meeting. The congregation acted more like an audience than participants. Although Willard Cantalon's message on the world money market wasn't full of spiritual food, Don came away with the idea of giving his own "State of the Union" message someday. On the way home, our hearts were filled with gratitude for the way God was moving at the Chapel. We began reflecting on why there was a continual fresh move of God's Spirit in our services.

Right from the beginning of our church, we had expected the people to come to each service early, up to an hour, to pray for the service. Our altars were full of people praying for the services as much as two hours before starting time.

Another foundation block that invited God's Spirit to move was everyone came expecting to minister in whatever way the Lord desired, even if it was just to smile and greet the person next to them.

THE TRUTH SHALL SET YOU FREE

Everyone was encouraged to worship Jesus in singing. Music ministers learned all the words to every song, doing away altogether with songbooks. They were free to worship the Lord instead of singing to a congregation. We spontaneously changed the word "He," to "You," so we sang *to* Jesus instead of about Him. If people couldn't remember all the words, they sang in tongues, instead of not singing at all. To our delight, it was almost impossible for anyone to minister a song without everyone joining in.

Our services were full of thrilling testimonies recounting how God during the week had changed lives, because everyone was taught how to witness and lead a person to the Lord.

The congregation, eager to learn from the sermons and exhortations, brought their Bibles and notebooks to church and always took notes. Each service was taped, and most checked out the tapes of any missed meeting. Many in attendance listened to the services over again.

Children remained in services and eagerly participated. Even toddlers prayed for the sick along with their parents.

Our church was growing so fast we were both busy every minute of every day. Just six years after starting the Bible college with 37 students, we had 1,200 students enrolled. Weddings were scheduled every weekend, sometimes two in one day. On any given Sunday, you could count two hundred children under the age of two. We had baby dedications about every three months, which each time included forty to fifty babies.

All of our Sunday School classrooms were bulging at the seams. We had worked hard to lay a good foundation for the Sunday School curriculum, but it was just a skeleton. The Lord was giving us wonderfully talented teachers, however, and we hoped to develop materials and studies for every age level. Already the audio-visual supply room was taking shape; the teachers had visual aids to help make God's Word clear to even the toddlers. Accreditation was underway so we could start our own Christian School as soon as possible.

I marvelled at how much Don accomplished in a day. Besides preparing sermons, studying for and teaching Bible college, designing the buildings, writing the by-laws which defined the church government and how it functioned, he also outlined a plan for the operation of the Sunday School department and the Christian School.

As we drove home, we mused, "We want our church to experience the kind of camp meeting atmosphere we remember. Why not have our own camp meeting?" As we pondered the thought, we remembered a friend of ours who had an evangelistic ministry in Canada. We hadn't seen or heard of him for several years, even though we had supported his ministry financially. He was doing the work of a true evangelist, patterning his ministry after the New Testament church. His love for Jesus and compassion for souls drove him to the lost and hurting. He went to the little towns and Indian villages across Canada, bringing the miracle power of Jesus to those in need.

Brother Moore's testimony was a good example, because he relied on God for his entire ministry and life. God used him in mighty healing power and word of knowledge, and supplied his own financial needs in supernatural ways.

He told the story of how early on in his healing ministry the devil contested his faith. In an Indian village in Canada, a lady was brought to the meeting totally deaf. When she was brought forward to be prayed for, everyone was waiting to see what would happen, as they all knew her. They wanted to see if this man's Jesus was really who Brother Moore said He was. The devil worked on Don Moore's mind with doubts. He prayed for her once and nothing happened. Then the Lord spoke in his mind, "Are you going to let the devil get away with this? Are you going to let him rob you of the ministry I have given you? Are you going to let these people go away thinking that he is more powerful than I am?"

Don Moore walked back to the lady standing at the platform, bent down, put his fingers in her ears and shouted, "Come out, you devil! In Jesus' name!" The lady screamed, as she heard for the first time in her life. After that, the villagers streamed into the meetings with their sick loved ones, and the Lord proved to them that He is still King of Kings and Lord of Lords. From then on, Don Moore's healing ministry, especially to the deaf, was profound.

He told of the time he and his new wife were on their way to a particular village, when they pulled into an abandoned gas station in their little Volkswagen to sleep for a few hours. No sooner had they settled down to sleep, with Don taking the back seat, when the Lord spoke to him and said, "Back up the car." It really didn't make sense. They were way out on a lonely road parked in an old abandoned gas station with plenty of space all around them. Nevertheless, he knew he should obey the Lord, so he asked his wife to back up the car.

She sat up, started the car, and backed it up a few feet, turned off the engine, and settled back down to sleep. About ten minutes later, a semi-truck came barreling down the hill, out of control with brake failure, and crashed into the building right in front of them. Had they stayed where they were, both would have been killed. Don said, "Next time the Lord tells me to back the car up, I'm going to move it more than just a few feet; that truck almost hit the front of our car."

Time and again the Lord supplied their financial needs, sometimes at the last minute. Once, the evangelist was completely out of gas and out of money. He coasted into a gas station and asked for one dollar's worth of gas, not knowing how he was going to pay for it. Suddenly a little lady appeared at his window and, handing him a dollar bill, shouted, "Here. I was waiting at the bus stop and the Lord spoke to me and told me to give you this dollar. Oh, there comes my bus. 'Bye." With that, she was gone, and he never saw her again. He wished he'd had faith to request $5 worth of gas instead of just one!

We were delighted when our contact with Don proved positive. He was still doing the work of an evangelist, and he had to be in Seattle on business, so he could spend a weekend with us. We put the camp meeting idea on hold, and prepared for Don Moore's soon arrival.

* * *

The word spread quickly. Every available spot in the chapel had a chair in it. Our new balcony was filled, and extra chairs lined the aisles as well. Children sat on the floor or on the laps of their parents.

There was a young married couple sitting about four rows back with his mother and uncle. The four of them had come to the meeting at the invitation of Marty, one of our college students who had gone to high school with Rosemary.

Ralph and Rosemary, along with Ralph's mother and uncle, drove fifty miles to the meetings to see for themselves what God was doing. None of us knew that this was the first time Ralph had been in a church since he was eight years old, because a Sunday School teacher had let him down. She had promised each child a New Testament if they had perfect attendance for one year. After Ralph diligently showed up for one solid year, no one remembered the promise the teacher had made, so Ralph got no Bible and gave up on God.

In his junior year of college, his mother suffered a serious car wreck that left her in constant pain with a neck she couldn't move. As a result, she also developed a bleeding ulcer. With all the stress, including dropping out of college to care for his mother, Ralph became an alcoholic. Ralph brought his uncle as well, who had an incurable disease called neuropathy, which had already taken all the feeling out of his toes and fingers. The sharp pain this disease produces resulted in Ralph's uncle being addicted to morphine. Ralph reasoned, "If there is a God, as Marty claims, then I want Him to heal my mother and my uncle. I know what's wrong with them, and I'll know if they are healed." This time God was not going to let this boy be disappointed!

The air was full of expectancy, as praise to Jesus burst out of everyone long before the service was scheduled to begin. As Brother Moore stepped onto the platform from the prayer room, he didn't start his ministry to the body with his own personal testimonies. Instead the Lord used him in the gift of the word of knowledge. Although he hadn't talked to anyone in the congregation, he began calling out specific needs in the body.

First he proclaimed, "God is healing someone's neck right now." Ralph's mother turned her head and looked at Ralph.

"Mother, you turned your head!" Ralph whispered with astonishment. "Are you healed?" Brother Moore asked Mrs. Alskog to come to the platform, as tears filled her eyes. He laid hands on her and prayed. Every bit of pain left her body and there was no stiffness left in her neck. Her ulcer was gone, too. As she started back to her seat, Don Moore called her and said, "The Lord isn't finished with you yet. He wants to fill you with the Holy Spirit." She raised her hands to the Lord, and began speaking in other tongues.

Next Don Moore said, "Someone's ankle is being healed. Please stand up and come forward." Ralph's uncle went to the altar and when Don Moore prayed for him, all feeling returned to his hands and feet instantly. He was totally healed! His doctor had told him he wouldn't live over six months, but eight years later (my last contact with the family), he was perfectly well and alive.

Then Brother Moore said, "There's one more with a spinal condition that the Lord wants to heal." This time it was Ralph's turn. After Ralph was instantly healed and delivered from alcoholism, Don Moore asked him, "Have you accepted Jesus as your Savior?" Ralph replied, "No," so Don led him in the sinner's prayer. Ralph's body shook through the remaining part of the service, under the power of God.

Both Ralph and his wife, Rosemary, came to Bible college. Rosemary worked in our accounting department for many years, while Ralph worked in the administrative department, involved with the construction that never seemed to end.

Several years later, Don Moore came back to Seattle and visited our church, not to minister, but to seek God for direction. He marvelled not only at the increased numbers (our congregation was five times larger), but also the spiritual depth. He said, "Everyone I talk to manifests knowledge in the Word with spiritual understanding. They are all able ministers."

* * *

Lester Sumrall's ministry to our body proved to be a blessing as well. We met Brother Sumrall at a conference in Dallas, Texas. After Brother Sumrall preached his last sermon, both Don and I felt it would be wonderful if he would come and minister at the Chapel. Don wrote a short note and passed it up to him on the platform. We joyfully thanked the Lord when he kindly accepted our invitation. We were awed that this great man of God, whom we had admired and supported his ministry to the Philippines, would come to our small congregation when he was used to preaching to thousands. It was overwhelming.

Upon Brother Sumrall's arrival, he felt the Lord wanted to have signs following Don's ministry. Brother Sumrall laid hands on Don, and the Lord blessed Don with a healing ministry that resulted in legs being evened in length as God touched and corrected whatever the problem was in the hips or back that caused one leg to be shorter than the other. Over the years, the congregation watched hundreds healed in this manner.

One lady named Sandy got her miracle just before she entered Bible college. She said, "That evening the pastor asked those who were suffering from back pain to come forward. The pastor had me sit down in a straight chair. He held my heels out and measured my legs against each other. With my back straight against the chair, my left leg was almost three inches shorter than my right. I already knew why: a congenital back problem, the toboggan accident, and the fall at the restaurant had created a twist in my hip that caused my leg to draw up. As soon as Pastor Don prayed, I felt an instant energy, like electricity, surge through my leg. I was amazed, even scared.

My eyes were wide open and I saw that left leg shoot out to the normal length. I jumped. I realized that for the first time in thirteen years, there was no more tension in my back. I twisted back and forth and moved around—no pain!" The congregation roared with praise to God.

Sandy said that for the rest of the evening she cried for joy and that night slept on her back. Amazingly, it was the most peaceful sleep she had ever had. (This healing is fully documented with medical records and doctor's reports in Community Chapel's booklet, *Healed by the Great Physician*.) Sandy, an accomplished opera singer, became one of our music instructors and also taught voice lessons.

Before Lester Sumrall closed his last meeting at our church, he predicted our church would expand and cover the whole hilltop. He also warned Don, "Be careful that someone doesn't spoil the very special and unique work being accomplished at the Chapel."

* * *

Don was right in his prediction that the Pauline Epistles class would give Tom a platform for sowing discontent among the students. Two students in particular came to Don with their concerns. One was Lanny (our future son-in-law) and the other was Petra, who was also getting her degree in psychiatry. She felt Don should sit in on the class. "The message Tom is getting across to the students is transmitted more by his actions and tone of voice," she said.

It wasn't long before a critical and superior spirit cropped up among the student body. Some of the criticalness was aimed at me, disapproval of the way I looked and dressed. Some college girls stopped wearing make-up altogether.

Don began teaching a series in Sunday School defining legalism.[3] He also preached sermons on legalism citing examples from church history how the church as a whole has been coming out of legalism since it's birth in the New Testament. Week after week he continued, until the forty-some students who were supporting Tom dwindled to twelve.

Tom felt he could no longer support Don's doctrine. He left and formed his own church called *The Church of the Narrow Way.* There was much heartache and sorrow, in the twelve who left as well as in us. Don had done all he could to save the flock from the horrible doctrine of legalism. *Little did we know how far we had to go to get free of it ourselves.*

I don't know all the problems Tom's church went through, but in time it was dissolved, but the love and respect between us remains. While Tom's church was still intact, they encountered a lady who was possessed by demons. She was not delivered after much prayer, so they contacted me to ask if I would pray for her. I invited Tom to bring her to an afternoon prayer meeting I had with a few of the ladies of the church.

The day before she arrived, the Lord showed me the demons and how they would behave. He also told me exactly how to deal with them. When I announced to the prayer group what was going to happen and that there would be demonic manifestations, I gave them a choice to leave if they felt fearful. Two left. I instructed the rest, "Stand as a wall of praise; no matter what happens, your expression of faith by praise will do more to force the demons to leave than shouting at them." As soon as the girl entered the room and the door closed behind her, the demons manifested exactly as the Lord had shown me.

First the demon of sarcasm spoke out of her mouth. Rolling her eyes back in her head, the demon said, "Oh, here we go again." The Lord had told me this demon would manifest first, but I was to ignore it, as it was a weak demon that was used as a front to shield the other two, the demons of fear and hate. The Lord had told me, "This weak demon will leave when the others go." I ignored the sarcastic demon and told the girl to kneel. The demon of fear filled her face and threw her across the room. I rushed to her side as she hit the floor.

The other prayer warriors stood around me and praised the Lord as I held the lady's face and forced that demon to look me in the eye as I commanded it to leave in Jesus' name. After only a few minutes, I saw the demon of fear come out of her and hover over her. I addressed it again, pointing my finger at its location, "Leave the room in Jesus' name." It shot up to the ceiling and over to the opposite wall. Again, I pointed my finger at it and commanded it to go back to its source, never to return to this vessel again. It shot out of the room, and I knew she would never have to worry about that demon again.

When I turned back to the girl, who was lying relaxed on the floor, I knew the battle was not yet over, because of what God had shown me. Again I took the girl's face in my hands. Immediately her eyes filled with hate. Through clenched teeth, she began to curse. The two men who had asked to be there held her down as I commanded that demon to silence and told it to leave her in Jesus' name. I saw, as it left, the demon of sarcasm departed, and told them both never to return.

I looked into the lady's eyes—they sparkled with happiness. She grabbed me and hugged me, exclaiming, "They're gone! They're gone!" We laughed and cried at the same time. I said, "I know, I know!" I kissed her on the cheek, as the praise team were literally jumping up and down shouting, "Thank you, Jesus!" I spoke in her ear, "Honey, now that you are empty of those unclean spirits, let Jesus fill you with His Holy Spirit." She raised her hands and began speaking in other tongues almost immediately.

> *Just as she had been a manifestation of demons, I know I was manifesting a strong angel of authority. It was he who rebuked those demons and saw them leave. The angel just used me to do it, so I got to say what he said and see what he saw. I can take no credit for what happened. It was the Lord who set her free.*

She was completely delivered and filled with the Holy Spirit within about fifteen minutes. I stepped outside to tell Tom, "She's lying on the floor with the glory of the Lord on her face, speaking in tongues." I didn't see Tom again for many years, and I don't have a progress report on the lady's spiritual growth. It was hard for me to walk away from her that day and leave her to the care of another. It wasn't as if we didn't have enough lambs of our own to care for, however. In fact, the Lord sent us someone to fill Tom's position in the office even before he left.

* * *

Roy and Margaret heard about our church from Keith and Joanne who went back to Wisconsin. They met Roy in a church they attended for a while. Roy, a soft-spoken man in his forties, had been in a Pentecostal church all his life and in the ministry as well. At the time Keith met him, Roy felt his spirit was dried up. He hadn't spoke in tongues for years, and he longed for a fresh touch from God.

Unknown to me, Roy had put a fleece before the Lord: "Lord, if You will set me free so I can feel Your Spirit again and speak in tongues when I visit Community Chapel in

THE TRUTH SHALL SET YOU FREE

Seattle, I will take it as a sign from You that You want me to move my family to Seattle and become part of the Chapel." With that prayer, Roy flew out for a weekend of services.

It was Sunday night before the evening service—Roy's last meeting—that he knelt in the crowded prayer room where I was praying before the service. The Lord spoke to my heart, "See that man over there, kneeling at that chair?" I had to turn completely around, as I was facing the wall and the chairs were in a row in the middle of the room. Immediately, I knew the man the Lord was talking about. He had his head down, holding it in his hands with his elbow propped on the chair. I said, "Yes, Lord. I see him."

The Lord said, "I want you to go lay hands on him."

I argued, "Jesus, I can't do that. He's the minister from Wisconsin. He's an old-time Pentecostal. I'm a woman, and women just don't go up to a man and lay hands on them."

I prayed a while longer before the Lord spoke to me again. "I want you to go lay hands on that man before the time runs out."

"Okay, Jesus, but I'm scared. I don't know what to pray. I will if You want me to; and if this isn't You, then at least I'll know I was willing to obey You."

I went over, stood behind Roy, and placed both my hands on his shoulders. The power of God shot through us like lightning. Roy's head flew back, his hands shot into the air, and he started speaking in tongues. I joined him in my prayer language, and someone turned the lights up signaling the start of the service. Neither of us could move because the power of God was too strong. After everyone else left the prayer room, my husband came in to see what was keeping me from the service. As he entered the room, the Lord spoke through me with a message in tongues and interpretation for Roy.

Before the service closed that night, Roy testified from the pulpit about the fleece he had laid before the Lord, and how God had answered it. Roy went back to Wisconsin, got his wife and two daughters, and moved to Seattle. I don't recall how many different positions Roy filled before he left the Chapel, but I know he worked as the office manager for many years, until there was a disagreement concerning switching the accounting system to a new computer technology. I wasn't involved in the dispute, but I was grieved to know that Roy and Margaret left the ministry with wounded hearts.

* * *

God used an entirely different method to supply us with a wonderful Bible college Dean, who was perfectly cast for the role.

An older gentleman was in the University district one day when he heard a group of our young people singing and testifying. He was so impressed with the glory of the Lord on their faces and their sincerity in wanting to bring people to Jesus, he offered to buy time on a local radio station so their songs and testimonies would reach more people. Mike, the leader, set up a tape recorder and some microphones in one of the Sunday School rooms, and in this makeshift studio, recorded some fifteen minute sessions with him playing the guitar.

The broadcast reached a retired Marine Air Force colonel and his wife who had just moved into a home on Dash Point, about 25 miles south of the Chapel. Ken was out in the back yard when his wife, Jill, came running out the back door shouting, "Ken, come quick! You've got to hear what's on the radio. I think it's what you've been looking for."

As Ken came through the kitchen door, the fifteen minute program was just ending, so he didn't get to hear it, but Jill had written down the name and address. Taking his wife's word for it, Ken and Jill came to the very next service. They knew instantly this was where God wanted them. Ken testified after he became our Bible college Dean, "My only regret in retiring from the military was that I would no longer be able to work with the young men. Now the Lord has given me a whole church and college full of young people to love."

The best word to describe Ken's life and ministry among us until his death in 1990 is "honorable." He served his Lord and church with the same loyalty and devotion with which he had served his country during his military career. Ken refused to take a salary in all his years of service at the Chapel. It wasn't beneath his dignity, either, to be a student himself. He graduated from our Bible college with both a Bachelor and Master of Theology degree.

* * *

In spite of the setback when Tom and his group left our church, Lester Sumrall's prediction that the Chapel would "cover the hill" came to pass. Our growth soared.

People from all over the United States, as well as other countries, filled the pews. Each life testified of the miracle-working power of God.

One tall young man was convicted after a service and literally fell off the pew and started crawling on his hands and knees toward the altar, groaning and crying as he went. I rushed to him and prayed the prayer of salvation in his ear. As Ron heard the words, he shouted them out to the Lord and was wonderfully saved. When Don came and prayed with him, Ron received the Holy Spirit. He knew then that he could no longer be the manager of one of the hottest night clubs in Seattle.

Soon after enrolling in Bible college, Ron was part of a team that went to Expo '71 in Texas, where our Bible college booth attracted a lady from Kansas who went back home and was used by the Lord to bring close to forty students to Bible college. As soon as we had a student graduated and capable, a fellowship was started in that area which grew into a church. Another outreach team went to Iowa, and from a small home Bible study fellowship, sixty students came to Bible college.

As people increased, ministries flourished. A Ministries Office emerged, which included new convert counseling, home Bible study fellowships in almost every area of greater Seattle, prayer meetings, healing ministry, big brother and big sister ministries, help for new and single mothers, wedding coordinators, engaged couples' counselors, etc.

Witnessing teams went to college campuses, parks, centers, jails, and door-to-door. We established a food and clothing bank for those in need. Besides the Bible college office and all its departments, we opened a Christian School, a full-time youth ministry department which planned activities and services for the teenagers, Sunday School with a full-time staff plus 150 volunteer teachers, and a maintenance and security department which included coordinating the building projects.

Our publishing department grew until it was fully staffed and equipped, capable of editing and printing books, complete with colored graphics and photos.

Everyone contributed to the ministry—the vision I'd received of the fruit arbor became a reality. Radiant faces full of joy were everywhere as people served Jesus with all their hearts. Our church doors were rarely closed.

Of all the multitude of talents, none were more grand than the ministers in music. The commitment these gifted musicians made to Jesus made it possible for Him to anoint their voices to proclaim His greatness. By the inspiration of the Holy Spirit, they gave us hundreds of songs. As we progressed from one move of God's Spirit to another, the new songs from music ministry fit exactly what Jesus was doing in our lives. Nor were the children left out; new songs for them were recorded by our children's music ministry.

With our fully equipped music studio, we produced quality tapes filled with the songs born of the Spirit. Our once-a-month Gospel in Song services, held on Saturday evenings, drew visitors from all over the Northwest.

A prayer ministry was launched. In the second semester of our Bible college, through my personal crises, Jesus gave me a key to intercessory prayer that changed my prayer life.

Wallowing in self-pity, I ran to the prayer room, crumpled in a heap, and whimpered, "Jesus, I hurt so bad . . . ." Suddenly, my prayer shifted, and I heard myself saying, "But this time I want to know what is on Your heart, instead of coming to You with what's on mine—

You already know how much I hurt. This time I want to know what causes You pain."

I began worshipping Jesus, and it wasn't long until I felt as if Jesus joined my heart to His. I experienced His grief over His church nationwide. I learned to cast my cares upon Him, freeing my spirit and mind, so Jesus could use me to intercede for whatever He knew needed prayer at the time. It was a simple lesson in how to put faith to work.

Shortly after this experience, a lady named Chrissie—who, along with her family, came to the Chapel after the Lord rescued them from a hippie community—was at the back of the church after a service. The Lord spoke to Chrissie's heart, "Go up where Barbara is praying and kneel beside her and pray." With fear and trembling, she obeyed. We soon became very close and dear prayer partners. The Lord used us as if we were one voice with Him. Our spirits were joined in what seemed to be the fulfillment, at least in part, of Jesus' prayer in John 17 when He prayed, "Father, that they may be one as we are one."

As time went on, Chrissie and I prayed together several times a week. Many times our understanding was unfruitful, but our spirits were keenly aware of what was happening. One of us would speak a statement in tongues that was clearly a question, and the other would speak the answer in tongues. Sometimes this went on for an hour. Sometimes we could tell by the tenor of prayer that we were battling in a warfare against the demons of Satan's kingdom. When the battle was won we would spontaneously break out in a victory song in perfect harmony—a real miracle for me, not having much musical talent.

THE TRUTH SHALL SET YOU FREE

It wasn't too many weeks until others joined us. After the services, the small prayer room was so crowded one more person couldn't possibly squeeze in. The triumphant songs in the spirit were heard all over the building, as well as the battles, all spoken in tongues.

Soon prayer groups were formed, until almost everyone joined one of the prayer meetings scheduled at various times during the day, every day of the week. Even though these prayer meetings were two to three hours long, the desire to pray increased, so we started having prayer retreats that lasted anywhere from three to five days. Every department and ministry of the Chapel had a prayer retreat at least once a year.

Prayer was the heart of the church, and the Word of God the backbone. Because Don had spent an average of six hours a day since he was eighteen studying the Bible, we were blessed with an abundance of knowledge in the Word of God. The truth of who we are in Christ, our relationship to Jesus as His Bride, and the ministry of the universal church in the last days before the Rapture, was the focal point of all the teaching and preaching. No doctrine of the Bible was left out, but they all pointed to our relationship with Jesus.

* * *

Our church and Bible college grew and expanded, along with the Christian school which included preschool through grade twelve. The first building was remodeled and added onto continually. It was jammed with one thousand people by the time we purchased thirty-six acres just west of the original site and built a large auditorium with the beginning seating capacity of 2,000. The building was designed to be expanded, increasing the seating to nearly 8,000. We also built a separate educational building and a college housing complex. The original five-acre parcel remained in constant use for the Bible college, administrative offices, publishing department, and music studio.

We paid for the thirty-six acres by an interest-free loan from a member of our church, but now, for the first time, the Chapel was in debt. We started the building project, but had to acquire a bank loan in order to complete it. Moving into the new sanctuary didn't stifle the move of God. In fact, God was about to do something that surprised all of us.

Chapter Fourteen

"Satan, I Declare War on You!"

"Your adversary, the devil, as a roaring lion, walketh about seeking whom he may devour."
(1 Peter 5:8)

"Pastor, we are having the most phenomenal thing happen back here in our church," Keith, pastor in Wisconsin, told Don over the phone. "Actually, what started the whole thing was a statement I made at the end of a sermon," he continued. "I spoke to the devil and said, 'Satan, I declare war on you!' Pastor, it was like the devil came out of hiding so we could see him to fight him. But we found out his army of demons is actually hiding in God's people.

"That's right. A few days ago, a lady in our church, a good sister in the Lord, came to our home, and within a few minutes she started manifesting an evil spirit. That demon spoke out of her mouth with terrible cursings. I knew it wasn't she, so I started rebuking it in Jesus' name. Before long, it left her, and she was so glad to be free. Then, all of a sudden, another demon manifested through her, so we rebuked that one. Anyway, after about three hours of this, she was totally set free of all the demons that had been plaguing her. Now she doesn't have hate, anger, and bitterness well up inside of her.

"Since that happened, we have been praying for people constantly and, Don, God's people are getting delivered and set free of things that have been in their lives for years. It's as if I have a new church, Pastor. The manifestations are awful, but the victories are sweet. Finally, the people are able to live overcoming lives. We just didn't know we had these demons that were causing us to act and think in ways that we hated. Don, after this started happening, someone gave me some books on the subject, showing from the Bible that Christians can have demons."

By the end of the conversation, Don agreed to study the subject in the Bible, and invited Keith and Joanne to come to Seattle to testify about what God was doing in their church. Both Don and I had been taught that Christians couldn't have demons actually manifest through them. We believed a Christian could be tempted by demons and enticed by demons somehow, but they couldn't enter our bodies or minds. Only an unsaved, demon-possessed person had demons living in them. We were surprised at Keith's report.

As soon as Don opened the Bible and researched the subject for himself, he found plenty of Scriptural support for Christians being plagued by demons. One example is found in Matthew 16:23, where Jesus said to Peter, "Get behind me, Satan." Apparently, the devil had just spoken through Peter.

Before Keith and Joanne arrived, Don told our congregation he had been wrong when he taught that Christians couldn't have demons. He proceeded to teach a series on the subject, proving his old theology was incorrect. We ordered Win Worley's books, along with *Pigs in the Parlor,* and Don Basham's booklet, *Can A Christian Have A Demon?,* and made them available to purchase from our bookcounter.

When our people learned how God was setting people free, they were eager to get prayer and get delivered from thoughts and habits in their lives they had struggled with for years. Needless to say, a move of God of this nature is easier to direct if your church body has fifty people rather than fifteen hundred, but we formed prayer groups with a leader over each one, so every person in the congregation had the opportunity to be delivered.

One of the first ones to get delivered in our services was a lady who came up to me after Keith's testimony. The service had only been dismissed for ten minutes when I caught a glimpse of Darlene out of the corner of my eye while I was talking with someone else. Immediately I saw wild hate in her eyes and she couldn't stand still—she was in such torment. I sensed there was going to be a long battle ahead, so I motioned for her to wait until I finished with the one to whom I was speaking. But the demons wouldn't let her wait.

They threw her to the floor. Immediately the power of God surged through me and I knelt at her head so I could speak to her in her ear. Of course, it took no time at all before a crowd of people formed around her. Having had experience in these things before, I asked everyone to proclaim the victory through praise. The demons twisted her body and screamed through her. I held her head, so the demons couldn't bang it on the floor, and spoke in her ear, "Darlene, no matter what these demons try to do to you, keep your mind on Jesus. They can't keep you from loving Jesus in your mind. Nod your head if you heard me and you will do it." She nodded. With that, the Lord gave me spiritual discernment and I called those demons by name, and each one left her. Each time a demon left her, she relaxed, smiled and proclaimed, "I'm free! It's gone!" It was about 45 minutes later when we hugged each other, both of us exhausted, but thankful to Jesus for the victory.

For many months after that, you could walk into the sanctuary any time of day until after midnight and find teams of prayer warriors battling against the demonic forces in the lives of their brothers and sisters. The people humbled themselves and submitted to prayer. They also sacrificed their time and prayed for others. Testimonies of mighty deliverances filled the services. We saw one lady's hands twisted with arthritis straighten out in front of our eyes as we were impressed to command a "demon of arthritis" to leave in Jesus' name. People were also encouraged to practice "self-deliverance," so we prayed against any demons we might have, and when we prayed for others, we asked the Lord to deliver us at the same time. After this initial plunge into deliverance, it became a part of the ministry at the Chapel.

I clearly remember I had a manifestation of a demon that was so contrary to me I knew I had to get rid of it immediately. I went to Chrissie, my prayer partner, and confided, "Chrissie, this feeling comes over me and when it does, I can't stand to touch or be close to Don. It's awful!"

"Oh," she said, with perfect confidence, "That's a husband-hating demon. I got delivered from that one. You just lie down here on the floor and don't do anything. I'll pray for you."

It was a different experience for me, because I was the one who always prayed. I had a hard time just letting her do it, but every time I tried to help, she stopped me. Once I surrendered to her prayers, that demon left me and I never had that problem again. It was a good lesson for me to be on the other side for once, and "submit to one another in love" (Ephesians 5:21).

* * *

The devil's plan for Don was exposed when Chrissie, myself, and others were praying for him. In my mind, I saw a scene in which the Spirit of the Lord was talking to a powerful evil spirit who was sitting at an executive's desk in a dark, cave-like room. The Lord commanded the demon to come out into the light and expose his plan to ruin Don and his ministry. I was made to know this demon was the master planner for Don's destruction, and he was over other demons who would carry out his plan.

I wasn't given any knowledge regarding the other demons, only that they existed, but this master demon was so angry at God's command, he fumed and fussed as he and his desk were moved out into the light. Once the light hit him, he seemed to lose all his power. The words I heard him say were, "His [Don's] mind is our biggest threat. We will get to his mind through drugs, and he will fall."

On the surface, this statement didn't make sense. Don had been a Christian all his life. He had never touched a cigarette, or tasted beer or other alcohol. He certainly couldn't be tempted with cocaine, LSD, speed, or marijuana. The first aspirin he ever took was after we were married, when he had an impacted wisdom tooth. He discovered he was allergic to aspirin, because he broke out with a terrible case of hives.

However, right after, the whole episode with Tom—who left the church over the doctrine of legalism—the tremendous strain on Don took its toll. He got a bad case of shingles. If I had to designate one point that could be called the beginning of this master demon's plan to destroy Don, I would point to this time, because with the development of pain in his back from the long hours he spent at his desk studying, often until 2:00 a.m.—coupled with the stress and tension of the ministry—he found a temporary release through pain killers. When the doctor discovered the blisters extending from his side to halfway across his stomach, he knew it was shingles. The fear of what kind of damage had been done to the nerves haunted Don and increased the tension. The doctor added muscle relaxants to the Tylenol III (codeine) tablets.

The pain was terrible, and he was miserable. To get Don away from his desk, we left for Vancouver. I was driving, of course, since he was on drugs. He took another codeine tablet even though it was too soon after the last one. About fifteen minutes later, he took another Valium. Before we got to the border, he took yet another codeine. Without realizing it, he had overdosed and began hallucinating. Because of the terror he experienced,

"SATAN, I DECLARE WAR ON YOU!"

he was more scared than I that night, but the incident didn't stop him from taking his prescribed medication the way he wanted, instead of the way the doctor ordered. Don made up his own rules, rather than follow the doctor's orders.

After the shingles episode, Don's body couldn't take as much stress as before, so our breaks became more frequent, only now by the time we left he was usually taking heavy doses of pain killers and Valium, or other forms of relaxants which made him more vulnerable to seducing, perverted spirits..

I can make excuses for him, saying his resistance was low, but I have no excuse for myself, except to say I'd been taught to obey my husband. I rejected my own true feelings, and did what my husband wanted me to do, that is, most of the time. Sometimes I wouldn't; then I'd feel guilty.

One time I actually got out of the car and walked away. Don let me go. I was several blocks away by the time he caught up with me. A truck driver stopped and offered me a ride. I almost got in, to get as far away from my husband as possible. Instead, when Don pulled up beside me, I got back in the car and after a couple of hours of silence, I was right back by his side again. The worst nightmare, however, happened in Las Vegas.

* * *

The day started out innocently enough. We had arrived in Las Vegas the afternoon before, taking advantage of a special rate on airfare and hotel accommodations. Vacations were not paid for by the church. Neither of us were interested in gambling, but we both enjoyed poolside rests. As I stepped into the shower that morning, Don left the room to get a dry towel, wearing only his knee-length robe.

I thought, *Surely he won't have any temptation with the maids on our floor, because we just finished making love.* Yet no sooner had he returned to the room and got into the shower himself, when there was loud knock at the door. With my towel still wrapped around me, I called, "Who is it?" Another loud bang on the door. They shouted back, "Police! Open up!"

Oh no, I thought, *this time he got caught.* I responded, "I'm sorry, but I can't open the door. I'm not dressed, and my husband is in the shower."

Another loud knock. "Get dressed; we're coming in!"

I pleaded, "Can't you please wait? My husband will be out of the shower in just a minute."

By now the police were talking to the other hotel guests who had gathered in the hall to see what all the commotion was about. At the next loud knock, Don yelled, "Just wait! I'm going to get dressed, and then I'll open the door. I'm not going anywhere; we're on the 22nd floor!"

I hid in the bathroom when Don opened the door and stepped into the hall. He never came back into the room. I didn't know what happened or where they might have taken him. About a half-hour later the phone rang. It was Don. "Jean, listen to me. I promise you, before God, I didn't do it. You've got to believe me. They are taking me to the police station. Come and get me out as soon as you can. Don't believe the reports; I didn't do it."

Stunned, I asked, "Where are the car keys?"

"SATAN, I DECLARE WAR ON YOU!"

"Oh, they're right here in my pocket. Just a minute." I heard him ask if he could bring me the keys. They said I would have to come to the guard station to get them.

"I'll be there as soon as I can," I promised. We hung up. I had no idea where the guard station was or where the police station was. I wasn't even sure I could drive the stick-shift car we had rented. The first thing I did was pray. "Jesus, help me to do the right thing. Lord, I hope you can use this to free Don of the terrible demon that drives him to do these things. Lord, is he innocent or guilty this time? Should I defend him?"

I didn't get any answers from the Lord, but at least I wasn't panicky. *Well,* I reasoned, *The first thing I have to do is finish dressing. Then I'll call the operator and find out where the guard station is.*

When I reached the guard's room and recovered the car keys, I asked, "How do I get to the police station?" With a smirk on their faces, they gave me wrong directions. I ended up on the wrong side of town. When I finally did find the right building, I couldn't find parking except in the metered section. I didn't have any money for the meter—Don had all our cash in his wallet (I didn't carry a purse on vacations). I parked the car anyway, hoping I wouldn't end up in jail, too.

I waited in the police station for nearly an hour before I was ushered into a small room where two police officers handed me five typed testimonies from housekeepers at the hotel. Fortunately, I couldn't read them, because I had left my glasses in the hotel room. The officers were reluctant to read them to me, so they merely explained, "Your husband has been booked for indecent exposure based on these five witnesses." I stared at them, shaking my head.

THE TRUTH SHALL SET YOU FREE

I asked, "Can I see Don?"

One said, "He's not here; he has been taken to jail."

I couldn't believe it! Involuntary tears streamed down my cheeks. They sympathized, "We're sorry, ma'am, but there's nothing we can do. You'll need to get a bond to get him out of jail."

"How do I do that?" I asked, bewildered.

"Look in the phone directory under 'bonds.'"

I sighed, "Would you do me a favor? Could you get a message to Don and let him know what I have to do to get him out, and that I'm working on it, so he won't worry?"

"Sorry, ma'am. We can't give messages to the inmates. This isn't a hotel. But there's a pay phone in the lobby, if you want to call a bondsman from here."

Getting up to leave, I replied, "No, thank you. I don't have a quarter. I'll go back to the hotel and call from there."

Back to the hotel. The first bondsman I dialed couldn't help me. "What you need," he said, "is a good criminal lawyer. He gave me the name of one he said was the best in town.

As I waited for the lawyer's answering service to put me through to his home—it was Sunday, so the office was closed—I prayed. "Jesus, what if this gets back to the church—that their pastor is in jail?" I laughed aloud. Then I thought, *Oh, no, this really is serious! Lord, please don't let this news get out, and please help me to make the right decision about hiring a lawyer.*

The lawyer agreed to meet me at his office right away if I could pay him a $700 fee in advance. I didn't even have a quarter! Don also had the charge card. I asked

"SATAN, I DECLARE WAR ON YOU!"

the lawyer anyway, "Will you accept a charge card?" He reluctantly agreed. Now I just had to convince him to either wait for the card until he got Don out or take the card information from the hotel. I got a copy of our account from the hotel desk and met the lawyer in his plush office. After getting the card approved, he told me, "Go back to the hotel. I will call you as soon as I get Don released. I'm sure I'll have Don out in a few hours"

Was I relieved when that hotel phone rang! I had no guarantee the lawyer was going to do what he said. The only credentials I had was the bondsman's recommendation.

Wouldn't you know it, on the way to pick up Don, my car ran out of gas? Right in the middle of an intersection as I was making a left turn! Somehow I managed to push the thing over to a side road. Finally a nice man came to my rescue. Upon discovering the tank was empty, he offered to take me to a gas station. He even bought $3 worth of gas for me. I couldn't bring myself to tell him I was on my way to get my husband from jail.

Finally I arrived at the door where Don was to be released—he wasn't there! *Surely he would wait for me*, I thought. *Maybe that lawyer was a phony after all, and he's cashed in on our $700.* After waiting for half an hour, I went around to the front of the building. No one there could help me. I drove back to the hotel to call the lawyer. Don was in our room. He hadn't been told I would meet him, so he took a taxi.

He wasn't interested in hearing what my day was like; he just wanted to know how to get out of this mess. I told him, "We have an appointment with the lawyer in the morning."

He said, "You did the right thing retaining him."

We got something to eat, the first for me all day. Over dinner, Don told me what a nightmare it had been for him to be stripped, given coveralls to wear, and put in a cell with everyone else. He was angered when the policemen who went through his wallet found a picture of me and said they were going to my hotel room to "keep her company while you're in jail." I shuddered, thinking, *I'm not safe in this city.*

We sat in the lobby after dinner, and Don told me he had spent the day praying and how much he hated his weakness. Softly, he added, "I feel like such a failure, unfit before the Lord to be a pastor. Yet I know the Lord has called me and given me a pastor's heart, fully knowing all my weaknesses."

He reflected on how much he had suffered from condemnation. "That's why," he said, "I preach so vehemently against letting the devil condemn you when you have repented. I can identify with the young men in the assembly who have strong sex drives, because I feel the same pressures they do. I can't talk about this with anyone else for fear they will lose respect for me."

I looked up into his tired eyes and sensed he had to tell me something I didn't want to hear. He studied the pattern in the deep red carpet, and his shoulders slumped under an invisible weight, as he confided in me about his struggles to break off a recent affair.

"It was like a force driving me to see her," he said, as if saying it would push back the force. He said the affair stopped short of adultery, because he was deathly afraid of committing adultery. He admitted, "I know I'd be an adulterer if I wasn't a born-again Christian, because the lustful enticement is so strong."

"SATAN, I DECLARE WAR ON YOU!"

Too weary to respond and numb by the day's events, I listened in silence, but every confession stabbed my already wounded heart. When we returned to our hotel room, I doubled over with gut-wrenching agony. Without realizing it, I had again let myself be his scapegoat, giving him an excuse for his behavior.

> *Do you suppose this may be the reason Don suffered from condemnation? He never felt forgiven, even though he repented repeatedly.*

In the lawyer's office the next morning, we learned the legal procedure. The lawyer asked Don to take a lie detector test. The results of the test were negative, even though Don knew he wasn't guilty. The tester said it was possible for Don to fail the test because he was so nervous about it that they couldn't get an accurate reading. Their comment was, "His conscience is too sensitive to give the machine the right data." We were able to go home after the trial date was set. The lawyer got the charges reduced to a misdemeanor, so Don never had to go back to stand trial.

We returned home and put the whole thing behind us. No one at church knew anything about it. Jesus, in His great mercy and grace knew Don would soon get delivered from that horrible unclean spirit.

It happened when another dear man in our church who struggled with the same temptation came to our home one day, white as a sheet, asking to speak to the pastor in private. When the man left, Don told me he had

THE TRUTH SHALL SET YOU FREE

been arrested for indecent exposure and was afraid of a jail sentence. I happened to ask if the man's wife was with him. Don said, "No; that's where he made his mistake. He should use his wife, so he'd have an alibi." Suddenly, a light went on inside my head. *So that's why Don uses me!* Anger and pain raged in me. It was too much to bear—in one awful instant, I chose not to believe what I'd just heard—I just couldn't deal with it.

    I am forever grateful to that young man for being humble enough to come to his pastor for help because a few days later both men, like the Apostle Paul in Romans 7:24, cried out, "*O, wretched man that I am! Who shall deliver me...? I thank God, through Jesus Christ our Lord.*" "Where sin abounds, grace does much more abound" (Romans 5:20). Don prayed and rebuked those demons with all the fury of heaven against the devil. In God's mercy, He redeemed them (Isaiah 63:9). Both Don and the young man were completely delivered, and neither were ever tempted like that again.

* * *

    Don's deliverance, however, didn't keep his heart from getting too involved with women in the church, so the Lord gave me a vision concerning Don, me, and the ministry. In my mind, I saw a tower-like structure being built that was made of bricks. It wasn't finished, but was already quite high. The two bricks at the base symbolized Don and me. The foundation was deep and solid, and I knew that represented Jesus. The whole structure, however, was leaning a little to the right, with one small part leaning more than the rest.

"SATAN, I DECLARE WAR ON YOU!"

The Lord showed me what needed to be done and what would happen if it weren't. He said, "These two bricks at the base (referring to Don and me) need to be adjusted so they fit perfectly on the foundation." He showed me the adjustment by first moving Don, who needed more of an adjustment than I, and then He moved me. He said, "If this adjustment can be made now, none of the building will be lost, and it, too, will go in line. If the adjustment is made later, it can still be made, but this part of the structure will topple." This time as I watched the adjustment take place, the portion that leaned the most fell off—not with a crash, but each brick fell, some together, some separately.

Then Jesus said, "If the adjustment isn't made, the whole structure will come down before it is finished, because there is no way it can be completed." I saw it come crashing down. When I shared the vision with Don, he commented, "I don't know how it applies to you. It's me who has the problem with girls and not you. You don't need to change; you're not involved."

I said, "Honey, I don't know how I'm involved, all I know is the Lord gave me the vision, so there must be something wrong."

I used to testify, "I don't know who I am outside of being Mrs. Donald Lee Barnett. I have no other identity other than being whatever my husband wants me to be." I knew how his mind worked, how he thought, so much so that he let me make many decisions in his stead, because he knew I would do exactly what he would. I even tried to get my mind to think like his.

A few times his frustration with me, because I didn't think like he did, reached a point where I broke emotionally, and my body quivered for hours. We never yelled and screamed at one another, and just one time, other than the judo hold incident, did he ever hit me.

Nothing more was said about this vision, and about a year later the small part toppled over—we first lost two families, then seven. But before its final fulfillment, the Lord gave us many more chances to see and make the adjustments. I received some insight into my problem at a prayer retreat.

* * *

In a vision, Jesus showed me a beautiful diamond. He was holding it with both hands under His chin. Jesus let me feel how He felt about this diamond. It was large enough to fill His hand. As He held it close and loved it, I saw how beautiful it was and how much pleasure it brought Him. It wasn't until Jesus turned it just a little that I noticed the flaw. It was amazing—the flaw didn't keep Jesus from loving it or receiving pleasure from owning it. I burst into tears when Jesus spoke in my mind, "This diamond is you."

To think that Jesus felt that way about me was overwhelming. In His wisdom, He had waited to reveal to me whom the diamond represented. With all my self-hate and insecurities, I would have never been able to experience how He felt about it. When I could speak, I asked, "Jesus, what is the flaw?" He said, "It's your love for your husband."

I was baffled! I had no idea my love for Don was a problem. Then Jesus said, "If you will give your love for him to Me, I can fix it." With that revelation and without hesitation, I said, "Yes, Lord, You can have it, You can have it. And I give You the love I have for my children, too; and for the church, too; and for my house, too—You can have everything I love."

Although I said the words, I really didn't know what it meant to give my love for Don to Jesus. I didn't know there was coming a day when I would know if I had indeed done what I'd prayed. Don couldn't accept the validity of this vision, because he knew I was completely devoted to him.

Don, in his own way, tried to make the adjustment in his love for the church. When God made him a pastor, he felt that God gave him a shepherd's heart. He testified that he never thought he could be a pastor, because he didn't think he could preach. In spite of his speech impediment, he knew God had called him to teach. Everyone who sat under his ministry agreed he had a unique gift of explaining the Word of God. Even those new in Christ came away with an unusual depth in the Word.

He said, "When I was a teacher, I had a love for everyone in my class, but I never felt a need to hug them. Once I became a pastor, God gave me such a love for the people, I feel like I just have to hug them and express it every way possible." He hardly ever left the pulpit without telling the congregation how much he loved them. He wasn't as generous with his hugs to the men as with the ladies; nonetheless, they received an occasional hug, too. The only ones with whom he had a problem were the crippled or retarded; but God gave me a special love for them, and I went out of my way to hug them.

Don's love transformed a rambunctious, rebellious eight-year-old boy who always gave his parents and the ushers a hard time. This boy saw the pastor in the bathroom one time and asked some questions. In the answer, the pastor hugged him and called him "pal."

The next time Don's glass of water at the pulpit needed to be filled, he asked if his pal would fill it. The boy literally ran to the pulpit, grinning from ear to ear, to get the glass. After that, this kid became Don's shadow, ready to do anything for him. His behavior changed, because now he was accepted as the pastor's friend. He even took it upon himself to police the drinking fountains, making sure other children didn't squirt one another, as he had done in the past.

Problems kept cropping up, however, when Don's hugs and attention became excessive. It started out innocently enough. Like the eight-year-old boy, the ladies needed love and acceptance. Routinely, these relationships were brought back into balance before any serious involvement took place, and Don would, on occasion, have a meeting with a segment of the women, attempting to make them aware of his weakness. As hard as it was, he usually felt better afterwards, and was stronger not to yield to the temptation.

Jesus, however, had a plan for all of us, to rid us of the spots and wrinkles (Ephesians 5:27) and burn up all the wood, hay, and stubble (1 Corinthians 3:11-15), because His Word declares He will have a church without any spots or flaws! We at the Chapel had the knowledge of the Bride relationship and the Manchild ministry of the church in these last days. Everyone was working toward and dedicated to the day when all that God had given us could be shared with the whole body of Christ: all our wonderful music; all our children's music; all the Sunday School les-

"SATAN, I DECLARE WAR ON YOU!"

sons, Christian school curriculum, and teen programs that we developed; all the Bible studies, sermons, Bible college classes; all the books and booklets published—everything was, one day, whenever the Lord opened the door, going to be used for His glory. Jesus was leading us, one step at a time, into a position where He could take us from the fruit arbor He'd shown us in the vision into that dazzling white room, which was a love union with Him.

Chapter Fifteen

Who is the Son?

"All things been handed over to me by my Father, and no one knows who the Son is except the Father, and who the Father is except the Son, and anyone to whom the Son wills to reveal Him."
(Luke 10:22)

By 1982, our congregation had increased to over two thousand adults. Besides the church in Wisconsin, additional satellite churches sprang up in Kirkland, Tacoma, Olympia, Spokane, Yakima, Vancouver and Victoria in Canada, Kansas, New Mexico, two in California, two in Montana, and overseas in Greece, Switzerland, Sweden, and the Philippines. Our pastor's extraordinary wisdom in the Word of God was passed on to all the excellent Bible college teachers and other wonderful scholars in our body, of whom some became the pastors of these satellite churches. Their combined congregations numbered around two thousand.

Never have I seen such dedication and devotion to God, His Word, and His body—almost to a person, each was 100% sold out to God. The church, and God's purpose for us in the last days, was the life of each member.

The love and respect shared among congregations and leadership seemed unparalleled. Most faithfully gave tithes plus offerings, while eagerly volunteering time and talents to ministries. With amazement we watched the Spirit of God bring us all into the same wave after wave of His Spirit, whether it started in the Seattle church or in one of the other congregations.

By this time the Lord had—through many prophecies and visions—given us three very powerful promises: 1) Jesus was going to manifest His very presence to us; 2) Jesus' presence would bring judgment; and 3) we were going to experience a baptism of love.

With God's promise to bring judgment, our pastor preached sermons dealing with handling God's judgment properly.[4] The pastor showed, for example, that Adam and Eve, when confronted by God, both blamed someone else (Genesis 3:11-13). When King Saul was confronted by the prophet Samuel, he lied (1 Samuel 15:20); but when Nathan the prophet told King David, "Thou art the man" (2 Samuel 12:7), David confessed and repented.

In one of these sermons, the pastor told of a revelation one of the intercessors received from the Lord while praying for him. She said the Lord showed her Jesus was coming to the Chapel, and when He did, He would bring judgment that would start with the pastor. Don stated, "I don't know exactly how it will happen, but I am praying I'll have a humble attitude."

God had also promised our pastor a profound experience in the Spirit. Many months before it happened, it was confirmed by several people, independent of one another. Not only I, but other prayer groups that prayed for their pastor weekly, had experienced the same thing:

the Lord had something special for Don. We left to go to a prayer retreat with the elders, which by this time numbered eighteen plus their wives, and over a dozen intercessors. Along with others, I felt in my spirit that sometime during this four-day retreat the Lord would do what He had promised. None of us were disappointed.

* * *

The presence of the Lord was mighty among us from the very first day of our elders' prayer retreat. After three days and nights of solid prayer, breaking only to eat and sleep, it happened. As everyone filed back in to the large prayer room, the presence of God and His angels had already filled the room, almost as if someone had sprayed the room with a fragrant dewy mist. Reverently, we knelt, laid our hands on our pastor, and softly prayed in tongues.

Then, in unison, without a cue from a director, we heard bubbling forth from our own mouths an harmonious melody paralleled only to the grandest symphony. It had to be that an heavenly choir of angels had joined us. If you could have heard that melody, you would have known it was a song about a journey—not a march, although it was definitely victorious—but rather a smooth chariot ride in the sky. Everyone sensed our pastor's spirit was being carried upwards.

Afterwards, the pastor said he felt as if he represented the whole body of Christ, not just himself. "I know now," he said, "just how important to Jesus is every single member, because I felt an acute loss if even one voice stopped or if one elder removed his hand for even a moment. Every single member is so important to Jesus—if for a second, someone is missing, He feels great anguish and pain."

After about forty-five minutes, Sandy, an intercessor, expounded on God's love in a clear soprano voice. Each of our voices blended into a beautiful harmony as we joined her. That heavenly sound is forever ingrained in my consciousness. The song of God's love continued into the second hour, but our pastor wasn't aware of time, because his spirit had been carried up into the throne of God. Later, Don said, "I can relate to the Apostle Paul when he said (in 2 Corinthians 12:2) *'whether in the body or out of the body, I cannot tell: God knoweth, such a one caught up to the third heaven.'* I knew my soul was still here in my body, because I could still feel and hear, but the beautiful spiritual experience was so all-consuming that I wasn't aware of anything else."

At the end of the third hour, just as the experience was over, the song ended. Don opened his eyes and wept. He struggled to relate to his surroundings, and asked, "Where is my wife?"

He hugged me. He hugged the others. He was too emotional to speak. He felt his own arms. "Is this me? I'm so puny." He burst into tears again. "I don't want to come back! Everything is so shabby here." He stood up and Marvin, an elder, held him as Don's whole body shook. He cried, "I can't stand it here; my hands and arms are so puny. My body is puny. Everything is shabby. I don't want to stay here."

For the next half-hour, Don walked around the room as if he were lost and on a strange planet. He kept repeating, "It's so glorious there and so shabby here. Everything is strange here. I'm so puny. I don't want to live in

WHO IS THE SON?

this body." As soon as he thought he had his emotions under control, he burst into tears again. "It's glorious there. It's glorious there."

Someone opened a Bible and read 1 Corinthians 12:4-5: *"How that he was caught up into paradise, and heard unspeakable words, which it is not lawful for a man to utter. Of such a one will I glory; yet of myself I will not glory, but in mine infirmities."* Don lamented once more, "Oh, Lord, I'm so puny." He sat down, held his head, and wept.

Don tried to tell us what had happened to him, only to discover there was no way to explain what the eternal realm is really like, because there is nothing on this earth to compare it to. It became clear why the Bible speaks of what won't be there, such as no sorrow, no pain, no tears, rather than what is there. The pastor had always taught that the description of the New Jerusalem in the book of Revelation was figurative and not actual, because the Bible says it hasn't entered into the heart of man what we shall be like, only that we *shall be like Him for we shall see Him as He is.* That's what had happened to Don.

"Just as it is written, 'Things which eye has not seen and ear has not heard, and which have not entered the heart of man, all that God has prepared for those who love Him.' For to us God revealed them through the Spirit; for the Spirit searches all things, even the depths of God." (1 Corinthians 2:9-10)

Our pastor had seen Jesus—the glorified Son of Man—as He is, and now there was no way to tell us what he had seen, because it wasn't a vision of a personage, but rather it was an experience. He had experienced Jesus as the glorified Son of Man in His eternal position in heaven. There was no earthly adjective or likeness to describe it. All Don could say between sobs was that it was far more glorious than he had ever imagined, but the awesome truth of Who the glorified Son of Man is was the reason God gave the experience.

While Don was in the experience, he found himself asking the Father, "Who is the Son?" He knew the question was not one he thought to ask, but that it came from God. The Father pointed to Don—who was representing the whole body of Christ—and said, "You are the Son." Instantly, Don saw all the elders and everyone praying in the room down below on earth, and the Father said, "There is the Son." In that joyous occurrence, God established forever in Don's consciousness the irreversible revelation of Luke 10:21-22, where Jesus prayed: *"I praise Thee, O Father, Lord of heaven and earth, that Thou didst hide these things from the wise and intelligent and didst reveal them to babes. Yes, Father, for thus it was well-pleasing in Thy sight. All things have been handed over to Me by My Father, and <u>no one knows who the Son is except the Father, and who the Father is except the Son, and anyone to whom the Son wills to reveal Him</u>."* [author's emphasis]

The wonder of it all was beyond expression! After our pastor actually sampled being one with Christ as equal heirs (Romans 8:17), and tasted our unending eternal position in heaven, he didn't adjust to this inferior earthly environment for days. In fact, he doubted his ability to function as a mere human being. He said, "Everything here seems abnormal; we're limited in every way—mentally, physically, socially. But "over there" seems normal. We know, we see, we experience—it's limitless! It's the way we were created to be. I know, in time, I'll probably feel like this is normal, and that eternal realm will seem strange. But right now 'over there' is normal." Don said he saw the heavenly host of angels and he sang with them. The song he sang spoke of taking God's love to the people below on earth, the same song all of us were singing while he was in the heavenly realm.

Our church was packed the following night, as word spread fast about what had happened at the elders' retreat. The service started with Sandy singing the song the Lord had given to carry our pastor's spirit into the experience. Don, still too emotional to stand, sat on a chair placed beside the pulpit, and he related the details to the congregation. The pastor carefully laid a foundation from the Word of God, including the Scriptures that show we are one body (Ephesians 4:4) of Christ (Ephesians 4:12) and that Christ is the head (Ephesians 4:15). He encouraged the congregation with Ephesians 3:17-20: *"So that Christ may dwell in your hearts through faith; and that you, being rooted and grounded in love, may be able to comprehend with all the saints what is the breadth and length and height and depth, and to know the love of Christ which surpasses knowledge, that you may be filled up to all the fulness of God. Now to Him who is able to do exceeding abundantly beyond all that we ask or think, according to the power that works within us."*

The pastor emphasized he did not feel unique or special because Jesus gave him this experience. Rather, he was given it so he could tell everyone the truth of who we are in Christ, and express God's love for us so each member could be "filled with all the fulness of God."

Many in our congregation listened to the tape[5] of that service over and over again, each time realizing afresh our awesome position and privilege of being made into the image and likeness of God, to be one with Jesus and one another. As the truth of Don's experience took root in many of us, an incredible thing happened.

For me it began on a Saturday afternoon at a one-day elders' retreat. Only four of us were left in the room when the Spirit of the Lord asked me "Are you really willing to become one with Jesus—to be one with the Son of Man? Are you willing to feel as He feels, to experience as He?"

As soon as I said, "Yes," I instantly knew I was entering into what that dazzling white room in the vision (see Chapter 11) symbolized. It seemed as though my whole being was melded into Jesus, the glorified Son, so that His feelings and emotions were mine. I felt as He did but I didn't lose my own identity. Therefore, I felt how Jesus feels and how I feel at the same time.

I experienced Jesus' love for the Father and, at the same time, His love for me. I felt as Jesus feels when He gives me His love, and I felt how He feels when I receive His love. When I gave my love to Jesus, I felt Him receive it. I felt the Father's love for His Son and for me, and I felt Jesus and me, as one, giving our love to the Father, then I felt the Father receive our love. It was incredible beyond description.

This experience wasn't in the heavenly realm as was Don's. Rather, it happened right there, not as a vision, but in me as a Christian. I was experiencing Christ in me, the hope of glory (Colossians 1:27). I had memorized this verse when I was a child, and always believed it, but now it was real. I experienced it—Jesus and I were one. I knew why I had indeed come short of the glory of God (Romans 3:23). Even though I was filled with the

WHO IS THE SON?

Holy Spirit and been used mightily by Him in prayer and in the gifts of the Spirit (1 Corinthians 12:4-12), including visions, revelations, and specific leadings, this intimate union with Jesus, the glorified Son, surpassed everything.

> *Now that I know how Jesus feels when I express love to Him, I never get so busy I don't take time to meet with Him where he dwells (Ephesians 2:6) for the sole purpose of loving Him and giving Him the satisfaction of having me receive His love. This intimate exchange of love is the very core of my life with Jesus. It's the reason He died for me and it's my reason for living.*

Before I left that one-day retreat, the Lord spoke to my heart, "If you can cause the people to believe that I love them just as they are, they can experience Me in ways they never dreamed possible." After sharing this wonderful revelation and experience with the congregation, hundreds of us were launched into a whole new dimension in the Word of God.

The truth in John 1:14—*"And the Word was made flesh and dwelt among us (and we beheld His glory, the glory as of the only begotten of the Father), full of grace and truth—"* became a reality. The Word was not only about Jesus, but Jesus was (and therefore is) the Word.

It was like light streaked across the congregation. Everywhere—in the prayer room, in college classrooms, in the library, in the halls, at home, and in the church services—people experienced specific verses or phrases in the Bible, feeling at those moments as if their spirits were the Word. They were feeling as Jesus does, because He is the Word.

Imagine how Jesus felt as a young man when He read the Old Testament and knew He <u>was</u> what He was reading. When He read Jeremiah 23:6, "...*and this is his name whereby he shall be called, THE LORD OF RIGHTEOUSNESS"*, Jesus realized He *was* righteousness. Jesus didn't just speak wisdom, He *was* the wisdom of God (1 Corinthians 1:24,30). Jesus not only gave love, but He *was* love, for God is love (1 John 4:8). Is it any wonder that the soldiers who came to arrest Jesus in the garden fell back as dead when Jesus, revealing His true identity, simply said, "I AM"?

Lanny, our son-in-law and a teacher in the Bible college, experienced whole verses at a time. The best way I know to describe it is to say he would live that passage of Scripture as if it were he. This sometimes went on for days or even weeks. All who experienced this walked reverently through each day in the holy presence of God, being continually conscious that they were interconnected with Jesus, feeling how He felt as the fulfilled Word of God.

One brother named Dan, a scholar of the Word, laid on the floor after a service and, holding his sides, laughed for over an hour, repeating the words, "Oh, the joy!" as he experienced Hebrews 12:2—Jesus endured the cross because of the joy set before Him.

I, too, had a similar experience with the same verse, but instead of laughter, I cried. I know now how Jesus endured the torture of the cross, and why He admonishes us to count it all joy when some fiery trial besets us (James 1:2). When we don't have our own joy, we can experience the joy of the Lord (John 15:11).

Jesus also allowed me to know the event He is looking forward to the most. I was surprised at first, that it was not the Rapture of the church or even the great Judgment Day. As soon as I had the experience, I could certainly understand why these events were secondary to Jesus. His joy will be full when He can deliver the kingdom to the Father (1 Corinthians 15:24). The purpose for which He was born will be fulfilled in that moment. I pray that you, too, will have the same opportunity as I had in feeling how Jesus feels about this event. It's impossible to express in human terms. It's mind-boggling to realize that we will be there to be a part of it, as we are one with Him and equal heirs as well.

While Lanny was experiencing whole passages, usually in the Old Testament, I, along with others, sometimes experienced only one word, such as "grace" or "tenderness." I remember one dear sister, her tear-soaked face glowing, repeated the word "wonderful" over and over for the entire four-hour worship service.

Imagine how Jesus felt on the mount of transfiguration. Over the years, I had heard many wonderful sermons on this subject, but none of them compared to the glorious event when I tasted the sensation that flooded Jesus when, as a man, He came face-to-face with Moses, (Mark 9:4) the Lawgiver, knowing that He was the Fulfiller of the Law. All I have to do today to bring the experience back is think on it.

It, along with all the others, has become a part of my relationship with my Friend and Bridegroom, Jesus. Many times I have asked Jesus to let me experience how He felt about meeting Elijah on that day, but He hasn't as yet allowed me that privilege. I have tried to imagine it in my mind, but I can't conjure up the real experience, which proves to me that these things aren't something I can dream up on my own, but must come from the Spirit of the Lord.

After the pastor's initial experience with the glorified Son, he wrote a narrative on the life of Christ. He spent months at his desk researching the clime and times of that era and correlating the four Gospels to form one continuous story. For many weeks we eagerly walked through the life of Jesus with our pastor as he read the descriptive account each Sunday morning. The excitation of feeling Jesus' earthly journey brought both rushes of joy and tears as the narrative unfolded.

Our publications department published the series in tape form[6] and since then, Don has written narratives on every major character in the Bible.

As with the Apostle Peter—who, after he experienced Jesus' transfiguration (Mark 9:5) and wanted to build booths so they could stay there—the Lord never allowed us to "camp" at any one of the moves of His Spirit. He wanted to take us from glory to glory (2 Corinthians 3:18). How else can we become a manifestation of His glory if we never experience it by seeing Him as He is, knowing as He knows, feeling as He feels?

Jesus had taken all of us who could believe and receive into a position of being one with Him, at least in a measure. All of us who experienced Jesus in this way longed to continually live that way, and we were about to enter into what God had called us to: the most incredible move of His Spirit the church has ever experienced. Everything, however, that could be shaken would be shaken (Hebrews 12:27) with His love. Were we ready?

Chapter Sixteen

From Glory to Glory, We Shall Behold Him

"But we all with open faces beholding as in a mirror the glory of the Lord, are changed into the same image from glory to glory, even as by the Spirit of the Lord."
(2 Corinthians 3:18)

    Two years before we began experiencing what I'll call the move of God's love, Jesus showed me He wanted to give it to us, but we weren't ready. Another year went by. Then the Lord tried again to get us prepared by telling us to get our marriages in order. I prayed, *"Lord, I don't want just my marriage fixed, I want to have our church fixed as well."* I was aware of many of the relational problems in the corporation.

    As the months passed, again and again the Lord admonished us, through sermons and prophecies, to work on our marriages and all relationships. One of the sermons the pastor preached was "Piling Oily Rags Up by the Furnace."[7] The point being all the little things in our lives we had not dealt with became a potential danger. If we stacked them up in the basement of our hearts, when the fire grew hotter and hotter, the rags would spontaneously burst into flames and burn up the whole house.

> *Looking back on those days in my own life, I can say I didn't realize everything that needed to change in my relationship with Don, and unfortunately, he still doesn't see most of what was wrong. Consequently, the teaching on authority and submission, and what was practiced in the husband-wife role was a far cry from what I now know is the Lord's will.*
>
> *These roles were also prevalent in the elders' and congregation's relationship to their pastor. With the desire to be spiritually mature, many unwittingly suppressed valid personal needs. Without realizing it, we were working to build an edifice that would look appealing from the Christian world's point of view. Perhaps we were seeking the most elusive goal of all: acceptance and respect from those who had rejected us. But the Lord could see all the wood, hay, and stubble that needed to be burned up.*

How did God step into our lives with His refining love? The answer may surprise you as much as it did us.

* * *

At our Sunday School and Christian school teachers' retreat, spontaneously the teachers began dancing their worship to Jesus!

When the teachers returned on Friday, they filled the evening service with their testimonies. One Christian school teacher reported, "Just weeks before this retreat, the Lord had given one of our school administrators a little song (at a prayer meeting) proclaiming, 'We will leap, and we will prance, we will twirl, and we will dance.' At the retreat, just that happened. It was not planned, nor had we expected anything of the like. It was beautiful! Barriers began breaking down. Freedom in the Spirit abounded. So joyous was this experience, we brought it back with us to the assembly. Uniquely, we had all experienced a common knowledge, without previously sharing it one with the other. That knowledge regarded the pleasure of the Lord toward us as we, like King David, danced uninhibited before the throne of God" (2 Samuel 6:14).

Their unity, exhilarating joy, and excitement were contagious. That Friday night, over fifty percent of the two-thousand member congregation stepped into new freedom and danced, expressing love and worship to Jesus.

Don and I were not at the retreat, nor in the Friday evening service. We were in Hawaii. Word travels fast, however—the very next day Jody, an airline stewardess, hand-delivered a tape of the Friday service when she stopped on a layover on her way to Japan. Upon hearing the tape, I knew it was anointed of God, but the pastor was uneasy, even scared. As we discussed it, sitting under a beach umbrella overlooking the ocean, Don's uneasiness increased because the Lord had done it at a retreat where he wasn't present.

I commented, "Honey, maybe God couldn't start this with you because of how we were brought up believing dancing was evil. Maybe He had to start with someone else, so you would be forced to look into the Word of God on the subject."

We recalled how God, being faithful to His Word in Amos 3:7—*"Surely the Lord God will do nothing but He revealeth His secret unto His servants"*—had a year ago shown me in prayer that worship in the dance was missing in His church, even though His Word told us to dance (Psalm 150:4). God's Spirit revealed to me how He longed to have His people free in their spirits, so He could receive from them worship in the dance. Satan, being fallen Lucifer who had been the angelic being over all music in the heavenly realm (Ezekiel 28:13,14), had now, in his fallen state, claimed possession of this form of worship.

When we returned the following Sunday, before he had searched God's Word, Don brought perspectives which, when followed, left only a handful worshipping in the dance. Lanny told me, "Barbara, your own comments that Sunday were also very conservative, and I had a negative reaction to them. I thought, 'If only you could have been here, you wouldn't think that.'"

> *It's true I feared my ability to dance; it was an unknown area. For the first time, I was scared I might miss out on what God did. But I suspect my comments to the congregation were born out of my unhealthy position to Don as his enabler.*

It wasn't hard for Don to find dancing as a form of worship in the Bible. As soon as he studied the subject, he had enough material to preach a series of sermons on the topic.[8] Then the Lord gave Don a supernatural dancing experience that convinced him it was of God.

At noon on Tuesday at the end of a prayer meeting, with six ladies left and one man, we stood and joined hands with the pastor to thank the Lord. Spontaneously, we burst forth with singing in the Spirit. In no time, we raised our hands to the Lord in praise. Suddenly, our pastor started spinning across the floor. Startled, we opened our eyes to see our pastor moving around the room with his eyes closed, twirling as he went. Everyone was delighted except him. He was scared! He felt out of control.

As soon as he said, "No, Lord," he stopped. Once stopped, he would say, "Yes, Lord," and be propelled around the room again in the same motion. Later, the pastor testified, "Whenever I'd say, 'Yes, Lord,' and yield to Him, my body would take off, spinning around the room. Then I'd be afraid I was going to slam into someone, so I'd tell the Lord, 'No.' Immediately, I stopped moving. Then I'd want to experience it again, because I didn't want to hinder the Spirit of the Lord from doing what He wanted to do, so I'd say, 'Okay, Lord.' Then I'd find myself whirling around the room again. I felt as if my body was moving with an angel at the controls. Brother, you'll know it's not you when it happens; you're out of control. It's scary! It's wonderful! I know it wasn't me. It was God."

Now the pastor was excited. He said, "That experience made a believer out of me!" Don admitted he was skeptical until he experienced it himself, saying, "Now I can understand how men like John Sherrill couldn't believe in speaking in tongues until God baptized him, and he spoke in tongues himself. That's how this dancing was for me. I guess God had to do it so I'd know it's real, and is it ever wonderful! Glory!"

The pastor wanted all the elders to enjoy the same experience. He scheduled an elders' retreat. The whole focus was praying to free the elders to dance. Lanny and I watched with delight when George, our music director began dancing as if he had just been deluged with gallons of God's love. One afternoon Don had a major breakthrough and wouldn't stop dancing even though his muscles ached. He became a big proponent of dancing and came back from the retreat ready to get out of God's way and let it happen in the church.

The Scriptures that convinced the pastor to encourage the congregation to worship Jesus in dancing were the ones that ordered God's people to dance, such as Psalms 149:3 and 150:4. This was an important truth for us, having been raised in Pentecostal churches where dancing is believed in, but only if the Holy Spirit does it supernaturally, without the believer initiating anything. The Word of God, however, reveals we should dance; we didn't have to wait until the Holy Spirit came upon us and supernaturally moved our bodies, although this might, at times, happen, as was the case with Don in the prayer meeting.

Along with this truth, the pastor taught the congregation they were responsible for the dance movements, and not the Lord. He admonished the congregation to avoid sensual dancing, but he also encouraged them, assuring them that many of their dance steps would be the same as what they had done before becoming Christians, because some movements were natural to the way God made us.

During the very next worship service after the elders' retreat, the platform filled with praises to God in song, as first one teacher, then another, stepped forward and, with a glowing radiance, worshipped the Lord by dancing. It was spontaneous and beautiful, sending waves of rapturous praise swelling through the congregation. It was heartwarming. After the service, during what we called post-service worship, people swarmed to the open space at the front of the sanctuary and flowed into one harmonious expression of love to Jesus accompanied by Music Ministry's songs born of the Spirit.

> *As I observed this holy scene taking place in front of me at the pastor's front pew, I imagined that this sight surely equalled what happens in God's throne room when all the angels worship and cry, "Holy, holy" (Hebrews 1:6). I thought, Surely this is the beginning of the baptism of love Jesus promised us. This is an experience in the "white room" of the vision Jesus gave us at the beginning of the Chapel.*

With Don's increased freedom in the dance, he wondered why he had gone so long in his Christian walk without it. At last he had a wonderfully fulfilling way to express his love to Jesus; it made up for his lack of musical talent. I wanted to experience this new expression, too, but I doubted my own physical ability, so the Lord sent someone to help me. When everyone entered into post-service worship, a brother showed up, stood behind me, and tenderly sang until I got up enough courage to dance. Cautiously, I moved my feet. At each new movement I tried, he laughed with joy and praise.

An hour before each service, I went up the back steps from my car, to a hallway away from the crowds and danced worship to the Lord. Somehow this brother found me and began singing. As this continued week after week, that back hallway seemed to me as if it was transformed into a heavenly garden full of sweet fragrance, as I danced in worship to my beloved Jesus. The brother joined me in dancing his own expression of joy, and our united dance brought the presence of Jesus in an unimpeachable way. In awe, we whispered, "Holy, holy, holy."

By the time the church service started, the beauty of holiness was so real we couldn't stand still. Ecclesiastes 3:4 declares that there is a time to dance, and this was it; if we hadn't danced, we would have dishonored our Lord. The urge to express love and worship to Jesus compelled the congregation to dance. No directive was needed from the pastor. Many of the most skeptical were convinced this was an heavenly visitation. The people's faces glowed with countenances of ecstasy, knowing their worship was received by Jesus.

In past years, many Christians had confided in me, "I tell Jesus I love Him, but I don't feel anything. I don't feel my love for Him, and I can't tell if He is receiving my love. Furthermore, I don't feel His love. I know He loves me, because the Bible says so, and I know I love Him. I want to please Him, but is it out of fear or love? I wish I could feel His love."

By some miracle which I can't explain, dancing their love to Jesus freed many in the congregation to feel the emotion of love, both theirs and God's. It made an astounding difference in all of us. Remember how the Lord had told us "if the people will only believe that I love them just as they are, they will experience Me in ways they never dreamed possible"? Well, that's what happened—our love for Jesus exploded!

All doubts vanished about whether Jesus really loved us or received our love. Faces glowed with joy. People even walked differently—that is, if they walked at all—they bounced and skipped their way to their cars after services, with heavenly music dancing in their heads. In fact, hundreds reported that in our minds we heard songs sung in the Spirit as though an heavenly choir of angels were there, even while we slept. This went on for months. The spiritual phenomenon was glorious! Perhaps this was an example of Ephesians 1:3—*"Who hath blessed us with all spiritual blessings in heavenly places in Christ."*

Our already wonderful worship services were transformed. With each new song spontaneously sung under the Holy Spirit's inspiration, the congregation loved our beloved Jesus with dancing. No one wanted to go home; the presence of the Lord was too wonderful. People stayed until 4:00 and 5:00 a.m., making use of every available space to worship Jesus with songs directed toward Him.

When a song was sung or heard on a tape, it was like a magnet pulling us into holy heavenly places. At home, we had to leave the stereo off, so we could get our work done. It was common to see people stagger to their cars drunk with this sensational new wine wherein, the Bible says, there is no excess (Ephesians 5:18). Every morning, the Bible college chapels reverberated with the joyous presence of God's love, as students danced worship in a line, up and down the aisles. The glory of the Lord's presence fell like rain, and no one wanted to miss out.

One day after teaching my last classes for the day, a girl skipped her way to me. Joyfully, she took my arm and said, "Come with me; you've got to hear this!" She ushered me into the college tape library to hear the tape of Greg Thiel's (a teacher) class. The tape had nothing on it but the sound of laughter and praise, because as soon as Greg stepped to the podium to begin the lecture, the power of the Holy Spirit had slain him. He laid on the floor and laughed the entire hour. Every time he attempted to get to his feet, the Spirit of the Lord came upon him and he hit the floor again.

At all hours, every day, people were in the Chapel worshipping Jesus. A Christian School teacher sent this report to her missionary friends:

"The dancing has been by far the most profound experience of my Christian walk. Through the months, I felt a continued need to express myself in the dance. In fact, I would get out of bed in the middle of the night and dance up and down my hallway—all by myself! One day, I danced for ten solid hours, from morning until night, and felt myself acting out, as it were, a spiritual vignette of sorts. It was one of the most profound experiences of my life as I danced in anticipation of the coming of the Lord and adorned His pathway with fragrant rose petals. At the time, each movement was deliberate and thrillingly real to me".

"There were times I've danced and sensed that the Enemy was being defeated. It was as though there was no way whatsoever for the Enemy to break past the angelic hosts camped round about me, protecting me as I danced my love and praise to Jesus.

"Sometimes my dancing was so locked into Jesus that everything else faded into oblivion. Once, while dancing in the Lord's presence, I found myself in a wonderful, royal white room. I felt as the Shulamite, dancing before King Solomon and giving Him great delight! This experience was very intimate—a personal love dance between me and the Lord. From that time forth, I have been a different person. My love relationship with the Lord is on a plane I had never previously realized.

"One night, as I was dancing, I got set so free that I began leaping and twirling. Instead of dancing with my eyes closed and locked into Jesus, I began opening my eyes and sensed God's plan for me to dance not only before Him, but also in the presence of His wonderful Body. Since that time, this has been my experience. I have no reservations whatsoever about leaping across the front of the church. I even did so when my Lutheran parents were here visiting from Virginia; it seemed so natural. I am beginning to see what it can mean to worship the Lord with all my heart, soul, mind, strength, and body. Also, I feel that through the vehicle of dance I'm learning to discern the Lord's Body in a new way. Barriers and intimidations are crumbling to the ground, and we are finding a place of love and acceptance one for the other as never before. It is such a delight to hear one after another share sweet, precious testimonies of how their personal relationship with Jesus is being enhanced and how the Enemy is being defeated through the vehicle of dance.

"Each vessel dances uniquely before the Lord. Each time we dance, it is an act of faith. I don't know the steps until I "jump right in"; and the steps vary so that I could not even recall the steps I did months before. I can't do it "by memory." We see what appears to be love dances, dances of great joy, victory dances which are *powerful beyond words, and many, many more dances by different vessels in the Body who yield to the Lord in this unique and wonderful way.*

"I have been dancing for one-and-a-half years now, and it is always new and fresh. It is as vital to my daily walk with the Lord as prayer and Bible devotions. If I couldn't express my love to the Lord in this full, free way, I would honestly feel grief. It is pure before the Lord— nothing sensual. There is no need to train. The Spirit brings the movements spontaneously. We need only to yield. My experiences along these lines are countless."

Nor did God leave out the children. My little granddaughter, only two at the time, told her daddy, "If I fall asleep, Daddy, before the service is over, be sure to wake me up when you start dancing, because I want to follow you." I remember Lanny waking her at about 1:30 a.m., after the sanctuary had cleared out enough to make room, and Wendy, in her long nightgown, worshipped the Lord, dancing behind her father as he circled the entire sanctuary. The glory of the Lord radiated from her face, as an occasional tear fell from her eyes—and mine. I thanked the Lord that He knew how to bless the little children today just as He did when He sat them on His lap.

* * *

At our collective churches' camp meeting in 1985, Pastor Keith from Wisconsin told us how this move of God's love was affecting him and his church in Wisconsin.[9] With a radiant face, he mounted the platform, bounding up two steps at a time. He couldn't force the broad smile from his face.

"I wouldn't trade anything for what I'm experiencing now. The last few days have surpassed anything I've ever experienced. I'm so thankful for what God is doing. I feel a new power, a new boldness. Some things I've experienced are so glorious, they are hard to explain."

He sighed and laughed at the assenting spontaneous response from the packed assembly.

"Since God has been moving this way in the last number of months, our church back in Wisconsin has been totally transformed. This move has done what none other has—the people are different! My! People come in the church and they either run out the door or they start dancing. The gray line is rapidly disappearing; people are either hot or cold. I'm so excited about this move!

"I have a little problem, not with the move, but with the love aspect—the problem is that I have such a love for people. I love you. I love Don Barnett. I've loved that man for twenty years. I've loved him fervently, but I've never been able to express it. It's as if there have been hoards of black demonic forces between here [Seattle] and Wisconsin that caused me to feel like I didn't fit, I didn't belong. But in the past few months, as I heard testimonies from Seattle, I knew this was it. I've never had one doubt since. I've been waiting twenty years for this—actually all my life—and I want to get right in the middle of it. My life has been transformed. My, my, my! I've had experiences. I've had dreams. I'll just share one.

"I was standing in our church with the Spirit of the Lord on me, and I was in glory. A hand touched me on the shoulder and began ministering to me. I thought, Oh my! What kind of an anointing is this and who is it? I was almost afraid to look. I thought, Who in our assembly has that kind of an anointing? I turned and *looked*—*I was looking right into the face of Jesus. As I looked, he didn't say anything. He took me and slowly turned me around until I faced him. I was looking into His eyes. It was a most glorious experience! He pulled me to Himself and kissed me on the cheek and said, 'I love you!' Then He kissed me on the other cheek and said, 'I love you!' Of course, I woke up immediately!*

"These are the kinds of things that are happening. I've experienced, while sleeping, what seemed to be spirits of the brethren. It's as if they dance through me. I've heard of angels doing that, but people's spirit have done it.

"We have listened to the teaching and music tapes from Seattle. We have services going on from morning until night every day. We start at 5:30 a.m. People keep coming. I try to get in on at least three prayer meetings a day. Others are doing the same.

"I haven't been dancing very long, but I knew if I started dancing, everyone else would, because the people will follow their pastor. So I sat there and thought, the responsibility is on me—what am I going to do?

"You know, God in His sovereign ways knows how to bypass all our hindrances and inhibitions. I believe God sent angels into our church. The Bible says we entertain angels unawares, and I'm certain now that we do. As a matter of fact, they may have operated through us and we haven't realized it.

"God sent an angel—I had been dancing only six months, when God sent this angel one day in the service as music ministry was singing. A certain young lady was dancing when suddenly I was caught up almost like into a vision. She faded out—becoming almost transparent—and I perceived the angels worshipping before God. It was as if she became like an angel, and so did all the others worshipping in dance. Angels began to go

not just sideways, but up into the air, increasing in speed until they were going so fast they became streaks, passing through one another.

"In that glorious moment, the Lord showed me that in His presence, this was what He was looking for. He was looking for worship in movements that bring glory to Him. It was marvelous! I never want to go back to the way we were."

Suddenly, Keith began to yodel! Joy and praise shot through all three thousand of us; spontaneously, the whole crowded assembly bounded from their pews and expressed uninhibited jubilation unto the Lord.

* * *

One Friday evening during the service, an extraordinary spiritual event happened that was a foretaste of what Jesus had in store next for His church.

A brother, under the inspiration of the Holy Spirit, walked to the piano, sat down, struck a chord, and began singing, *"When I ponder on the grace of God ..."* Instantly, a power surged through me that felt like God's grace in the form of an invisible substance consumed me, transforming me into the Bride of Christ. Without hesitation, I glided and twirled across the floor with speed and grace as if floating on a billowy white cloud. Before I realized it, a brother joined the dance and as the song continued, every move we made expressed how Christ was wooing His Bride, forever covering her with His marvelous grace.

In one glorious instant, nearly the entire congregation had their "spiritual eyes" opened and understood the drama unfolding before them, as the sacred song imbedded itself into our consciousness.

It's Much Too Wonderful
(c) 1993 by Jerry Hebert

When I ponder on the grace of God
The Son of God who died for me
My heart is filled with gratitude
For all that He has done.
    I'm filled with love for him, Jesus my Lord
    I want to praise him, Jesus my Lord
    Forever and ever, Jesus my Lord
    I want to worship him
    I love him so—I love him so—Jesus my Lord.
When I think of all he's given me
What he bought on Calvary
My mind is filled with ecstasy
The love of God toward me.
    It's overwhelming, Jesus my Lord
    I want to praise him, Jesus my Lord
    Forever and ever, Jesus my Lord
    I want to worship him
    I love him so—I love him so—Jesus my Lord
To imagine that he's called me
To live with him at his loving side
I can't understand such a glorious call
The king of all kings desires me.
    It's much too wonderful, Jesus my Lord
    I want to praise him, Jesus my Lord
    Forever and ever, Jesus my Lord
    I want to worship him
    I love him so—I love him so—Jesus my Lord.

The three of us (the musician, the brother, and myself) knew without a doubt that holy angels had manifested through us. The congregation sensed it, too. All of us had, by this time, been thoroughly taught by our pastor and teachers about the ministry of angels. We understood angels minister through people unawares (Hebrews 13:2), and God has given His angels charge over us (Psalm 91:11). I had, on many occasions, known the presence of angels, and, after the Lord led the congregation into the ministry of deliverance, the manifestation of angels was not uncommon.

The spiritual phenomenon that was about to burst upon us, however, was not primarily the manifestation of angels, but rather real, tangible, life-changing experiences with the glorified Son, Jesus, our Bridegroom, and us, as His Bride. We were going to experience a spiritual courtship of sorts—the fulfillment of the Song of Solomon. And when did it start? As soon as we opened our eyes!

* * *

Sometimes I wonder if the Lord didn't put the book of the Song of Solomon in the Bible especially for His Church in this age when all the signs of our times point to the soon fulfillment of 1 Thessalonians 4:16-17—*"For the Lord Himself will descend from heaven with a shout, with the voice of the archangel, and with the trumpet of God; and the dead in Christ shall rise first. Then we who are alive and remain shall be caught up together with them in the clouds to meet the Lord in the air, and thus we shall always be with the Lord."*

Every detail of King Solomon's courtship with Abishag is a type of Jesus preparing His Bride for her

THE TRUTH SHALL SET YOU FREE

heavenly abode. The Shulamite in the Song of Solomon was the most beautiful maiden that could be found in all the land and was brought to the palace from the country village of Shunam, for the express purpose of heating up King David's dying body (1 Kings 1:1-4).

But David died before their marriage was consummated; consequently, when David's son, Solomon, inherited David's kingdom, making him king of Israel, this beautiful Shulamite became his. Solomon loved her immediately, but she needed to be groomed and educated to the ways of the palace. Abishag was thrilled that this handsome new king wanted to make her his choice one out of all the queens, concubines, and virgins he'd inherited from his father, David, but she knew her sun-darkened skin from working in the fields needed time to become fair, befitting a queen (Song of Solomon 1:5,6).

As the love story unfolds, we find a reflection of ourselves as the choice one of Jesus, our heavenly Bridegroom, and how He loves and woos us into an intimate spiritual relationship with Him all the while servants of His kingdom (daughters of Jerusalem, Song of Solomon 1:5) help groom us and prepare us for our heavenly palace.

As unbelievable as it may seem, the spiritual application of the book of Song of Solomon became an undeniable experience, as God took us into the next phase of our spiritual journey. Hundreds of us experienced how it felt to be His heavenly Bride—not just by faith, believing we were because the Word of God says Jesus will have a Bride (Revelation 119:7), but we actually experienced being her, feeling as if we were her, all the overwhelming emotion of it, living it day after day, for months.

Furthermore, and even more astounding, we experienced being a manifestation of the Bridegroom—not that we became Jesus, because that is not Scriptural, nor is it, or will it ever be, possible. But we do, according to many texts of Scripture, have Christ dwelling in us. In John 14:23, Jesus says, "My Father will love him [referring to mankind], and we will come and make our abode in him [mankind]." Jesus also said, in Revelation 3:20, "Behold, I stand at the door [of man's heart] and knock: if any man hear my voice, and open the door, I will come in to him and will sup with him and he with Me."

It seemed incredible—unbelievable even—that we could experience how it felt being the Bride of Christ, with all our sins and imperfections. But I'm sure, too, it must have seemed impossible to Solomon's kingdom that Abishag could be their queen. We find in Song of Solomon 5:7 that even the watchmen smote her and wounded her, and the keepers of the walls took away her veil.

But even though Abishag, with her faults and imperfections was despised by some, King Solomon loved her. His eyes saw beyond her blackness, so he loved her, and as he did, she changed. All the habits of her old life were gradually replaced with the graces and splendor of a queen. Near the end of the book we see Abishag's confidence in herself has changed from what it was in chapter one. In chapter seven, verse ten, she says, *"I am my beloved's, and his desire is toward me."*

In Song of Solomon 7:11-13, she goes on to beckon him to come and receive her love. Abishag is so confident, she says, "Let us get up early to the vineyards to see if the tender grapes appear." She wanted to look after his kingdom with Solomon. She reminds me of Revelation 22:17—*"And the Spirit and the Bride say, 'Come.'"*

If God waited to move until He had a perfect church, He could never take us from glory to glory. Only Jesus qualifies as a perfect one. There is "none righteous, no not one" (Romans 3:10). Only the righteousness of Christ allowed us the spiritual phenomenon that happened. The fact that Don, me, and others had made mistakes, sinned, repented, and sinned again, and even had weaknesses and sins some of which we weren't aware, didn't mean God couldn't or wouldn't use what we had and what we were.

Perhaps this is why God recorded some of men's shortcomings and sins in the Bible (e.g., Noah, Eli, David, Achan, Moses, Peter, Thomas, Paul, etc.), so we wouldn't give up on ourselves when we sin, and leave our calling in Christ. Furthermore, they help us to realize that God's ministers are people just like us—sinners saved by grace. The ministers not only need our prayers and support but they need us to not put them on high pedestals, expecting perfection from them. Too many times this has fed a false expectation which keeps ministers isolated from their people, fearing that if some fault in their lives were found out, the people would either reject them or lose faith in God. (One precious babe in Christ saw me in a grocery store once. Horrified, he exclaimed, "Do you shop?" He turned and walked away, shaking his bewildered head.)

> *I wondered if this next move of God was going to affect our souls as much as our spirits. It did! Our weaknesses and sinful ways were exposed. Was this the beginning of God's promised judgment?*

Before God sent this next move, revealing Jesus and His Bride, He gave us a very solemn warning. God told us what He was about to do.[10] He also exposed part of the devil's plan. Even though God's Spirit anointed me to give the message, it applied to me along with everyone else.

* * *

As I stood behind the pulpit that Friday evening, I knew I was expressing God's heart, and a holy hush swept through the assembly. God warned us: *"Satan has a plan to destroy this church from within."* God told us the devil's attack would be very subtle and we would need to be united in prayer and heed God's Word. He said the enemy was planning to destroy us by twisting our love and the unity the Lord was performing among us. God caused me to experience how awful it would be.

Through a flood of tears, I exclaimed, "I saw the demonic forces come, and I felt their power; I felt what they want to do to you and me—the hurt, the tearing apart of marriages, the anxieties, jealousy, turmoil, and pain. But most of all, I felt the pain and sorrow the Lord Jesus would experience if we allow the enemy to overtake us."

God's heart continued to pour through me as He revealed the devil's plan. In summary, He told us the devil would cause some to be threatened by what God did. Demons of fear would grip their hearts making them afraid to yield to Jesus' pure love and therefore they would miss what God wanted, and leave. Again, the Lord warned us these forces would be so subtle that those who closed themselves off would think they were wise in doing so.

On the other hand, a spirit of pseudo-love—bringing erotic, exciting feelings, something we would have a tendency to welcome—would try to seduce us. Demons of lust, enticement, and seduction would flood in, looking for weaknesses in us so they could entice us to illicit affection and sex, illegitimate fascination and expressions of love.

Demons of jealousy and self-pity would take advantage of any old wounds and hurts that were left in marriages. All the dissatisfaction in our marriages and lives would surface, giving both God and Satan opportunity. The choice was ours. Out of fear, we could seek to save our lives, and miss the most incredible move of God in the church's history; or, we could yield to the enticement of the flesh; or, we could obey all the counsel of God, remain in His love, and be perfected (Ephesians 4:13). God had warned us, and He would warn us again, and again.

God told us, "Pray for angels of purity." Some of us took Him seriously.

* * *

"Open your eyes, open your eyes," many of us heard the Spirit of the Lord whisper, as we were dancing before Him.

One sister said, "When I obeyed His voice and opened my eyes, lo and behold, I saw the body of Christ all around me, dancing their worship to Jesus. And I, too, was one member who helped make up the whole! Jesus wasn't just with me in my prayers and worship, He was also with me in my brothers and sisters. A rapturous ecstasy flooded my being—I was in the midst of His mystical body (Ephesians 5:27) on earth; and each of His members radiated Christ's love and glory through their smiling faces and joy-filled eyes."

Jesus said He was going to manifest His very presence to us, and this was how—in our brothers and sisters, His body on earth! Hadn't His Word declared, "Where two or more are gathered in my Name, there am I in the midst of them" (Matthew 18:20)? We had always believed it by faith, but now, when we opened our physical eyes, they saw the spiritual. 2 Corinthians 3:18 became a reality right before our eyes—*But we all with open faces beholding as in a mirror the glory of the Lord, are changed into the same image from glory to glory, even as by the Spirit of the Lord.*

Unspeakable joy billowed over us as the phenomenon spread to the hundreds who entered into worship. It shot like a laser beam to every satellite church, making us one in the Son (John 17). The Lord had suddenly come to His temples, bringing the spiritual fulfillment, at least in part, of the prophecy in Malachi 3:1, and a host of angels accompanied Him.

The angels ministered to us and through us in such a real sense, that we felt them move in us and through us, and even saw them in one another, as they went about fulfilling their commission, teaching us how to dance, sing, worship, and minister to one another. The angels' assignments weren't just to help us experience those heavenly places. They also set about to "gather out of God's kingdom all things that offend" (Matthew 13:41).

Yes, with Jesus' presence came the judgment He had also promised (1 Peter 4:17), fulfilling the rest of the prophecy in Malachi 3:2-6. Never had we dreamed that God's judgment to us would come through our brethren with such love, compassion, mercy, grace, tenderness, and unexplainable joy and glory on one hand—and, on the other, the sufferings of Christ, agony, pain, grief, and unbelievable craving. The dicotomy: we experienced thrilling joy one minute and unbearable agony the next. Although the circumstances in each life varied, the experiences had a common thread: all were in the Lord's glorious refining fire.

No wonder the devil showed up with hordes of demons. This move of God was an unprecedented threat to his anti-Christ plan, and as a good strategist, his main target was the pastor, then the elders, and on down the line. As the battle raged, we were thrust into not only glorious relationships with Christ and His Bride, but also powerful deceiving demonic manifestations, because Satan was after the darling of God's heart.

For me, right when I experienced the most wonderful thing that had ever happened in our marriage, the spiritual battle exploded.

Chapter Seventeen

What Is This Love?— Ecstasy and Agony

"Till we all come in the unity of the faith, and of the knowledge of the Son of God, unto a perfect man, unto the measure of the statue of the fulness of Christ."
(Ephesians 4:13)

I don't know how the term "connection" got started, but it certainly describes what began happening. After many of the congregation opened their eyes while worshipping, and, in a very real sense, perceived one another as members of Christ's body, Jesus—assisted by angels—began connecting our spirits one to another in love. Romans 12:5 and Ephesians 4:16 became reality which affected every part of our lives. It was marvelous beyond description.

In a Sunday evening service, right before the pastor preached, I got "connected" to my husband's spirit. For me, it was the most wonderful thing that ever happened in our marriage.

THE TRUTH SHALL SET YOU FREE

A brother gifted in music stepped to the microphone and began singing *Beholden to You*. I felt the Holy Spirit draw me like a magnet; I began dancing. Tears, sprung from my thankful heart and streamed down my cheeks. I felt as if as if every word of the song was part of my life in Jesus, and my dance expressed and gave each melodious truth back to my beloved Savior:

Beholden to You, for all that You've given me.
Beholden to You, in all that I do.
Beholden to You; You make me so happy.
I just couldn't live a day without You.
    Praise God, at last I've found the way.
    Jesus, Your gentle hand holds mine.
    Amazing grace You give to me
    Has made my life divine.
Beholden to You, for all that You've given me.
Beholden to You, in all that I do.
Beholden to You; You make me so happy.
I just couldn't live a day without You.
    Your way is clear; I'm going home.
    Jesus, Your sweet love is all I need.
    The joy I have here in my heart
    Fulfills my every need.
Beholden to You, for all that You've given me.
Beholden to You, in all that I do.
Beholden to You; You make me so happy.
I just couldn't live a day without You.[11]

As Stu sang the song for the second time, it happened! I felt a form dance close to me. To my utter amazement and delight when I opened my eyes, it was Don! In one supernatural instant, all his previous disdain for my form of dance disappeared. Joy flooded over me.

WHAT IS THIS LOVE?—ECSTASY AND AGONY

As our eyes met, our movements were perfectly synchronized. Every detail of our steps and the motions of our hands and arms fit together. I know an angel helped me, as I don't possess that ability. I was never able to dance with him that way again.

For ten minutes we worshipped, twirling and turning, forming unique patterns, each expressing how thankful we were to Jesus, because, in spite of our sins and shortcomings, God's marvelous grace covered us and forgave us. He had removed our sins as far as the east is from the west and He remembered them against us no more (Psalm 103:12).

I felt both Don and me feeling beholden to the Lord for all He had given us and done through us. I felt the Lord's heart towards Don, beholden to him for Don's long hours of study day after day, how he had set up the Bible college and the whole corporation, and his love for the flock. I felt the Lord beholden to me for my position in Him and the body. I felt myself express to Don how I was beholden to him as my husband. Then, I felt Don honoring me, beholden to me for my ministry to the body.

In those few moments of time, feeling one in the ministry with my husband, I felt dignity; I felt honored; I felt respected. Suddenly, I recognized whatever had died in my spirit when I was excluded from Don's closed prayer meetings with select intercessors was restored. When we sat down at the end of the song, Don held me, and I wept and wept. I hated to have him leave me and walk up to the pulpit to preach. The only thing Don mentioned from the pulpit was how much he enjoyed the dance. However, for me the experience didn't go away.

My love for Don exploded into new heights. All the excitement, the limerance, the thrill of touching him was not only restored, but was more intense than ever—I was propelled into ecstasy! I felt as giddy as a teenager experiencing love for the first time. It was wonderful!

* * *

A week after Don and I had worshipped to the song, "Beholden to You," we went on a retreat with the elders and intercessors. This retreat proved to hold both agony and ecstasy for me. Don was unaware of the agony I endured, because he was in such ecstasy. The only pain he experienced was in his body, as he used muscles he hadn't used for years, dancing before the Lord.

The Lord used a particular elder's wife to worship the Lord with our pastor in the dance. Through that spiritual experience, he was set free to accept the Lord's love for him and to know how much he was loved and accepted by the congregation. The change in our pastor was easy to see. He was happy. He was free. He was full of joy. His face shone with the glory of God. He smiled all the time. He couldn't sit still. He had to dance, whether his legs and back were hurting or not.

Don testified that while he was worshipping with a sister, at one point she became a blur and all he could see was Jesus. He felt as if his spirit was going to leave his body and go to that heavenly realm again, but it didn't have to, because Jesus was manifesting Himself through Terri, fulfilling the Scripture "Christ in you, the hope of glory" (Colossians 1:27). Then as Don danced with another sister, he felt Jesus' love as if it was pouring through

WHAT IS THIS LOVE?—ECSTASY AND AGONY

him to her. As soon as she accepted how much Jesus loved her, she was placed in a new dimension in her relationship with Jesus.

Other elders and their wives shared similar experiences, as their spirits were joined with others at the retreat. One elder literally bounced up and down as he told how he got delivered of legalism that kept him from believing God loved him. Then he had danced with his wife, and the experience was so powerful it completely transformed their marriage.

One morning at the retreat, as some ladies were praying for Don, an elder began to worship the Lord, dancing in an open area one step down from the fireplace. Soon another elder joined him, then another and another, until every man there was involved in a powerful expression of love to God and one another. It impacted us ladies so much that we joined hands and began dancing out of sheer joy for what the Lord was doing.

Two married ladies, both intercessors, came to me with a most unusual story. "Barbara," one shared, "We have had the most wonderful thing happen to us. Even though we have known one another for years and prayed in a prayer group together, we have never before experienced anything like this. We've always loved one another, but were never really close. Now we love one another fervently!

"It's as if Jesus took us and made our spirits one with Him and God's love. It's wonderful! We can't stop loving Jesus and one another. We love everything about each other. It doesn't make any difference that our backgrounds are different, we just love one another. I love everything about her; everything she says or does is just wonderful to me. And when she tells the Lord how much she loves Him, I can hardly stand the feeling of gratitude that overwhelms me. It makes me happy beyond words. In fact, sometimes I have to tell her the joy I feel from her love for Jesus is too much for my emotions to handle."

Her friend chimed in, "That very same thing happens to me! There are no sensual or homosexual feelings whatsoever; yet, it's so hard to leave each other and go home. Oh, another thing—we love each other's families, too. Her children are so precious and dear. It's like we love each other's children as if they are our very own. There isn't anything we wouldn't do for them or one another. For the first time, we are really loving our neighbor as ourselves, as Matthew 5:43 commands. We have no problem sharing anything the other one needs. In fact, it's such a joy to be able to help with housework or anything else."

They looked at each other and laughed, "We don't know how God did it, but it's so wonderful we never want to go back to merely loving like we used to. Our love for Jesus has increased a hundredfold, too, and just hearing each other's voices brings joy beyond compare. All of a sudden our lives—even the mundane tasks such as laundry and vacuuming—are wonderful. We don't want to do anything to lose this wonderful place we have found in God."

It wasn't long until hundreds of us experienced the same wonderful phenomenon.

* * *

WHAT IS THIS LOVE?—ECSTASY AND AGONY

The song that dominated this retreat was "Beholden to You." Every time it played all the emotions flooded over me again, and the longing in my spirit to worship again with Don was so acute it was physically painful. It caused me to understand how desperately Jesus longs for our expressions of love. I now know how much He treasures each attempt we make to open ourselves to Him just to express love and worship Him. I made new commitments to "love the Lord my God with all my heart and all my mind and all my soul," the first commandment.

Although Don—who couldn't bring himself to dance with me again—was oblivious to the agony I was going through, Lanny wasn't. He knew of a certain individual in music ministry whom God had used to minister to me in the past, so he made arrangements for that person to come out to the retreat. Through his powerful expression of worship and prayer, Jesus came to me with deliverance and comfort. We never sat down and talked. The only communication we ever had was expressed in the dance, but the Spirit of the Lord was so powerful in each movement, they brought me to my knees as the demonic spirits attacking me fled.

> *Perhaps if the criticism Don had about my shape in earlier years had been dealt with and resolved, we wouldn't have had this open door for the demons to gain access and thereby prevent us from God's intended spiritual union.*

On Thursday morning of this retreat, Sandy—one of the intercessors with a beautiful soprano voice—came to Don and me and said, "Pastor, I'm here because I'm scheduled to pray with you this morning, but all week the Lord has impressed me that I am supposed to pray for Barbara. I don't know why, but I'd like to pray with her instead of you today. The Lord has given me a song for her."

As soon as Sandy began singing in the Spirit, my spirit was drawn up into the throne of God, as if it was being carried there on the notes of the song. In a vision I saw an image of a face representing the Father. He blew a very thin stream of air that looked much like a fine white jetstream, wispy and fragile. It streaked down from Him to almost where I was on the earth. God said to me, "Are you willing to come to me on a whisper?"

By now I was crying, and although I didn't know how I could possibly get there on this "whisper" from the mouth of God, I said, "Yes, Father, I'll come to You on the whisper blown from the breath of Your mouth."

Of course, I asked Him who or what the whisper was, but He didn't tell me. Neither did I know when it would come, so I excitedly started looking for my "whisper" from the Lord.

Every time I worshipped the Lord in the dance with someone or prayed with someone, I searched to find a special wispy signal from the Spirit of the Lord through their spirit that would put me in heavenly places with Jesus. It didn't happen at that retreat, nor at the church services that weekend when Don and others testified of all the wonderful experiences they'd had with Jesus.

* * *

WHAT IS THIS LOVE?—ECSTASY AND AGONY

After the initial experience in worship with my husband, the longing in my spirit to be a part of his prayer meeting was so intense it was actually painful. Feeling more united in the ministry than ever, I even wanted to be included as the intercessors prayed for him, but Don didn't want to give up the intimate expressions he felt he needed, and my presence would hinder him, he said. So I stayed away. And, because of the wrong role I'd assumed, always feeling responsible to protect his image, I never told anyone why I wasn't right there by his side whenever they prayed for him. Don wasn't missing my spirit like I was missing his, so he didn't have the same need for me.

Over the next few months, I told him again and again, "Something is dying in me again, and I don't know what to do about it."

Feeling helpless, he finally sighed, "Take it to the Lord; it's your problem, not mine."

I suspected the devil was raging against what God had done in me when, after a while, Don wouldn't let me touch him at all.

Then, for the first time in our marriage, he established a "line" in the bed. I was to stay on "my side."

Our marriage problems didn't stop God, although I'm sure that was what Satan hoped for; he is the accuser of the brethren (Revelation 12:10), always contesting our salvation, trying to make the blood of Jesus null and void.

In the meantime, I kept searching for my "whisper" from God, thinking perhaps it could be just a glance, a wink, or maybe a smile even, from my husband, but it didn't happen. More and more people, however, were having life-changing experiences when they broke through the barriers of low self-esteem, self-hate, insecurity, and condemnation because of legalism, plus other hindrances that kept them bound from feeling accepted and loved by God and the brethren.

* * *

While searching for my "whisper" from God, in one worship service, I felt compelled to dance across the front of the church to where a black brother was standing with a look of anticipation on his face, as if he wanted to jump into the joyous expressions of praise he was staring at, but his feet seemed glued to the red carpet. As soon as our eyes met, it felt like angels streaked through me, much like an electrical current. The brother's face lit up as if a light had been switched on—and did he ever dance! His feet were moving as fast as lightning in fancy steps that would compete with the finest dancers in Mexico. The amazing thing was my feet were doing the same thing; I'm sure it was angels.

Because this brother felt accepted by me, he was set free, and after that he didn't need angels to help him. This man, along with other black brethren in our assembly, blessed all of us immeasurably with their gifted dances of praise and victory.

As wonderful as this dance was, it wasn't my "whisper" from God. On my way back across the auditorium, I spotted another precious brother, an accomplished piano and organist, who had for many months been in a state of chronic depression. It seemed that all life had been sucked out of him, and for months he hadn't touched the piano or organ. In one victorious instant, as our eyes met,

WHAT IS THIS LOVE?—ECSTASY AND AGONY

he was set free! We laughed and laughed, we hugged, we danced. From that moment on, that young man began writing songs inspired by Jesus, and these songs, plus the hundreds more from other gifted musicians carried the move of God's love. Again, I sensed there were angels moving through us, but this, too, was not my "whisper" from God.

I wasn't the only one experiencing an interchange of angelic ministry, however; it was happening all over the assembly. Imagine in your mind's eye, a large auditorium furnished totally in red, filled with over two thousand adults plus children. The platform is bulging with over one hundred singers and they are no longer singing with their eyes closed and hands raised toward heaven, because they have found that Jesus doesn't dwell in the rafters! Now their feet move and their hands reach out, keeping rhythm with their voices as they send the message of Jesus' love through their energized songs.

For the entire song service of one-and-a-half hours, no one stays in their seat. Everyone, including the children, is singing and dancing their love to Jesus. As they look into one another's eyes, they see more than a human soul, they see Jesus there, looking back at them. Some laugh, some cry, some crumple to the floor, some stagger about as if drunk. Over and over again, many of us found ourselves doubled over with laughter for hours as our spirits were made one with the joy of the Lord. Oh, the glory, the joy, the fun, the excitement was remarkable, but that's just what you could see on the outside.

Something far greater happened on the inside. All desire for worldly pleasure melted away. We had found our heart's desire; it was Jesus in His temples. People walked out of the meetings barely whispering, because they knew their lives had been changed by the holy presence of God.

If you were pastor, you can imagine the job you'd have trying to keep everyone in a church this size "in the middle of the road" without restricting them from receiving from the Lord. Also, how do you keep the unbelievers, the fearful and skeptical, from leaving before they can be convinced from the Word of God preached to "taste and see that the Lord is good" (Psalm 34:8).

I remember during the outpouring of the Holy Spirit in the late sixties and early seventies, some of the Lutheran pastors who got filled and spoke in tongues held two services: one the traditional Lutheran way and one for the charismatic believers. This current move of fervent love was as hard for the uninitiated to understand as it is for an eight-year-old boy to comprehend what it feels like to fall in love, especially when he "hates" girls. At any rate, our pastor admitted these were uncharted waters for him, and he established guidelines that fluctuated and changed as the move progressed.

Nevertheless, it seemed to be the hardest for the old-time Pentecostals. One proclaimed, "This looks like a ballroom dance floor." Do you know who had the easiest time? The new converts! One young lady went into the prayer area after the sermon, gave her heart to Jesus, got filled with the Holy Spirit, came back to the sanctuary and danced her newfound joy to the Lord. She simply assumed this was the way the Christian life was supposed to be. And she was right!

* * *

WHAT IS THIS LOVE?—ECSTASY AND AGONY

As the weeks passed, flowing into one heavenly visitation from the Lord, the devil showed up—or perhaps he was there all along. The Bible tells us in Zechariah 3:1 that when Jesus presented Himself before His Father, Satan stood at His right side. We can't expect to be the exception and not have the devil show up. This move of God certainly included us being presented to the Father. The difference between Jesus and us, of course, was the devil couldn't find anything to work on in Jesus, but he had no problem finding flaws in us.

My concern for Don grew as a result of my misguided belief that I was somehow responsible to keep his womanizing addiction hidden.

> *How sobering to have, and therefore live, beliefs that affect hundreds.*

My entire life was molded by the concept of "he who hath found a wife hath found a good thing" (Proverbs 18:22). That's what I was—a good thing—for my husband to have and use in any way that fulfilled him, promoted him, enhanced him, or pleased him. My pleasure came by doing and being whatever he needed and wanted.

Unwittingly, this concept was imbibed by not only other married couples, but by the elders and congregation. The elders, it seemed, became an extension of the pastor's will, and consequently, so did the congregation at large. Recently, a woman confided in me, "There were times when I would sense that the pastor had problems, but then I'd pass it off and go on." I suppose loyalty, like love, had created its own image of what the congregation saw.

I became anxious when the pastor scheduled private worship sessions with individual ladies almost every weekday morning and asked me to work at the church after teaching Bible college instead of coming home to our office, because he wanted to invite them to enjoy lunch with him in the lovely setting of our black, white, gold, and chrome dining room overlooking the refreshing waterfalls in our garden. He also asked me to prepare their special meal before I left the home every morning.

I reasoned, *If this is what God wants the pastor to do in this move of God's love, then wouldn't it stand to reason He'd want the rest of us to experience it, too, and do the same?* My concern drove me to my knees; I prayed, "Jesus, I don't understand everything You are doing in my husband. Am I jealous, because he's not including me?"

It was in this context that I got an inkling of what was my flawed love for my husband, which Jesus had shown me in the vision of the diamond over a year ago. I began realizing I was wrongfully protecting my husband from exposure for womanizing. My excuse was the ministry, that it wouldn't be hurt. Even though I didn't understand the full extent of my sin, nor realized I was Don's enabler as well, I repented for preventing the Lord from doing what He needed to do in Don's life. I purposed not to get in the Lord's way. Perhaps the Lord had to give me a glimpse into my problem before He could send me the "whisper" He'd promised, because it happened just a few weeks after I set up a temporary office on the east campus.

* * *

WHAT IS THIS LOVE?—ECSTASY AND AGONY

I should have known the slightest breeze from God would be incredible and overpowering, but I was looking for some barely detectable thing to happen that would require a lot of faith to really believe in or see. I got just the opposite!

It was late, really late, after a wonderful Sunday evening service. All day I was filled with the marvelous presence of God, and the aftermath of joy following an outstanding prayer time earlier that week. For hours, I worshipped the Lord with others. At 1:00 a.m., in spite of the lingering presence of the Lord, I turned to walk to the door, when I looked up and, behold!—a man walked toward me, smiling—all I saw was Jesus! As our eyes met, I whispered, "Jesus!"

Without changing our gaze, we danced in worship. Every move made an incredible imprint on my spirit. I could hardly remain on my feet. I perceived that every step I took was received by him, and I repeated over and over, with abounding adoration, "Jesus, Jesus, Jesus." I was aware of no one or anything else—only Jesus.

Jesus was there—with me—looking into my eyes and seeing everything I was. With all knowledge, He still gave me unconditional acceptance. I looked into his eyes and I saw Jesus my Friend, my Savior, my Lover and Bridegroom! I was experiencing Jesus with skin on! We never touched. Our spirits merged—we became one.

The song ended. Overwhelmed, I staggered to the wall. Another song began; he came to me and we worshipped again. When that song ended, he said, "Thank you, Barbara," and backed away to the door. I slumped to the floor in complete joy and ecstasy.

I knew from his piercing eyes, full of love for me, that Jesus knew me, everything about me. He understood me and He loved me. Oh, how He loved me! He knew I loved Him, too—He had received my love. Contentment filled my being. The sound of His voice saying my name echoed in my mind as if a million trumpets had announced my name throughout all of heaven. I had never known such joy, such peace, such acceptance, such contentment. The tears that trickled out the corners of my eyes felt like golden drops of joy, as I repeated His name over and over, "Jesus, Jesus. . . ."

It was 3:00 a.m. before I could walk down the stairs to my car. I knew that Jesus, the glorified Son of Man, had—in union with another human being's spirit—manifested Himself to me, and by doing so, our spirits melded into one. I was certain the Father had answered Jesus' prayer of John 17:21—*"That they may be one as we are."*

I thought, Surely this is the mystery the Apostle Paul refers to in Ephesians 5:31-32—"*...the two shall be one flesh; this is a great mystery, but I speak concerning Christ and the church."*

Heavenly music never left my mind day nor night, and over and over I experienced the union with Jesus and the man's spirit whom I learned was named Bob. Actually, one of the elders' wives told me his name when I excitedly told her what had happened. I longed to hear his voice again—to me it was like the voice of Jesus—but I wondered if I would ever get the chance.

It just so happened the following Saturday was an all-day church fellowship at Lake Retreat. As I rode in the car alone with Don, it was wonderful just to be with him, because my encounter with the manifestation of Jesus

WHAT IS THIS LOVE?—ECSTASY AND AGONY

only made the experience I'd had with Don more alive to me than ever. I hadn't yet told Don what had happened to me, but I felt volumes of love for him; it was delightful just sitting close.

> *It seemed that my encounter with Jesus through a member of His body had somehow expanded my own soul, giving me a greater capacity to love. It gave me hope that my flawed love for my husband could be fixed.*

As we drove into the parking lot at Lake Retreat, I decided to tell Don about my experience, "Oh, the reason I was so late getting home Sunday evening after service was because I had the most incredible experience with Jesus that I've ever had." He looked at me with fear-filled eyes. Trembling, he asked, "You got a connection?"

Before I could answer, he continued, "Don't tell me about it. I don't want to know who it is or anything about it."

"Honey," I said, "But it's not about a person. It's about...."

He interrupted, "I don't want to know about it. I can't handle it. If you have to talk about it, talk to Lanny."

As soon as we got out of the car, Don spotted one of his connections and hurried off to greet her. As I walked onto the beautiful wooded grounds surrounding the lake, the elder's wife pranced up to me all excited. "He's here! Bob's here! I saw him here."

Almost afraid to know, in case the spiritual phenomenon could only happen through worship in the dance, I asked, "Who is he? Where is he? I don't know if I'd recognize him again. I know I'd know his eyes and his voice."

"He's right over there, see, sitting on the hillside with all those people," she chirped, pointing in his direction. "See?"

I couldn't tell which one was he, but I hugged her and thanked her for being so excited for me. I walked out to the end of the dock, stepped out of my shoes, sat down, and put my feet in the water.

This was such a pretty lake, mirroring the Northwest's evergreen trees surrounding it and the billowy white clouds in the sunny sky. Children were swimming nearby, and some were paddling around the lake in boats. I could hear the sound of our music coming from the meeting hall, and I reaffirmed my commitment to the Lord to release my husband, because I didn't understand why he wasn't thrilled that I, too, had a "connection."

My spirit and mind were praising the Lord when I turned to my right. There, sitting beside me, was Bob. I hadn't heard him come up behind me or sit down. He said, "Hello, Barbara," as our eyes met. His face was aglow with the presence of Jesus.

I wondered if anyone else could see what I saw. I didn't even know this young man, yet I felt as if I knew him perfectly, and it seemed as if he knew me. Neither of us felt any need to talk; the fellowship we were experiencing in our spirits was far beyond anything we could verbally express. The glory of God radiated through his eyes, through his voice, through every gesture, as he represented Jesus, the Son of God, to me.

I don't know how long we sat on the dock before Don came up and sat down behind us. I turned my attention

WHAT IS THIS LOVE?—ECSTASY AND AGONY

to him, and before long I was engrossed in something Don was saying to one of the children nearby. When I turned back to Bob, he was gone. Just as suddenly as he had appeared, he left, but now I knew the members of Christ's body could be an outward manifestation of Christ who dwells within, not just when we worshipped Jesus, but in our daily encounters with one another, as well.

* * *

Through continued dancing before the Lord, I was propelled into a realm in God's spirit that became reality for many others whose testimonies paralleled my own. It seemed like God pushed aside the curtain of time and we danced into a vast realm that had no end, a foretaste of heaven while still on earth.

Could it be the earnest of our inheritance to come, spoken of in Ephesians 1:14,18? Verse 13 and 14 state that the Holy Spirit is the earnest of inheritance, and in 1 John 2:27 we are promised that the Holy Spirit, rather than man's teaching, will lead and guide us into all truth. Ephesians 1:18 makes it clear that the eyes of our understanding will be enlightened "that we may know what is the hope of His calling, and what are the riches of the glory of His inheritance in the saints."

We not only saw Jesus in one another, but we also got a foretaste of 1 John 3:2—*"Beloved, now are we the sons of God and it doth not yet appear what we shall be: but we know that, when He shall appear, we shall be like Him; for we shall see Him as He is.* Also, *For now we see through a dark glass, but then face to face: now I know in part; but then shall I know even as I am known"* (1 Corinthians 13:12).

When we saw and felt Jesus' spirit in one another, we experienced how it felt to be like Jesus: to feel like He does, to love like He does, and to know like He knows. In this vast spiritual realm, seated in heavenly places with Christ Jesus (Ephesians 2:6), we found ourselves capable of melding with everyone there all at once. I know none of us will ever have to line up in heaven to see Jesus—or anyone else, for that matter—because we'll all be one.

When I experienced that vast realm, I sensed how God longs to have His people free of every fear and hindrance that keeps us from having the earnest of our inheritance. Sometimes I get an acute longing for heaven—homesick even. Not for the glitter and gold of mansions, but for the fulness of Jesus and His glorified body which are His saints. Oh, the ability to know one another, to experience everyone in Jesus all at once! To experience the fulness of God in one another (Ephesians 3:19; Colossians 1:19)—that's heaven! I also know in a very real way, that we are not complete without one another, as Hebrews 11:40 declares.

To explain the spiritual phenomenon is like trying to tell a person who has lived in the tropics all his life what ice is like. How do you begin? You can't say it's cold, because he doesn't know what cold is. You can say, "Water gets hard, so you can hold it, and when you put it in your mouth, it turns back into water," or "The lake gets so hard, you can walk on it." But he'll never really know until he experiences it for himself.

We find the Apostle Peter describing his experience on the mount of transfiguration (Matthew 17:1-9) in 2 Peter 1:16-18. Peter said, ". . . we made known unto you the power and coming of our Lord Jesus Christ . . . we

WHAT IS THIS LOVE?—ECSTASY AND AGONY

were eyewitnesses of His majesty." In other words, Peter had a foretaste of the glories of Jesus. Perhaps what we at the Chapel experienced could be likened to a transfiguration of sorts. The outward image became a manifestation of Christ who lived inside, and supernaturally melded our spirits together. There is a provision in God for all of us to know one another after the spirit, because God's Word commands us to "know no man after the flesh" (1 Corinthians 5:16).

Sometimes this transfiguration experience happened to both individuals simultaneously, so both of them saw a manifestation of Jesus in each other as they worshipped. Other times only one of them experienced the other as being the glorified Son of Man. Still others experienced being the glorified Son, and when they did, they felt Jesus in them loving that person and feeling as He feels about them. It wasn't uncommon, especially at first, for one person to experience being a manifestation of Jesus without their partner feeling it or knowing how to receive it.

The most powerful unions were the ones where both felt themselves being a manifestation of Jesus and also experiencing the other person being the same to them. Coupled with that would be a union of the two human spirits in Jesus, which resulted in—for one thing—an unbreakable bond that goes beyond the human realm of time. Almost always, for those experiencing this kind of union where the three become one, we found ourselves fellowshipping and in union with God the Father. Someone started calling these deep unions "mega connections" and the phrase was adopted.

I recalled times when the power of God was so mighty and faith was so high, we knew angels were manifesting through us to produce the highly precision dance that made a prophetic statement of God's glory that is going to fill the whole earth. After such a dance, sometimes involving over fifty people, we would shout, "It has been danced!" thus proclaiming the victory for God's people that Satan could not take away from them, because the dance had been a statement of faith.

These life-changing spiritual experiences affected the way I viewed other people, as well as myself. The level of our ability to communicate with one another is so inferior to that realm, there is no comparison, so I can't be too quick to make a judgment, thinking I really understand the person by his words and actions. After this initial experience, I had a new awareness of my own frailty and just how fragile everyone else is. A gesture, a flippant word, a sarcastic glance can all wound. I understand now why the Father longs for us to experience that realm, because when we can come into the depth of His love that this experience brings and it can become a regular part of our relationship with Him and one another—just as praying in tongues is a part of our prayer life—we will be the fulfillment of Jesus' prayer in John 17. Our reverence for one another and carefulness with their hearts and lives will be part of the outward fruit. Fulfilling the Scriptures that admonish us to "know no man after the flesh" (2 Corinthians 5:16); and to "know nothing among one another, save Christ and Him crucified," (1 Corinthians 2:2) will be no problem. It won't be by our own self-righteous works either, but it will be the fruit of continually "walking in the Spirit" (Galatians 5:25).

When we are experiencing this glorious realm, there is no problem loving one another fervently, and loving

WHAT IS THIS LOVE?—ECSTASY AND AGONY

the Lord God with all our minds, hearts, and souls, because there are no doctrinal or personality or racial or sex gender barriers there. I could see God's plan unfolding to unite whole churches, which were already one within their own body. As yet, we hadn't heard of other churches experiencing the spiritual phenomenon, however. Perhaps the prophecy given over me during the Latter Rain revival was the reason why God was giving us these experiences. Remember, He foretold that He would use me as a forerunner.

Surely God had us on a journey to experience an unfolding revelation of Himself, just as He had—at the start of our church revealed. It was a part of our calling. But being on the leading edge of God's move also put us on the front lines of the battle between God and Satan, and what happened next gave Satan a window of opportunity.

Chapter Eighteen

Angels Unawares, Holy and Unholy

"Let brotherly love continue. Be not forgetful to entertain strangers for thereby some have entertained angels unawares."
(Hebrews 13:1,2)
"The Son of man shall send forth His angels and they shall gather out of His kingdom all things that offend."
(Matthew 13:41)
"And no marvel for Satan himself is transformed into an angel of light."
(2 Corinthians 11:14)

How are these spiritual experiences going to affect our souls and daily lives, I wondered. Remembering the Lord's warning about the devil's plan to destroy us from within, I prayed for angels of purity, as Jesus admonished. Now that I had a powerful spiritual union, I determined to keep in touch with Lanny.

* * *

At the elders' retreat held just before the 1985 fall camp meeting, God set the stage for Don and me to restore our spiritual union, and at the same time be united with the whole eldership, including all the satellite pastors. Even the pastors from our churches overseas were there. The last evening of the retreat held on our own campus, men rolled a piano into the gym, anticipating the fresh new songs from the Spirit of the Lord. People poured into the gym, full of faith and hope after praying for three solid days.

The holy presence of God seemed to descend on us like a dense cloud covers the face of a mountain. One of the pastors literally ran to the piano and began singing, *"You've not been honored enough, Oh Son of Man...."*[12] As the sound filled the gym, it felt as if it also poured into all of us. Immediately, as if directed by an unseen hand, we all began dancing honor to the Lord. Don hastened to an elder's wife from the church in Tacoma. As he took her out to the middle of the floor and started dancing with her, something else happened to the rest of us. Instead of worshipping with just one connection, we were carried into groups. The momentum grew, and a circle formed. George, the music director, with whom both Bob and I had a strong union, knew by the Spirit of the Lord that I should join my husband. As the three of us danced, he said, "Barbara, you need to be in there with Don.."

I said, "Oh, no I can't. That's his new connection."

George said, "She'll understand. We'll take care of her. God is doing something special here. You belong with Don."

Suddenly we were whirling in the circle that was forming around Don. Bob, George, and other elders caught the mounting momentum from God's Spirit and moved in closer to Don. The circle tightened. They separated Don's connection from him, and I took her place. This whole procedure happened without missing a single step or movement of the dance that by now included over two hundred people. Everyone was empowered by the awesome presence of God, as we whirled and turned, gaining speed.

The circles tightened as the song honoring the glorified Son resounded throughout the gym. God was supernaturally uniting our spirits corporately. The power of God in that gym was indescribable. Surely there must have been hundreds of angels there, directing our whirling, leaping, and turning in circle after circle, as the whole group was propelled around and around, circling the entire gym.

It seemed as if our spirits were whirling upwards in a cone shape much like a tornado in reverse—instead of coming down to touch the earth, we were spinning upward to touch heaven. Every movement honored Jesus, the glorified Son of Man, whom we saw in one another's eyes as we sang, *"You've not been honored enough, Oh Son of Man...."* Afterwards, many agreed that it was as if we were experiencing being Ezekiel's vision of the wheel in the middle of the wheel, or what we today would call a gyroscope (Ezekiel 10:10).

When I looked into Don's eyes, they seemed horrified that I was there instead of his connection. Then I saw fear, mixed with disgust. He said, "Where's my connection?"

I said, "Don't worry. The elders took care of her. She understands."

As the circle moved in tighter around us, he said what I thought was, "I gotta go lay down." Sometimes after he danced a short time, his back hurt and he'd have to lie down.

I responded with, "Please wait. God is doing something special."

He said, "I have to go," I said, "You don't want me here, do you?" He shook his head.

I felt stinging pain in my spirit, as if a sword had pierced me and ripped out a big portion of my being. It made me nauseated and dizzy. Reluctantly, I danced my way through the circles, being careful not to disrupt what the Spirit of the Lord was doing in the rest of the elders and their wives. They looked puzzled and couldn't understand why I left Don.

When I reached the outside circle, Bob was there. As we separated ourselves from the circle, an elder's wife dashed over to me and said, excitedly, "Oh, Barbara, you should be in there with Don." I managed a weak smile, and with my eyes brimming with tears, shook my head. Bob took my arm and said, "Let's go outside for some fresh air."

I stumbled out the back door and we sat down on a boulder at the edge of the woods that bordered the back of the building. I didn't have to tell Bob what had happened. He knew. When he said, "I'm sorry," I replied, "I'm sorry, too. He just didn't get it—Don just didn't understand what was happening." Bob knew I was speaking to Jesus, so he didn't respond.

I don't know how long we sat there, looking up at the stars, before Bob said, "We better go back in now." I lost something in my spirit towards my husband that night that I couldn't get back. Proverbs 18:14 says, "The spirit of a man will sustain his infirmity; but a wounded spirit who can bear?" When we returned to the gym, I was so numb everything was a blur. The circle had disbanded, and Bob disappeared into the crowd to worship with someone.

Don seemed oblivious to the fact that we had just missed going where Jesus wanted to take us, and he had absolutely no idea what had happened to me. Later he told me his concern was for his connection. He blamed me for hurting her by coming in and cutting her off from their dance. I reassured him, "It will never happen again, because now I don't feel a need to worship with you; whatever it was that was dying in me is now dead." I never again missed not dancing with my husband, nor did I have any desire to pray for him, either alone or in his scheduled prayer meetings.

Without my knowledge, the stage was being set so every detail of my life could be fixed. The glory of it went way beyond my grandest dreams, and the pain was as excruciating as the glory was marvelous. God had been preparing just the right vessel all his life for the assignment.

* * *

At about 1:30 in the morning after a Friday evening service, I said to Lanny, "I don't know what is wrong with me. I am sitting here after just experiencing one of the most wonderful times in the Lord I could ever hope to have, and yet something is missing. I'm not satisfied; I ache inside for something else from Jesus. Is it because

Bob wasn't here to experience it with me?" Lanny let me talk. I continued, "I just don't know. I didn't need to have Bob here to have the experience I just had, but still...."

Just then, out of the corner of my eye, I saw a man walking across the sanctuary in the middle aisle which was still crowded—nobody wanted to leave the presence of God. I interrupted myself, grabbed Lanny's arm, and abruptly asked, "Lanny, who's that?"

He looked and questioned, "Who's who? There are lots of people there."

I pointed to the man whom my spirit had seemingly shot out to and said, "Him! That one! Right there!"

"Oh," Lanny said, "That's Jerry. He's a fine brother. I believe he's in his last year of Bible college. Wonderful man, always makes good comments in my classes. He's married, has a couple of kids. I'd trust you with him; he's really solid. Did you hear how he came here to Bible college?

"After hearing about our Bible college four years ago, Jerry got a ride with a truck driver coming to Seattle from Minnesota. He wanted to check out our college before moving his family here. Without knowing where we were located, the driver arrived with his cargo in Seattle, pulled off the freeway and into a deli. Jerry went to the phone and dialed the college office. Our Dean answered, and guess where Jerry was? Three minutes away at Len's deli." Lanny laughed, "That's right! Jerry had just enough time to come and check us out. God directed the whole thing."

"That's a wonderful testimony, Lanny," I sighed, "My spirit practically leapt out of my body when I saw him."

"Well," Lanny said with a wink, "If you want to worship with him, just go cruise the chapel in the afternoons after Bible college. Jerry spends every spare minute that he's not studying or working, worshipping the Lord in the chapel."

Just as I said, "Lanny, you know I'm not a cruiser," Wendy, my four-year-old granddaughter woke up and came to get her daddy to worship the Lord with her.

After the next Sunday night's service, Lanny went to Jerry—a six-foot-tall man with an athletic build, in his middle thirties—where he was standing with his eyes closed and his hands raised. Making a fist, Lanny reached up and rapped on Jerry's chest as if to say, "Hello, can I interrupt you?" When Jerry opened his eyes, Lanny said, "Do me a favor. Go dance with Barbara."

"You mean the pastor's wife?"

"Yeah."

* * *

The next Sunday morning, after Sunday School classes, the pianist took his place at the piano and, in no time at all, people danced their worship to the Lord with joyful abandon. Suddenly, I spotted him. He was clear over on the opposite side of the church from where I was standing at the pastor's pew. Instantly, it felt as if my spirit flew to him like an electric current.

Jerry started dancing in my direction, weaving his way through the other worshippers. I felt as if my eyes were glued to him. I silently prayed...*Jesus, are You going to give me this one to worship You with? Of all the sons in Your court, he is the choicest one. The way he dances before You is so lovely, so pure, so exquisite! Does he even know I am here? How can I worship with one as princely* as he? *Every move seems to tell me of Your love and how much You love him. Dear God, cause him to know what I am feeling from Your heart for him.*

As soon as Jerry was about three feet from me, I knew it was Jesus in me that responded to the look in his eyes and the glow on his face. I joined him in worship, and my surroundings faded; I felt myself to be in the heavenly court of the King's palace dancing with His beloved. In one glorious moment, I sensed how our heavenly Father must feel about His Son and His great delight in having a Bride prepared for His Son who gave His life for her (Revelation 21:9). Later, I was embarrassed when I remembered that at the end of the dance, without stopping to think, I had kissed him on his neck.

When the service ended, Jerry returned and we danced in the post-service worship. We found ourselves right back in the magnificent heavenly throne room of God. At the close of that day, Jerry said to me, "I'll always be here when you need me; just let me know." *Lord,* I thought, *this man seems to know what my longings are even without asking me.*

You can imagine my surprise when the poolside phone rang at the Marriott Hotel in Palm Springs the following week (our Bible college break) where a number of us were staying and it was Jerry for me. He and his wife were in Victoria, Canada, on a little vacation themselves. He felt in his spirit such an acute longing just to hear my voice and called to see if everything was all right with me. When I asked him, " How did you find out where we were staying?" his only answer was, "Oh, I have ways." I received two more calls from Jerry before we returned home, and although I didn't tell him anything, he just seemed to know that all was not well with me.

> *How can I explain to you what transpired in my life and our church in the months that followed? Oh, the joy, the ecstasy, the heavenly visitations, the pain, the agony, the excitement, the miracles, the sorrow, the spiritual awareness and growth, the devil, the deception, the selfishness, the insecurities, the love—most of all, the love!*

* * *

This astounding unconditional love from God poured into us through our spirits. When the Lord moved on our spirits, either by His Spirit or through the ministry of angels, our spirits experienced a thrilling unconditional love for the person to which we had been drawn. It didn't seem to matter if they were male or female, married or single, black or white, old or young, fat or ugly, stubborn, rebellious, troublemaker, mean, or whatever—we loved them fervently! The experience in our spirits also affected our souls and bodies, causing us to feel overwhelming, exciting, joyful, marvelous love that was beyond any natural human expression.

The need to express this love or somehow transmit it to that individual became the vital issue. We felt desperate, to the point of agony, for the fantastic love—because we somehow sensed how God feels about us through one another. Now, by pouring His love through the members of His body, we were given a tangible visitation of God's nature, which is love. He gave us His love "with skin on." It came in the form of our brothers and sisters in the Lord, which, in turn, somehow expanded our own souls and released us to have brotherly love, the hallmark of this church age found in Revelation 3:7 (Philadelphia, which means "brotherly love").

There are many Scriptures that admonish us to have not only God's agape love for one another, but our own brotherly love as well. Scriptures such as Romans 12:10; 13:10; 1 Peter 3:8; 2 Peter 1:7; 1 John 4:16-21; 2 Corinthians 5:14; and John 13:34-35 were happily and joyfully obeyed: "*A new commandment I give unto you. That you love one another as I have loved you...*" "*By this shall all men know that you are My disciples, if you have love one for another...*" "*Be kindly affectioned one to another with brotherly love...*" "*Having compassion one of another love as brethren...*" "*Brotherly kindness, and to kindness, love...*" "*God is love, and he that dwelleth in love dwelleth in God. Herein is our love made perfect...*" "*There is no fear in love...*" "*He who loveth God loveth his brother also.*"

Let me tell you it was sheer delight, fun even, to love the ones to whom we were connected. But also, we experienced pain—agonizing pain. Why? Because God allowed us to "bear one another's burdens" (Galatians 6:2). Many testimonies paralleled mine. Supernaturally, we would know some detail about the person's life, and with the revelation, we'd experience the pain and agony suffered by that one as if we were living it, without any emotional block. Sometimes the pain was so intense, I'd hurt for days, realizing how much Jesus is "touched with the feelings of our infirmities" (Hebrews 4:15).

One lady testified, "I was driven to my knees to pray for my connection when the Lord let me see him as a child. All God showed me was that as a little boy he had gone through a devastating experience that left a permanent scar on his life which closed him off from being vulnerable to love. When we got together the next day, I told him what had happened to me in prayer. With no emotion, he told me how, when he was a little boy he had been wrenched away from his parents and taken to a boys' home.

"As he related the story, I experienced all the pain that he could not feel, and my compassion broke away the shell around his heart. He is actually a very tender and loving man, but nobody knew his real nature. Now, for the first time since his childhood, he's experiencing who he really is as God's child."

With events like this happening, you can see why it became necessary for us to spend time with our connections other than just worshipping with them in the dance. It was difficult to find times to be together so inner healings such as this one could transpire without causing a problem to those who hadn't experienced it. They couldn't relate to the need to express it, or in some cases, didn't trust the motives of the person who wanted to be with their mate. It was hard to accept someone else seemingly loving one's mate more fervently than he or she did.

In these early stages of the move, the in-depth studies on how the soul and body are affected by the spirit were very enlightening and vital to the church. We needed to understand from the Word of God what was happening to us. We were, to our "connections" at least, being the living epistles of 2 Corinthians 3:2. Many of us integrated into one another's daily lives, happily helping with every day chores and sharing whatever we had to give. One single forty-year-old lady declared, "I didn't know how much I'd missed until I got to be involved in my connection's family. The experience changed me and made me marriageable."

* * *

Have you ever seen the movie *The Bishop's Wife*? It's an old black and white movie about a bishop who was so busy in the ministry trying to make a name for himself, he neglected his family. In desperation, he asked God for help. He received the answer to his prayer in the form of an angel clothed in the body of a handsome man. His assignment was to do the tasks the bishop didn't have time to do himself. Even though the bishop had full knowledge that this was an angel, when he saw the thrill his wife experienced by having the angel meet all her unfilled needs, he became outraged at the angel and wanted his prayer cancelled.

In a sense, that movie depicts the way God ushered in His judgment of our lives and ministry at the Chapel. Every time I look back on those days, my eyes fill with tears of thankfulness to the precious loving plan our Lord had to perfect His body and fulfill His Word in us. Just like the movie, it took us a while to realize this move included the judgment of God that He had forewarned us of in 1982.

* * *

It was as if Jerry at times became a manifestation of my guardian angel. God began using Jerry to uncover the problems in my life, my marriage, and Don's relationship with the elders and members of the congrega-

ANGELS UNAWARES, HOLY AND UNHOLY

tion.. Time and again Jerry knew things about me: hurts in my past that I never shared with anyone, buried personality traits that never had a chance to be developed or expressed. A trip ten of us took to Hawaii over Christmas break presented an opportunity for God to bring these things up and begin dealing with them.

The Spirit of the Lord was gloriously around us as I began discovering who I was as a person. For one thing, Jerry let me talk—about whatever I wanted to talk about. He let me tell him all about Hawaii the way I wanted to tell it. I had been to Hawaii many times, but I had always had to let Don tell about our trips. Jerry didn't know this, of course, because he had never been around us.

It was hard for me at first. I was full of fear that I might say something wrong. Gradually it dawned on me that Jerry totally accepted me and he was even excited to hear me talk. I cried with joy.

> *If I would have known that Jerry's wife was an excellent conversationalist and has an exceptional command of the English language, I would have been too intimidated to ever say a word. She could keep any group of people spellbound and in laughter for hours.*

One evening we stood knee deep in the surf on Waikiki Beach, lost in the glory of God, not even daring to move, let alone talk. For over an hour, both of us were aware of nothing but the profound holiness of God.

Another new experience for me was deciding what I wanted to do. At first I couldn't do it. I'd say to Jerry, "You mean, just what I'd like to do, without considering what everyone else wants to do first?" When I put everyone else's desires and needs out of my mind, there didn't seem to be anything left. Then Jerry seemed to know a desire I had that had been suppressed for so long I couldn't even find it. Whenever I discovered something about myself, he would be so happy he would pick me up and whirl me around with delight, encouraging me to keep on searching for, and finding my own identity.

Before we left Hawaii, Jerry said to me, "You've always wanted to get your ears pierced, haven't you?" When he saw the surprised look on my face, he lifted my hair back off my face and added, "You secretly admire the beauty of earrings, but you have never ever let yourself even consider getting your ears pierced. Well, I think you'd look great with earrings and I think you should get your ears pierced." Smiling with joy as he imagined how I would look, he promised, "I'll buy you your first pair of earrings." It wasn't until the following May that I got my ears pierced. When I finally decided to do it, I lost the grip of legalism that had bound me and colored my judgments. Its roots went deep, clear back to the rules established by my church when I was growing up.

On another occasion, we were walking on the beach, when Jerry turned to me and announced, "B, you've always admired anyone who would go up in that parasail, haven't you?"

Surprised, I quipped, "How do you know all these things about me? I don't let myself even think about things like that."

Giving me a little shove in the sand, he avoided the question. "Come on, admit it. You would love to go parasailing, but you're just too scared."

"Yeah. But, Z, it is scary."

"No, it isn't. It's perfectly safe. You couldn't get hurt if you wanted to. You're strapped into a harness and the boat pulls you up into the air. Come on. Let's go talk to them about it."

As we neared their booth on the beach, I protested, "No, Z, I'm too scared. I can't."

"Well, it won't hurt to talk to them," Jerry said, as he pulled me over to the booth. "This lady really wants to go parasailing, but she's pretty scared. Can we buy a ticket and if she changes her mind when we are out on the barge...."

The attendant interrupted, turned to me, and smiled, "Oh, you'll love it. Lots of people are a little scared at first, but they all come back just thrilled that they did it. Hey, if you change your mind, I'll give you your money back. Do you want one, too, sir?"

Jerry laughed, "No. I've jumped out of planes many times. But can I go out on the barge with her?"

"Sure. They'll be back to shore in about an hour."

By the time the barge came in for another load, I was shaking with fear. The crew waited until I was the only one left. We had been on the water for two hours. I could wait no longer. I devastated Jerry by saying, "I can't do it. Even if our connection depends on it, I can't. You do it. I want you to do it."

As we headed back down the beach, Jerry shuffled along in the sand. With sad eyes, he said, "I guess I just can't help you, B. You won't trust me."

I interrupted, "Z, yes I do. I'll do it tomorrow."

"No, you won't. You'll just have to get someone else to get you delivered from that demon of fear. I can't help you."

I felt so sorry that I had let him down. I promised, "I'll do it first thing in the morning. Don't tell Don what happened. I'll do it, then we'll come back and tell him, okay?"

As we neared the condo, he said, "You won't do it."

I countered, "Yes, I will. You'll see."

I ran down the beach first thing in the morning and was on the first barge to leave the beach. As frightened as I was, I knew I had to defeat that demon of fear. As I soared into the windy air and rose 300 feet above the water, suspended in space, my knuckles were white from gripping the harness so tightly—but I was free. I was free from the fear that I had worn like an overcoat around my heart since I was a little girl. The tears of joy that filled my eyes were brushed away by the wind. I felt a new union with my Creator, as I surveyed His creation below with only the sound of the wind in my ears.

Jerry swept me up in his arms almost before the attendants could unbuckle the harness when my feet touched the deck. We laughed and cried together, as we ran back up the beach to tell Don. Jerry knew this deliverance was going to have a major impact on my life. Now I was free to discover who I really was, and he was excited for me. In the months that followed, I learned to ski and swim a little. I went snorkeling and scuba diving, hiking and catamaran sailing.

Bursting into the condo, I shouted, "Guess what I just did?" Before Don could answer , I added, "I went parasailing!"

Don's eyes grew wide, "You're kidding!"

"No, honey. I really did. You have to do it, Donald. It's so fun!"

I was like a bird in a cage that suddenly discovers the door has swung open. I was free to fly out and discover the whole vast world of my own personality.

As big as legalism and fear had been in my life, a bigger foe was the role I'd assumed that shaped my marriage. Almost like an addiction, I was possessed with being whatever my husband wanted me to be. I would have walked off a cliff, if he so ordered me. Before this trip to Hawaii ended, the Lord had pronounced the death sentence on an evil spirit and this concept began weakening. At this point, however, I didn't really know what had happened to me. I was just beginning to experience the difference, and some of it wasn't pleasant. The freer I got, the more fearful Don became.

My ability to handle the long "talks" that Don insisted on having with me every few weeks—usually following times that he spent alone with one of his connections was all but gone. I wasn't able to listen to his blame and accusations of me concerning why he had the problems he had. I found myself interrupting him, refusing to believe what he said about me. We ended up arguing, something we had seldom ever done in our thirty-seven years of marriage. I'd run out of the house to get away, because I was no match for his lawyer-like mind that picked apart every phrase I chose to use. On the next vacation the two of us took alone, I was trapped and couldn't get away. I broke emotionally. How can I forget how it happened?

* * *

We were riding in a rented car in Palm Springs. Don's intention for this vacation was for just the two of us to get away, for the purpose of working on our marriage. My assignment had been to write down the points of our relationship that I had problems with and wanted changed. I had spent the day carefully wording each concern, so as not to blame him. Don made it clear he didn't want any detail.

We sat in the sun at the pool. While Don drew caricatures of his connections and made them cards, I managed to get the list down on a 3 x 5 card. Of all places, Don chose to read the list in the car as we were driving to a deli for lunch. After glancing at the card while driving, Don settled into a long dissertation blaming me for all his problems, including why he couldn't hold the line with his connections. The longer he talked, the more hopeless I became, until—without warning to either of us—my body started shaking and uncontrollable sobs escaped from deep within. In this uncontrollable state, I thought, *Is this how it feels to have a nervous breakdown?*

Don shouted, "Jean! What's wrong? Stop! Jean! Oh, no! Dear God, what have I done? I've ruined my wife! Oh, God! Help me! Forgive me! Help her, Jesus, help her!" Reaching over and touching my back as I was doubled over with muscle spasms, he sighed, "Jean, what shall I do?" Now he was like a little boy. "Do you want me to call Jerry?" I couldn't answer.

He pulled into a parking lot. Spotting a phone booth across the street, he spun the car around and sped to it. Wouldn't you know there was a police car at the intersection? Instead of giving us a ticket, however, he told us how to get to a hospital in case I needed medical help.

When Don reached Jerry, I couldn't control the sobs long enough to speak with him, but he made it plain to

Don that Don wasn't going to reach me through the power of his intellect. Finally the sobs subsided, but my body trembled like a wounded puppy and I whimpered for days. I knew I couldn't take the chance of going on a trip alone like this for a long time. After the incident, I started stuttering whenever I was around Don. My heart condition, which very few people knew about, worsened, sapping my energy.

* * *

Don never seemed to experience what I did when we took our connections on vacations. For me they were filled with the holy presence of the Lord, besides coming alive and growing as a person. But Don usually came home more worried about the church than when he left. When we returned from Hawaii, we found out he had plenty of cause for concern. It seemed that a door had been opened to the devil, and his army of sexual demons were deceiving people.

Under the guise of spiritual healing and freedom from legalism, some connections were acting out the union of their spirits with anything from French kissing to intercourse. Others were trying to get their spirits united through sexual actions. Still others were having spiritual unions all right, but they were with familiar spirits. It was amazing how perverted demons found one another. We certainly couldn't blame God for failing us. Besides the clear warnings in His Word (Romans 2:21-22; 1 Corinthians 5:6-7; 6:12; Ephesians 4:27)—how many visions had He given us? Four to me alone, not counting what He had shown others.

A few weeks before that trip to Hawaii, God faithfully gave me an experience that uncovered the plan of the devil to make a mockery of God's love. While in deep intercession, my body started responding to what my spirit was experiencing. I felt my abdomen muscles contract as if I were about to give birth. There were no actual labor pains, just deep contractions.

As this continued, it became clear to me that our church was in a great spiritual battle between Satan and God. The devil wanted to destroy what the Spirit of the Lord had conceived in the church. The union between Jesus and His church had barely taken place among us; the fetus was not yet ready to be born.

What this union with Jesus was producing wasn't adequately nourished or formed to emerge from the protection of the inner workings of our church. This the devil knew. His wicked intent was to abort God's fledgling fetus. While in agonized prayer, it was as if I saw Satan jerk out the bloodied and bruised fetus. As he held it up, he laughed a hideous laugh as only he can. In defiance, he smirked at God and proclaimed to mankind, "See! This is what God's love produces!"

> *In my heart, I wondered if whatever the pastor had done with his connections in Hawaii had put the tool back in the devil's hands to ruin what God was trying to do.*

* * *

Crisis after crisis awaited us when we arrived home. Not only were some off course, some had jumped overboard. Some decided to leave their mates and marry their connections. Others jumped out of fear of losing their marriage if their mate got connected to someone other than them. In a desperate attempt to correct the navigation, the pastor called an emergency meeting of all those who had a "mega connection"—a spiritual union which remained consistent over a period of time and was deeper than any of the other unions of that individual.

After taking a survey, the pastor confessed to the group that he had "fallen out of the boat" himself and had to be thrown a life preserver to get back in. He had all of us kneel as he led us in a prayer of repentance. As we arose from our knees, he said, "Now, the past is behind us. I don't care what you have done. I'm only interested in what you will do from this point on. How many of you will promise me before God that you will follow the guidelines from now on?" Every hand went up. "Everyone who will do what this pastor asks, stand up." Everyone stood.

With that, Don set his outline on the podium and began reading the list of rules he had prepared. A lengthy explanation followed each rule, and before he was finished, he had left the door open for off-campus activity and intimate physical expressions (including kissing on the lips) without the intention of sexual stimulus.

At the close of the meeting, I looked at Jerry who was as puzzled as I. In a hushed voice, I said, "I don't think anything was accomplished tonight. Could it be he protected himself more than the church?" We slipped into the prayer room and prayed that the megas wouldn't take advantage of the liberty left to them, and that the Lord would help us to keep our union pure.

* * *

My work load had tripled. I was at the east campus from morning until late at night, trying to keep up with all the counseling needs. The devil's attack on our church was in full force. Just as the Lord had warned us, demons of dissatisfaction invaded the marriages. Spouses confided in their connections. Demons of self-pity and justification were right there to add fuel to the fire, taking advantage of our vulnerable state, right when God was breaking down the elements in our marriages that weren't His designed plan.

> *Looking back, I can see that our belief system on authority and submission both in the home and in the church structure was askew, and many marriages needed the same "overhaul" as mine. While living in the middle of the upheaval, however, it wasn't easy to see.*

My mornings left no time for me to do anything other than fix breakfast, which Don ate at his desk, prepare lunch for Don and his connection, pour over my lecture for my Bible college classes that day, shuffle through the mail, and rush to east campus to pray before I taught. That's one thing I couldn't do without—my prayer time before class. My mailbox at church was absolutely stuffed with urgent pleas for help, along with letters from those who were leaving the church out of fear of deception, the other satanic ploy of which the Lord had forewarned us.

There were also letters relating spiritual experiences that demanded evaluation. People wanted to know whether or not their experiences were from God. Don didn't want to give any counseling needs that pertained to this move to our minister of counseling, because he was having a great deal of trouble believing in it. Don also didn't want anyone to read the letters of resignation, for fear they would instill doubts in others' minds. Nor did he want to read them himself; it was too painful for him to handle the rejection. The only ones he wanted to handle were the ones who showed some possibility of being rescued by him. Otherwise they were up to me.

Jerry saw my impossible position. "B," he said (lots of people called me "B" because I always used just my initials on all correspondence), "You can't go on like this. You can't keep a handle on what's going on in people's lives. There's no way you can know the schedule or work load of the other ministers who are counseling. You don't know how many people are going directly to them, so you don't know if they can handle another case on top of what they're already doing. All these connections are starting to counsel one another. You don't even have time to read the reports from the counselors and other ministers. This whole area needs organizing."

Suddenly, a light went on. Practically at the same time, we said, "A counseling center! We need a counseling center!" I got happy. Jerry laughed, whirled me around, and we began to lay out the plan. I looked at Jerry. "Z," (I'd started calling him by his last initial when he used mine.) I queried, "I think you're the perfect one to set up and manage the Counseling Center. Would you be willing to do it?"

Jerry mused, "Well, I know what needs to be done, and I know I can do it. It won't be easy at first, but it's the only way to get this problem solved." As if to look into the future, he added, "It might be the very thing the Lord can use to save this move of God." Coming back to the present, he said, "I have to finish Bible college. That's why I moved my family out here. My wife and I have worked hard. She's really sacrificed, working full-time, and I've laid carpet while I've been going to school. My fourteen-year-old son, my three-year-old daughter, we've all sacrificed." Contemplating the future again, he went on, "I'll graduate in May and I've worked hard, so I could be in the ministry. I want to work with people. Now, maybe this is where the Lord wants me."

He caught the glow on my face as I listened to him express his heart to serve God's people. "B," he continued, "One thing I know for sure, and I've committed myself to it: for as long as I'm supposed to, the pastor and you take priority in my life." My eyes filled with tears, as Jerry explained, "I don't know everything yet that the Lord wants me to do, but He has shown me some things. One thing He showed me was that I was going to be a scapegoat." Now he got teary-eyed. "I don't know what all that means. I just know that's what He told me."

We sat there in silence for a few moments, knowing we were in the presence of the Lord, before I spoke, "Well, Z, you've edged your way into Don's heart like no other man. Don has never had a real man friend in his life. I hope he'll let you be that man."

Coming back to the issue at hand, Jerry addressed another concern. "How will the congregation handle you working in the same office with your connection? How about the rest of the staff? Will they all want to have their connections work with them because BB does? If you do it, they'll think it is the thing to do."

I protested, "But the pastor has told them over and over again not to copy...."

Jerry interrupted, "I know, B, but people do it anyway. They think whatever you do is somehow spiritual. I know you, the real you, probably better than you know yourself. But they don't. I didn't know you either, until God connected us. You were this beautiful, immaculately-dressed creature who lives in a spiritual realm with God and your every action is admired and imitated."

When I shrugged and said, "That's ridiculous," he said, "I know it is, but that's where the people are. The question is, can they handle us working in the same office together? You and I know it's all right—nothing sexual is going to happen—but if they try it and can't handle it, then what?"

It was true that my union with Jerry was unique, simply because I was the pastor's wife. God had a lot He wanted to do in me and Don and our marriage which, in turn, would affect the church. It took no time at all for Jerry's and my relationship to be equivalent to that of David and Jonathan in the Bible. The love we had for one another was greater than the love of a woman. (1 Samuel 18:2-3)

Just as God had used everything in Don and I when He started the church, so He was going to use everything in Jerry to pry open my heart so I could become the whole person that God had intended. Not only was Jerry connected to me, he had a connection with Don's spirit, too. Many times he expressed his love and respect for Don. It was as if Jerry became my life support system while I was being operated on by my Maker.

After the initial idea of a counseling center was presented to the board, it took a couple months to get the plans jelled and the finances worked out before the room could be ready. None of the senior elders or Don expressed a concern over Jerry and I working in the same office.

Before Jerry accepted the position, he sat down with the General Manager to whom he would be accountable and shared his heart. Without disclosing Don and my marriage problems, Jerry made it clear that whenever the pastor wanted his time, it would take priority in his schedule. The pastor and the General Manager agreed Jerry's wages wouldn't be docked for the time he spent with Don, including the pastor's vacations. All expenses for vacations were carried by Don and I, but Jerry couldn't afford the loss in salary.

You can imagine the added pressure on Jerry, as he was in his last term of Bible college and now getting the responsibility of organizing a whole new department for the corporation. In those few months before Jerry started his job at the church, I was thankful that he was working as a carpet layer in the afternoons whenever Jeff, who had a carpet installation business, needed him, because it gave me an escape from the tension between Don and me.

When anger toward Don would well up within me, I'd hop in my car and speed out to wherever Jerry was lay-

ANGELS UNAWARES, HOLY AND UNHOLY

ing carpet, usually a vacant apartment or house. Bursting through the door and in tears, I plopped down beside him. As he continued to install the tacking strip, I whimpered, "Z, I've had it!"

"Why? What's different today that wasn't there yesterday when you were fine?"

"Well, nothing, I suppose. It's been this way for a while now," I whined.

Handing me a carpet tool, he said, "Okay, then, you might as well make yourself useful while you're here. I could sure use your help. Here, I'll show you how to tuck carpet." Jerry never let me get away with self-pity. He didn't like the fact that Don was taking his connections out to dinner and then bringing them home and lying on the floor in front of the fireplace with them, but my feeling sorry for myself wasn't going to solve the problem.

* * *

Shortly after the Counseling Center opened, the phone rang. It was Don. He insisted that I come home. He had to talk to me. Jerry covered the receiver with his hand and whispered, "It's the pastor. He's had a secretary type up ten signs of a liberated woman. He wants to prove to you that you're a 'women's libber.'"

"Oh, Z, I just can't go through another long accusation session. Will he let you go instead?"

Turning back to the phone, Jerry asks, "Pastor, would it be all right with you if I came with Barbara? I need to know how you feel. Perhaps I'll be able to help." After a long pause, he said, "Okay, pastor. We'll be there at 2:00." He hung up the phone and smiled. "This will give me a chance to see if it's as bad as you say it is; and if it is, we'll figure out a way to keep you from going through it again."

The meeting lasted until 4:30. Jerry was shocked as he listened to Don's tirade, delivered in calm control. The worst thing was, Don didn't have the slightest hint of how he was destroying me. As we left, Don announced he was taking a connection out to dinner. Too devastated to even cry, I silently decided not to go home that night.

I slipped into a blank state of no feeling or caring, no concern for anyone or even my own safety. I ended up sleeping in my car in a secluded place on the water twenty-two miles from home. The only thing that brought me back to reality was my promised phone call to Jerry the next morning. He had decided on a plan.

Jerry vowed, "From now on, as long as it takes until you're strong enough to refuse to receive those accusations, I'll be your scapegoat. The next time the pastor wants to talk to you, I'll go." After that, Jerry would talk to Don sometimes as much as twenty hours a week. For the first time in his life, Don was letting a man in, and a friendship budded.

One time, Jerry grabbed Don and ushered him into a shoe store. "Pastor", he said, "We're going to get you a pair of tennis shoes. No wonder your feet and legs hurt. You're walking all over Disney World in those fancy dress shoes. Come on. You'll look better too. Those socks pulled up to your knees with your short pants makes you look like an old man." As soon as we left the store, Jerry picked Don up and whirled him around. Laughing with delight, we all literally bounced to the car. It was a first—our pastor in tennis shoes.

The talks that Jerry had with Don on these vacations sometimes lasted until the wee hours of the morning. They stretched out on the bed together like a father and son, and Jerry listened while Don went over all the reasons why I was the cause of his problems. Although on occasion Jerry broke through the shield of self-pity, the victory was short-lived. Don just couldn't accept full responsibility for his own behavior. The biggest case Don used against me became known as "the infamous black slip."

Jerry had just finished giving me a swimming lesson in the resort's pool when I, still dripping wet, tiptoed into Don's and my room. Evidently I surprised Don, because he rushed to the bathroom, but his connection was sitting up on our bed. My heart sank when I saw how beautiful she looked wearing shorts with newly suntanned legs. As she disappeared into her own room, I thought to myself, *Now what can I do to compete with that? I know....* I went to the drawer and got out a black satin half slip. Pulling it up over my almost dry swimsuit, I fastened a wide black and white stretch belt around the waist, making it into a strapless mini-skirt. It just covered the top of my bathing suit. I slipped into my shoes and walked out to the kitchen.

When Don came out of the bathroom, he looked straight at me but made no comment. As I walked over and sat down on the couch, he spoke to both Jerry and me, "I'd like to take my connection to this very fancy restaurant tonight, but it's pretty expensive, so it'll be hard for all of us to go. If it's all right with you two, we can all go some place together tomorrow."

I started to protest, "But Donald, if you take the car, there's no place out here within walking distance...."

Jerry stopped me, "It's okay, B, we'll find something. Pastor, you go ahead. We're just here for you. We want you to have a good time."

"Thank you," Don said. In a whisper, he added, "Jean, you know my connection doesn't have many clothes, so I'm going to take her to Sax's and get her a nice dress, okay?"

Totally deflated, I manage to squeak out, "Sure, no problem. Go ahead."

When — came out of her room, Don gave her a big hug and they escaped out the door. I looked up at Jerry. "So much for the black slip trick."

"I know, B, I know. He just doesn't get it." Before I had time to start crying, Jerry slapped his knee and added, "Well, come on. We're on vacation. No time to feel sorry for ourselves. Go put on some shorts and we'll go discover a new adventure."

The next morning, Don sat down and wrote me a six-page letter, accusing me of committing adultery with Jerry, because I wore that black slip. In the months that followed, no matter how many times Jerry and I tried to convince him otherwise, Don used it as the reason for his own behavior. Eventually I think half of Seattle knew of the infamous black slip.

Chapter Nineteen

A Dozen Red Roses

*"Brethren, if any man be overtaken in a fault,
ye which are spiritual, restore such an one
in the spirit of meekness, considering thyself,
lest thou also be tempted."*
(Galatians 6:1)
"...And if he repent, forgive him."
(Luke 17:4b)

As Don's grip of control on me loosened, he tightened his control over the church. Little by little, he narrowed the scope of musical expression. As a result, we lost some of our most anointed talent. Songs that had prompted the deepest worship were all but eliminated.

Fear and self-pity plagued Don. He escaped into denial and unreality, spending most of his time either drawing or with his connections. Then, right when he admitted to his prayer group of having a problem with lust, he convinced a doctor to give him shots and pills for impotence. I was shocked. After taking tests, Don had proven his problem was purely psychological. I could only conclude he hadn't told the doctor the truth. The medication didn't help our marriage. It wasn't going to matter anyway, once Jerry received a phone call one morning at the Counseling Center. Jerry prayed for almost a week before he knew he had to tell me about the call.

"B, I need to ask you some questions, but I don't want to take a chance on anyone overhearing."

We drove off-campus just to be sure. This was the first time I'd seen Jerry this solemn. The words crawled out of his mouth.

"I'm sorry I have to get you involved in this, but I don't know of any other way to confirm what I've been told. I count it as pretty serious when a girl comes and tells me the pastor has committed adultery with her." He glanced at me to see if I was okay, and continued, "How do I know she's telling the truth? It's just her word against his. So, I decided to ask her specific details, you know, like what did the pastor do when you finished? I figured I could ask you, and if your answers are the same as hers, then I'd know she was telling the truth." Taking my hand, he questioned, "B, are you all right? I hate to do this to you." His eyes filled with tears; he tried to lessen the blow, "You know we've suspected this for a long time now, but still, I have to have as much proof as possible before I go to Don."

I was so used to putting my own emotions on hold, I felt nothing except for Jerry. My eyes filled with pity, "Z, I'm so sorry you got caught in all this mess. What a terrible position to be put in, especially when you didn't do anything to cause it."

"It's okay, B. I'm probably the best one to confront the pastor. I'm thankful I was there to answer the phone. She was pretty torn up and probably would have talked to anyone." He hurried on, "I've met with her a couple times. She's going to be all right."

Afraid to hear the answer, I covered my face with my hands and whispered, "How many times has it happened?"

He reached over and removed my hands from my face and looked me in the eye. "Are you sure you want to know?" The awful truth started sinking in.

"I guess I just want a solution. Is she strong enough to break it off?"

"No, not really. She said they've tried but can't. That's why she called."

"Who is she?"

"The only reason I'm going to tell you is because I know how much you love her and you'll be able to help her."

"Is it L?"

"Yes."

"Oh, the poor dear! We are going to have to really help her through this, Z."

"I know. B, it's worse than I thought at first. It's been going on for many months now." Looking at me again, he added, "She says she thinks there's been others besides her."

Thinking of myself for the first time, I grabbed my head again and whined, "Oh no. I hope he doesn't have V.D. Z, you have to talk to him right away. Tell him I'm not going to touch him until he gets tested." Shuddering, I said, "Boy, I don't know if I can ever make love to him again." I mused, "Maybe this is why he couldn't stand to have me touch him and made me stay on my side of the bed."

THE TRUTH SHALL SET YOU FREE

I sat in a stupor as tears fell off my chin, "Z, what's it like to make love with more than one woman? You've had more than one woman. Your first wife died. How do I know Don won't be reliving these others while he's making love to me?" I choked, "Oh, Z, I just can't handle this."

"Don't worry about it now, B. I never think about my first marriage. It's not a part of my life now. I don't even remember it." Brushing the tears off my face, he asked, "Now are you ready to answer some questions for me?"

I managed a weak smile. "Sure, go ahead."

My answers lined up with hers exactly, so Jerry knew he was ready to confront the pastor.

"Z, how are you going to do this? Does Don know she told?"

"No. She says he doesn't suspect a thing. She's too scared to tell him. Besides, if she did, he'd just blame her."

"Are you going to have her there when you talk to Don?"

"No, I don't think I should. I want to make it as easy for him as possible. After all, he's my pastor. And besides, we've become pretty close. I know all the nitty gritty about your marriage. He's told me as much or more as you. If he won't admit it, then I'll have to get her. He'll probably want to see you, after I talk to him."

Shaking my head, I protested, "I don't want to talk to him alone. He'll blame me for everything."

"I know, I know. B, we have to trust the Lord to lead us. I just hope we can get this solved without the whole church finding out about it. So far, nobody knows but us."

"Z, are you going to put restrictions on him? You know this problem is bigger than just this. Oh, I sure hope the whole problem can be solved this time."

"I hope so, too, B. You know I'm committed to Don and you. Let's pray that it happens. I'll call Don right away and meet with him this afternoon, before he leaves for the pastors' retreat tomorrow in Spokane. It's a good time to confront him, right before the retreat."

Back at the office, Jerry was relieved when the pastor said he would meet him at the parsonage at 4:00. Jerry said, "You take me to the parsonage and drop me off. I'll call you if everything goes well. That way I have to stay there while you two talk because you will have to take me back to the office. If things are too tense, you'll have an excuse to get out of there."

I sobbed, "Okay, Z. I just don't know how I'm going to sleep with him tonight. I just don't know."

Jerry held me while I cried. "B, you don't need to try to deal with anyone else's problems today. I'll reschedule your appointments. You go into the chapel and be with Jesus. I need to call L; she's pretty scared."

"Oh, Z, please let her know how much I love her. And if she needs me or wants to talk to me, I'll gladly see her."

"Right now she'll just be relieved to know I'm meeting with the pastor today." Holding me at arm's length, he smiled. "I'm proud of you, B. For the first time since I've known you, you thought about yourself first before you thought about Don or the church. Well, almost first; you thought about me first, but that doesn't count. We are so one in spirit, we feel what one another feels." Lifting me off my feet, he quipped, "Hey, this is a victory day! The devil's on the run!"

THE TRUTH SHALL SET YOU FREE

Walking down the back stairs and letting myself in the back door of the prayer room, I locked the door behind me and laid face down on the carpet. "Jesus, help me. I'm exhausted." I fell fast asleep.

* * *

I jumped to my feet and looked at the clock. It was 3:30. I had slept almost an hour. I had just enough time to freshen up before taking Jerry to the parsonage. You can imagine how relieved I was when the office phone rang at 4:45 and it was Jerry's voice. "B, I'm here with Don and he wants to see you. Come on over."

I didn't have to ask Jerry how it went. I could tell by the tone of his voice. When I stepped down into the living area, Don was hunched over crying. He hesitated to even touch me, for fear that I hated him. Cautiously, I stepped toward him. He stood. Falling into one another's arms, we wept. He sat down; I knelt in front of him.

Bursting into tears again, he confessed, "I'm glad she went to Jerry. I've wanted to get out of this trap. I don't want to hurt you, darling." After blowing his nose, he continued, "I'm glad it's over. I've repented before God, and I repent to you. Can you forgive me, darling?"

I felt as if I were looking into the eyes of a little boy who had just been razor-strapped by his father. Reaching forward, I held him and we cried again. I sobbed, "Yes. We'll make it, honey. With Jesus, we'll make it."

Moving back from me, he began, "Jean, I actually wanted to get caught. In fact, I even hoped you'd catch me, because I wanted to hurt...."

Jerry stopped him. "Pastor, I think it's good that you are going to the retreat in Spokane tomorrow. It will be a good time for you to pray about your decision, and for Barbara to pray, too. I don't think it would be good for you two to talk about this any more tonight."

"Well, as a matter of fact," Don answered, "I was going to get with somebody for dinner and I'm almost late right now . . . Jean?"

"It's okay, honey. I have to take Jerry back to the office, and I have to get my lectures ready for tomorrow's Bible college classes anyway, so I'll grab a hamburger or something."

"Okay, darling. Here, let me hug you before you go."

Driving back to the office, I asked, "Z, how did it go? Did he admit to everything? Do you think he'll make it? He seemed broken, but will he leave her alone?"

"Don could see I had evidence, so he couldn't deny it. Yeah, he said she was right. He even added more. We'll just have to wait and see, B. I didn't ask him to submit to any guidelines. That's going to be the real test—will he be accountable? But this is the first step. We need to give him space to find out for himself that he can't make it without submitting...."

Interrupting, I complained, "Z, I can't live through another one. I want him to promise he won't be alone with her or anyone else."

"Now, wait. We have to take this a step at a time. I'm dealing with the pastor, here, and I'm just a nobody as far as he's concerned. I'm not even an elder. It's a miracle he even listened to me today. Now, first of all, you can too live through another one, B. Look how much you've already lived through, and by yourself, too. You didn't always have me for support. The Lord is going to see us through this. I know I can't lay a bunch of rules on the pastor, at least not at this point. I doubt, too, that he'll make it; and when he doesn't, you'll live through it. Then I can go to him with proof that he needs to submit to rules. We'll see what happens then. Oh, he did say he'd get tested for V.D."

Everyone in the Counseling Center was gone as we let ourselves back into the office. Jerry said, "I promised L I'd call her as soon as I could, then I want to go spend some time with my family."

"Thanks, Z, for all your help. You care about all of us so much. I know how hard this is on you and on your family as well. Especially when you can't tell them what's going on."

He beamed. "My wife is an absolute jewel. She's behind me all the way. We moved all the way out here and put our whole lives into this church. I don't want to see the pastor fall."

After studying for my classes, I closed up the office and drove home. I thought, *I'll raid the fridge. I'm sick of hamburgers.* Turning onto our street, I saw Don's car along with hers in our driveway, having already returned from their dinner date. I made a sharp right turn and headed up the street to Dairy Queen, too weary to care.

By the next day, the whole thing had caught up with Jerry as well. One look at me when I appeared in the door of the office after teaching for two hours convinced him. "B, we need to get out of here. I'm heading up to Mt. Rainier to hike. Wanna come along?"

"Great idea!" I shouted, slamming my notebooks down on the desk. "Let's do it. One rule...." We both echoed, "No shop talk."

I giggled with delight at the thought of the smell of fir trees in the fresh clean air. Just 45 minutes and we'd be there. Heading for the door, I said, "I'll run home and change. Meet you back here in 15 minutes." When I returned, we stopped at Jerry's, picked up his backpack loaded with all the usual supplies and drove out of town, not knowing just how significant this little outing was going to be.

* * *

We hardly said a word as we hiked up the trail for four miles, except when Jerry glanced back over his shoulder to ask, "Are you okay, B?" He was concerned that my heart wasn't acting up, as it had been doing a lot of that lately. We marvelled at the beauty all around us: different shades of green in the carpet of moss, contrasted with the ferns, and the towering fir trees at times almost blocking out the light. The sound of White River off to our left kept us constant company until we reached the day camp nestled in a clearing across from a ravine still holding the tip of a glacier as it stretched upwards toward the mountain. It was overcast, but we didn't mind as we continued up the side of the mountain.

Just as a furry marmot scurried into its home tunnelled in the hill, Jerry stopped. Stretching his arm toward the base of the glacier, he said, "Look, B, over there across the ravine. It's a mountain goat."

Spotting him, I exclaimed, "Yeah, he's a granddaddy, too. Look at his beard."

"Here," Jerry said, "I brought along some binoculars." Taking off the heavy backpack, he dug them out, and focused on the goat, "Wow, he's a big one!"

"Look," I said, now looking through the glasses myself, "Even though that side of the mountain is almost bare, he can still find food. He's eating little tufts of grass growing out of the rocks." The impact hit both of us.

At the same moment, we recalled what the Lord had shown Jerry: he was going to be a scapegoat. The awesome reality of seeing that old goat all alone way over there was very sobering. "That's me, B."

"I could end up there, too, Z."

I don't know how long we continued in silence before the fog started descending the mountain. Suddenly, we were at the base of the rocks that formed the face of the mountain. It was easy to see that a heard of elk had bedded down here, perhaps as recently as two days ago. With the stillness all around us and no protection, I began to pray in tongues, actually shouting.

Gulping deep breaths of the cool air, I released the anger, the hurt, and the insecurity that was built up inside me. Jerry didn't mind. No one else was there to hear me but God. I hollered out in tongues and heard the words echo back across the canyon.

Just as the fog was wrapping itself around us, I felt the presence of the Lord wrap Himself around me as if He were spinning a cocoon, made up of layer after layer of His security. When He was finished, none of my own defenses were left. I had expelled them all out in tongues, rendering me defenseless. Now His cocoon of security surrounded every inch of my being. I was safe. At the top of my voice I sang a song Mary Ellen had received from the Lord years ago:

Jesus alone is my security
Not anything I could ever do or be
He is my Rock, my Fortress is He
Jesus alone is my security.

This time I felt it to be true.

We scurried to get the wet gear stuffed into the backpack, started down the mountain and found the trail that led to the car. The security of Jesus continued to be my strength—even today.

* * *

The next day after Don returned from the pastor's retreat, the phone rang at the Counseling Center. The pastor wanted to talk to me in person. I got nervous. "Z, I don't want to give him a chance to blame me for his affair with —. He seemed pretty humble and sweet when we picked him up at the airport. I just don't want anything to spoil it."

"You're stronger now, B. You can hold your own. I think you should give him a chance. He says he's not going to accuse you; he just wants to ask you questions. Our phone conversation went really well. This time he sounded sincere. He wasn't full of self-pity. He's trying to understand what happened."

With a smile of encouragement, Jerry observed, "You can always get up and walk out if he slips back into 'there's-just-one-thing-I-have-to-say' mode." Half kidding, he added, "This will be a good test for you two, and it'll be a test for me, too, to see if I've been a success on this assignment."

After a fond embrace, Don took his usual position lying on the floor on his back with his legs up on a chair. I seated myself beside his feet, and he began, "Jean, I'm really trying to understand what's been going on. I don't want to accuse you. That's not my heart, but...."

THE TRUTH SHALL SET YOU FREE

As he launched into the infamous black slip incident, I thought, *How many times have I explained this to him? He always chooses not to believe me. This is going to be the last time I'm going through this. He does seem like he's trying to understand. Jesus, it would be a miracle if he accepts the truth.*

"...and so, Jean, I thought you committed adultery with Jerry. I would have never committed adultery with L if I had known that you hadn't committed adultery with Jerry. Anyway, I need to ask you, darling, have you and Jerry committed adultery?"

I leaned forward in my seat and looked Don squarely in the eyes. I repeated the words twice for emphasis, "No, Donald. Jerry and I have never committed adultery." Placing my hand on his knee, I continued, "Jerry and I don't have that kind of a relationship. It's not sexual. Even though he's twenty years younger than I, he's like a big brother."

Don interrupted, "I heard Jerry call you 'baby,' so I figured you were in adultery."

I tried not to smile. "Honey, Jerry doesn't call me 'baby.' You probably heard him say 'BB,' which he does sometimes, but mostly he just says 'B.'"

Don interjected, "It's not a big deal to me, because I call my connections honey, dear, baby, sweetie, all that; but it's just, well, it was hard for me to hear him call you 'baby.' I thought, They must be really close, but it's no big deal."

"Honey," I paused until Don looked at me, "Jerry doesn't call me 'baby.' Do you know why I put on that black slip? Let me tell you again: I was hurt because you had your connection using our bed like it was a lounge chair. She was young and beautiful. I tried to get your attention by wearing that slip the way I knew you liked it."

Rubbing his eyes and admitting to being sleepy, he said, "I'm really trying to understand." I thought, *His attitude is different.* I remarked, "You were sexually involved before the black slip thing ever happened."

Rubbing his eyes again as if to rub away the fog, he said, "Boy, if you're right, I owe you the biggest apology in the world." His lower lip quivered.

I slipped out of the chair, laid my head on his chest, and whispered, "Just 'I'm sorry' will do." I slipped out of the house just as he dozed off. On my way back to the office, I prayed... *Jesus, help my husband to think clearly. Protect his tortured mind from the effects of the drugs he's using. Help him to realize my actions don't govern his behavior.*

The next day, when I stepped into the church office after teaching my classes, I gasped at the splendor of a dozen perfectly formed red roses on my desk. My hands shook as I reached for the greeting card made by Don attached. It contained twelve promises, one for each flower. Each one stated what he would never accuse me of again. Moreover, he promised to pray over his new commitment each morning.

Without a moment's hesitation, I fled home and rushed into his arms. Together, we wept. I was filled with hope and joy. But this moment of reckoning was short-lived. Don's promises to me faded almost as fast as the roses. His mind was riddled with guilt and self-hate. It didn't take long for self-justification and self-pity to come to his rescue. He forgot how he had forced me out of his life. Instead he accused me of abandoning him. Rather than accept the truth, he chose to believe the fabricated story that he allowed to play over and over, day and night, in his mind.

* * *

L came to Jerry after a Friday night service. With racking sobs she confessed, "We've done it again. Can't you make the pastor stay away from me?" I followed as Jerry ushered her into a private room. Crumpling on the floor, she screamed, "I hate him! I hate him!" Gathering her up in my arms, I assured her of my love and support as the three of us cried out to God for His strength and direction. Before we left the room, Jerry determined to confront Don and plead with him to follow his own pastoral guidelines.

It was a heartsick man who returned from the parsonage after speaking with the pastor. Without needing to be told the answer, I asked, "How did it go, Z?"

Jerry moaned. "Not good, B, not good. The pastor's mind is in a totally different place than a few weeks ago. As brother-to-brother, I approached Don, pleading with him to follow the same Biblical directives that he, as pastor, had preached." Looking at me with amazement, he continued, "B, he told me he didn't have to, because he was doing fine now. I couldn't believe it. He denied he was in any trouble. I said, 'Pastor, I talked to L before I came over here. She said you did it this morning.' He looked surprised. He knew I had him.

"Then I begged him, B; I got down on my knees in front of him, and I begged Don not to be alone with women." Jerry held his head in his hands. "I told him his church was at stake; his marriage was at stake; but nothing moved him. When he retorted that I had no right to correct him, and started blaming you, I got up and walked out."

Minutes went by before Jerry spoke again, "The only thing I can do now is help L. If she can be strong enough to stay away...." His voice trailed off. "The problem is, there will always be another one."

"What shall I do, Z?"

"I don't know, B, I don't know. Pray. The Lord will show you; He always does."

"Yeah, I won't do anything until I know from the Lord."

* * *

One month went by, then another. More reports were put on my desk of connections falling into sexual sin, threatening marriages. Even the satellite churches weren't exempt. One lady wrote me a letter asking my opinion of what she thought might be a new revelation. She reasoned that intercourse with your connection could be justified as a type of the spiritual experience of becoming one in Jesus. Horrified, I immediately contacted her with a dozen reasons why this couldn't be a revelation from God, the most important one being that God's Word says, No! And the Spirit and the Word always agree. I breathed a sigh of relief when I learned she had waited to hear from me before she tried it.

But throughout our assemblies, the grip of deception tightened as if everyone was affected, just as Achan's sin affected the fledgling nation of Israel in the seventh chapter of Joshua.

> *Had the "leaven" in Don and I "leavened the whole lump" (Galatians 5:9)?*

Rumors started flying around that I said getting a connection was like having spiritual intercourse. I went to the prayer room and asked the Lord to show me what was happening to our people. Immediately my mind was filled with a scene, and the Lord unfolded to me the strategies of the devil to destroy us. I knew the destiny of our church hinged on whether or not we as a body and Don as our pastor would hear and do what God's Spirit was saying to us. I prayed...*Oh, God, I don't feel worthy or capable of bringing this to the congregation. Help me!*

I carried the weight of revelation around all the next day, waiting for the time to be right for me to bring it in the service that night. Jerry had once again heard from L. He said she had called while I was praying and said there were even more girls involved now, and she was ready to confront the pastor. She asked Jerry to be there, so he had made an appointment to meet Don after the service. She would be waiting in the meeting room.

Entering the service with a heavy heart, I breathed easier when I sensed the Holy Spirit hovering over us as if with outstretched wings, making it possible for me to release my own hurts and feelings of abuse, and freeing me to accurately bring what God had shown me. Never had He given me a harder assignment. The power of

God surged through me with such force I gasped for breath between each sentence like a marathon runner completing his last mile in a race. Although my body was shaking, I felt fearless. A solemn reverence swept over the congregation as I explained to them what the Lord showed me just the day before.[13]

In summary, the Lord had shown me the devil's scheme to sweep not just us but all people into his plan in these last days. Laboring under the impact of what I was saying, I continued. "The Lord showed me how the devil planned to use a person's natural responses to music and sex to accomplish his plan to make all peoples one. Suddenly I realized, no matter what nationality a person is, they are emotionally affected by music and sex."

Forcing back the tears, I said, "Then the Lord revealed to me that Satan had invaded man's sexual responses since the fall, and he had virtually controlled expressions of worship through music. What God created in man, when He made mankind to worship Him, has been tainted by the devil. But God is giving us a chance to be purified by ridding ourselves of all unclean spirits, so we can be truly one with one another and with Him. If we are going to come into a pure worship before God, we have to be free of all sexual demons, including those manifesting even in some marriages."

With force, I spoke hope, "But God wants to clean up our marriages and our spiritual connections. In His great wisdom, He has allowed these demons to attack us and now it's up to us—we can either turn from these enticing spirits, taking a stand against them, or we can yield to them and be sucked into the devil's plan." I gave a detailed account of all the Lord had shown me.

THE TRUTH SHALL SET YOU FREE

After this service, the prayer room was crowded with people humbling themselves before God. I excused myself from the people lined up to talk to me, asking them to see Lanny instead, and slipped into the prayer room to pray for the meeting taking place that very moment with Don, Jerry, and L. Noticing another girl who I knew was involved with Don and was also aware of the meeting taking place, I tiptoed over to where she was kneeling and knelt beside her. We hugged and cried to the Lord as she apologized to me and repented to God. I felt no blame for her, only pity, because in the experience the Lord had given me I had felt the power of the devil and knew I certainly couldn't "cast the first stone" (John 8:7).

I knew the meeting was over when Don marched into the prayer room and stood at my feet. The look in his eyes told me it wasn't my husband glaring at me, but a demon of hate. Without saying a word, Don spun around and left. I wondered if it would be safe for me to go home. I thought, *I need to talk to Z. He'll know.*

Leaving the prayer area, I hurried down the hall to the small counseling room. Hesitating for a moment, I cracked open the door. One look at Jerry sitting there holding his head in his hands with grief written all over his face told me the meeting had failed.

Within three weeks, it was as if the lid popped off. First one, then another, and another lady confessed to sexual involvement with the pastor. How could we let this go on? We weren't going to be able to keep it secret much longer. Jerry decided once more to confront the pastor. Don refused to see him. Jerry pleaded for an appointment. Don refused. Jerry was told to go to the general manager. Jerry tried. He was refused.

Almost two months had passed and I wouldn't touch my husband until he got another V.D. test. He didn't know why, because he didn't know that I knew about his other affairs. Yet he refused to see Jerry. Finally, in desperation, Jerry and I walked into the general manager's office. Our plan: Don't tell him any more details than necessary to convince him that Jerry had to get an appointment with Don.

Sitting across from his desk, Jerry began, "The last time I talked to the pastor, which was over two months ago, he told me he didn't need to follow his own guidelines. Since then, I have proof which shows me he does. Jack, I need an appointment with Don, but he's refusing to see me. The whole church could be at stake, plus their marriage. B can't take much more. I can't hold her together forever."

Jack seemed unperturbed. "The Scripture says you're supposed to have two or three witnesses. Do you have any witnesses? Have you personally seen anything?"

Jerry pleaded, "No, but we've got more than enough evidence from more than three women, a whole lot more."

Putting down his pen, Jack stated, "I don't want you to accuse the pastor just because some girls are saying things happened. This is pretty serious."

Finally, in desperation I leaned forward, insisting on Jack's attention, "Jack, we have material evidence."

It was the shock he needed. He switched from Don's side to ours, or so we thought. Jerry got his appointment with the pastor, but not before what Jerry called "Chapelgate."

* * *

The Lord tried to warn us, too. Just three days before it happened, Jerry arrived at work nervous. Removing the packet containing signed confessions—plus all Jerry's correspondence with Don—from the file cabinet behind his desk, he busied himself adding tape to the already stapled manila envelope. "B," he questioned, "Is there someplace else we can keep this? I feel like it's not safe here."

"No one else has the combination but you and Joe, right? Does he know what we keep in this file?"

"Not that I know of, but somebody could break in and carry out the whole file. I know this office is on the security system, but I feel nervous. Maybe the Lord is trying to tell me something. I've been uneasy all last night; I couldn't sleep." Stretching rubber bands around the envelope, he mused, "I can't keep it at my place and you can't keep it at yours. Maybe we should take it over to the airport and put it in a locker."

"Yeah, but how long can we keep it there? Isn't there a time limit on those lockers?"

The phone rang. We got busy. The file was locked back up in the cabinet. By the end of the day, we had forgotten about it.

* * *

Early Saturday morning, Don jumped out of bed, hurriedly showered, and was out the door, stating only that he had a meeting at the church. *Strange, I thought. He never schedules meetings on Saturday mornings; that's when he goes over his sermons for Sunday.* I had to be at the office myself at 9:00 to work on the new Bible college class, *Principles of Christian Counseling*, that would be taught in the fall.

At 8:45, Don came home as white as a sheet. He was so nervous he couldn't stand still for a minute. With quivering lips, he said, "Jean, I gotta talk to you and Jerry right away. Right now, it can't wait."

"Why?" I asked, amazed. "Jerry's been trying to get an appointment with you for over two months. Now all of a sudden you can't wait to talk to us? What happened?"

Ignoring my question, he asked, "How soon can you get Jerry here? This can't wait." His lower lip was quivering so badly, I thought he might be sick.

"Honey, are you all right? I can make some wheat hearts for you before I go."

"No, Jean, I can't eat. Just call me when you find out when Jerry can be here. I'll meet whenever he can."

Don returned to his study as I went out the door. He had spent the better part of 22 years at that desk, with vacations his only break. Right then I wasn't feeling any pity for him. Backing my car out of the driveway, I thought, *Wait until Z hears this—the pastor will see you any time you can fit him into your schedule. Quite a switch.*

I opened the door to the office and found Jerry was as pale as Don was when I'd left him. "Z, what's wrong?"

The words tumbled out of his mouth as he shook. "B, I can't believe it. Jack betrayed us. He and Don collaborated and got Joe [not his real name] to open the file. They broke into it this morning. The three senior elders were here. They each took their files and shredded them in the shredder! Don read his file and shredded it. Now he knows the names of all the girls and what they said he did." Jerry paced the floor in a state of shock. "I promised those girls privacy. They'll think I let them down."

Horrified, I managed to squeak, "How do you know this, Z?"

"Because I talked to Jack. He's right in there," pointing to the counselor's office outside our door, "He's talking to my assistant, Chris. He says they had a right to do it because they are the senior elders; the pastor didn't do anything illegal by destroying the files." Barely able to hold back the tears, Jerry continued, "If they wanted the files, why couldn't they be up front about it? Why did they have to sneak in here and get Joe to open the cabinet? Oh, B, if only we would have taken that envelope to the airport."

Beside himself with grief and bewilderment, Jerry concluded, "This is worse than Watergate. These men who are supposed to be my spiritual leaders, the ones I've trusted with my life and the lives of my family, those I've supported and given my tithes and offerings to—and now this. This is worse than the adulteries. What did they think I was going to do with the information? Couldn't they tell by the way we guarded the file we were trying to protect everyone involved? I was only trying to save my church, B, and your marriage, and the reputation of the women. I just can't believe it. I shouldn't have trusted any of them."

"No, it's my fault, Z. I told Jack we had material evidence. If I hadn't said that, they wouldn't have thought to raid the files. I'm sorry."

Jerry wasn't listening. He was trying to decide what to do next. I almost forgot that Don wanted to talk to us. Now I knew why.

On the way over to the parsonage, Jerry observed, "Isn't it amazing that now the pastor is anxious to talk to me after he knows I have confessions of his other recent adulterous affairs?"

All of a sudden, I remembered my card with the twelve roses. "Oh, no! Don shredded my card!" I sobbed, as if clinging to the card would change his behavior.

The pain in Jerry's face couldn't be hidden as the three of us sat in the living room. Don started crying. He bawled and bawled, but his tears didn't move me. I sat there like a stone. He volunteered to get another V.D. test, hoping that would please me. All I could manage was a shrug of my shoulders.

Jerry was the one who spoke, "Pastor, why did you do it? You could have asked me for the files. You knew I've tried for two months to talk to you. Couldn't you tell by the way I sealed your file that I was protecting you and everyone involved?"

Don glanced up at Jerry and shot an arrow right through his heart, "I don't trust you."

Jerry didn't say another word. There was nothing more to say. He got up and walked out. Before I followed him, I said, "Donald, you just destroyed the only true male friendship you ever had."

Don followed me out to the car, but it was too late. Jerry didn't believe his apologies. Why should he? He knew Don's track record.

Before the day was over, I knew what my next step should be. Monday morning Don found my letter on his desk. It was short and to the point:

THE TRUTH SHALL SET YOU FREE

Dear Donald,

I have taken my pastor's advice and followed the Word of God, which states if your brother who has sinned won't hear you, take one with you, and if he rejects him, then get two more, so I have chosen two elders, Scott and Lanny. They will be contacting you.

Your wife still,
Jean

* * *

The two elders got no further with Don than Jerry had. I panicked when, at an elders' retreat, I saw Don bring yet another new connection. I rushed to Jerry and confided, "This is unreal! He's not even supposed to have her here. I can't stand this. Look, Z, they are leaving. I'll bet he's taking her to the parsonage. Come on, Z, I'm going to go home and see if I'm right."

Jerry hesitated, "Now, B, are you sure you want to know? This may not be a good idea."

Through clenched teeth, I retorted, "I'm not going to let him get away with another one. You coming?"

Driving towards the parsonage, only a few blocks away, I broke out in laughter. "This is weird, totally weird. If ever I tried to convince someone of this saga, they wouldn't believe me. I can't believe this whole thing is happening either, but here we are living it. Look! There's his car in the driveway. What did I tell you?"

Jerry cautioned, "You don't need to go in and get hurt more, B."

"No, Z. I want to stop it before it happens."

Opening the front door, Jerry stepped in first. Suddenly surprised, while still holding the girl around the waist, Don asked, "What are you doing here?"

Jerry replied, "B had to get something, so I came with her."

Stepping in front of Jerry, I asked, "What are you doing here?"

Taking the girl by the hand, without answering my question, Don said, "We're just leaving to go back to the retreat."

As soon as the door closed, Jerry slumped into a chair and advised, "You're not going to control his behavior by spying on him, B. You'll only regret it later if you do catch him in the act. Remember, he told you once he hoped you would catch him, because he wanted to hurt you for causing him to do it in the first place." Visualizing what Jerry just said, I sank into the chair next to him. Speaking softly, he added, "You need to let Don go, B, and concentrate on taking care of yourself. Now, let's get back to the retreat before Don accuses us."

When Don and his connection disappeared from the meetings an hour later, I let it go. Jerry was right. I needed to think about my own life. That afternoon Lanny came to me with a sheet of paper in his hand. He said, "Here, B, someone gave me this. I think you should read it." As Lanny turned and walked away, I sat down and began to read:

LETTING GO

- To let go doesn't mean to stop caring, it means I can't do it for someone else.

THE TRUTH SHALL SET YOU FREE

- To let go is not to cut myself off, it's the realization that I can't control another.
- To let go is not to enable, but to allow learning from natural consequences.
- To let go is to admit powerlessness, which means the outcome is not in my hands.
- To let go is not to try to change or blame another, I can only change myself.
- To let go is not to care for, but to care about.
- To let go is not to fix, but to be supportive.
- To let go is not to judge, but to allow another to be a human being.
- To let go is not to be in the middle arranging all the outcomes, but to allow others to affect their own outcomes.
- To let go is not to be protective, it is to permit another to face reality.
- To let go is not to deny, but to accept.
- To let go is not to nag, scold, or argue, but to search out my own shortcomings and correct them.
- To let go is not to adjust everything to my desires, but to take each day as it comes, and to cherish the moment.
- To let go is not to criticize and regulate anyone, but to try to become what I dream I can be.
- To let go is not to regret the past, but to grow and live for the future.
- To let go is to fear less and love more.

Two days later, I got a chance to think and pray about it for four days, but not of my own choosing.

Chapter Twenty

The Scapegoat

"But the goat on which the lot fell to be the scapegoat shall be presented alive before the Lord, to make an atonement with him, to let him go for a scapegoat into the wilderness."
(Leviticus 16:10)
"For it is not possible that the blood of bulls and goats should take away sins . . . through the offering of the body of Jesus Christ once for all . . . there is no more offering for sin."
(Hebrews 10:4,10,18)

My heart had been beating irregularly most of the day, but when it sped up late in the afternoon, I became weak and dizzy. After the Counseling Center closed, I told Jerry, "I'm sure my heart will settle down, if I lie here on the couch a while. You go on home to dinner. Don's having dinner out, so I don't have to worry about fixing anything for him. I don't mind being here by myself. As soon as my heart clicks back in, I'll drive home." Jerry was nervous about leaving me, until I reminded him that the security guard would be here to check on me when he made his usual rounds.

Discovering that I was still there at 9:00 p.m., Jerry brought his wife Renee, a nurse, to check my pulse and blood pressure. Kindly but firmly, she insisted that we go to the emergency room at Valley General. Too weak to argue, I assented.

Four days and a battery of tests later, I was diagnosed as having a microvalve prolapse and a heart murmur. I laid in that hospital bed and cried, hoping my husband would come to see me, but he never did. I made excuses for Don when I clicked on the TV above my bed and saw Community Chapel was on it. The news media had learned about the first lawsuit filed in Pierce County against the church and Don and me personally.

* * *

From Don's point of view, he hadn't meant to go all the way; the pressure was too much, his body presented constant problems, forcing him on medication just to keep the pain tolerable. He worried over the declining finances of both the church and his own. When the cost of his vacations exceeded our bank account, he borrowed $8000 against his wages from the church just to keep the bills current. On top of that was the drastic drop in offerings, because so many people were leaving the church. It was getting harder and harder to meet the payroll and the $25,000/month payment on the bank loan, let alone putting money aside so the balloon payment of around $600,000 due in a couple years could be met.

Financial calamity didn't inflict on Don his greatest pain. It was losing those he loved and had ministered to for twenty-two years. It was hearing that marriage after marriage was breaking up. It was feeling that the Counseling Center was plotting against him to keep his connections from ministering to him. He worried over the satellite churches, as he heard reports of possible church splits and sexual misconduct, including this lawsuit alleging that our Tacoma pastor had seduced a lady under the pretense of marriage counseling.

And now there was the added worry that his own misbehavior would be dragged out into the open through this court trial. He admonished the people; in fact, he forbade the people to read the newspaper articles that began making headlines.[14] If they had TV's, which many didn't, they were instructed not to watch the newscasts. He appealed to the congregation's sense of fairness by complaining, "After all, if someone is telling lies about you, you wouldn't want me to read it. So, I don't want your minds to be full of lies about your elders and pastor." Many obeyed.

After the second lawsuit, which was a class action suit filed in the King County courts in Seattle, the insurance company cancelled its policy with the church. Although obligated to cover these lawsuits, the company was released from any obligation to cover any action which transpired beyond that date.

In an attempt to soften the impact, should his own behavior get revealed, the pastor's sermons took on a new slant. Week after week, most of the congregation responded with shock and disbelief. How could this happen? One known as a Bible scholar made light the results of sins of adultery. In addition, he taught that lying "in certain cases" was acceptable before God. I was horrified when he concluded, after reading about Jimmy Swaggart in the newspaper (something he wouldn't permit his congregation to do), "Jimmy should have lied."

THE TRUTH SHALL SET YOU FREE

Many in the congregation wondered, *Will Don not be accountable to anyone?*

When Don shamed and ridiculed the connections who weren't falling into sexual sin by stating, "You must be dead," I concluded, *This is a demon talking instead of our pastor.* The elders seemed paralyzed to do anything to stop him, except John and Lanny. They grabbed every chance to preach they could, trying not to undermine the pastor.

When Don announced from the pulpit that he had fired his two counselors, claiming they were cruel and insensitive and without compassion and love, and he was choosing another counselor named David, that did it. I turned to Jerry and whispered, "I've had it! I'm moving out of the parsonage."

* * *

"B, you'd be better off getting a restraining order against Don and you stay in the parsonage," advised Jerry the next morning, as we discussed the decision I'd made during the service the night before. Thinking of the future, he continued, "If you move out, you'll lose everything, whereas...."

"Now wait, Z," I interrupted, "This isn't going to be permanent. I'm just going to move out for maybe six months, just until Don comes to his senses and stops blaming me for all his problems."

Jerry sighed, "Oh, B, if you think you're going to change Don by you moving out, you're wrong. It's going to take a lot more than that. He's a sick man." Looking me square in the eyes, he added, "We've learned a lot studying for the new class this fall. You can't fix Don. In fact, you're part of the problem. You should leave Don for your own sake, for your own emotional well-being. And frankly, I think you should have done it a long time ago."

It was true. We had learned a lot through our research for the new class we were preparing to teach starting in September. Don had given his permission to offer the class called *Perspectives on Christian Counseling* only after everyone agreed it would be a team effort. The teachers would include Lanny, John, and David, besides Jerry and me. Don's fears were calmed by knowing that I was involved in preparing the material, because he trusted me to know what his mind was on any principles included in the lectures. Nevertheless, we were instructed to have an outline of all the subject matter on his desk in plenty of time for him to change anything in which he disagreed.

Of all the men on the team, Jerry was the one who had the heart to develop the class. His challenge was to spoil the "Egyptians," as he called it, without upsetting Don. Don's disdain for "worldly" psychologists and psychiatrists posed the biggest threat, as Jerry and I poured through the books in the University of Washington's medical library. All the excellent material we discovered that I knew Don would agree with, had it originated in his own head, we preserved for the class.

A source of information that also proved beneficial was books by Larry Crabb; his insights held major keys to understanding what was happening in our lives at the Chapel. It was a comfort to me to learn through these books that Don's problem was clearly defined and I wasn't to blame. I also learned that I had a responsibility to myself not to receive the blame.

I had to agree with what I'd read, "You know, Z, the harder I try to control Don's behavior, the more set in it he becomes. I've gotta move out so I can get well."

Jerry warned, "I'm telling you, if you move out instead of making him leave, you'll lose everything."

I argued, "But how can I do that, Z? The parsonage belongs to the church. It's not like it's my own home. Most of the elders don't know what's going on, and for sure the deacon board doesn't. If I get a restraining order against Don so he can't use his own study and library they've provided for him, they might kick me out."

He fumed, "If they knew what he's doing in the parsonage, they should kick him out."

"Well, Z, I have more than myself to think about here—how's the church going to take this, and all the satellite churches. And the court trials—the lawyers will have a heyday with this one. But you know who I'm worried about the most?" Before Jerry could answer, my eyes filled with tears, "David, my son."

David's condition had worsened to the point where he needed oxygen. I'd been spending as much time as I could with David, joking and laughing about his earlier teenage experiences playing chess. It was getting harder and harder to understand him, as his ability to speak was all but gone. I wondered how long it would be before Jesus took him home. Whenever it was, David was ready. I purposed to tell my kids about my decision first, before telling the church.

"Where are you going to move to, B? Where are you going to live?"

"What? Hmmm . . . well." The reality of my decision began sinking in. Thinking out loud, I said, "I'll contact Jody. Her place would be perfect, but I don't want it to be too hard on her. If it is, I hope she'll feel free to tell me.

"Hey, Lanny," I hollered, seeing him come into the Counseling Center, "Got a minute?"

"Be right there," he replied, as he went to deposit his college notebooks in his office.

Lanny stepped into my office and closed the door behind him. "Lanny, what would you think if I moved out of the parsonage?"

Without the slightest hesitation, he responded, "You have my blessings." Lanny is always short and to the point, "Are you going to tell Don or just do it."

"Just do it. I'll leave him a note telling him why and that I won't take any legal action unless for financial reasons I'm forced to. I'll keep the Mastercard and he can use the Visa. I don't think he'll cut off my money supply, because he knows any legal action would hit the newspapers."

"That's a good deterent, at least for a while. You certainly have Scriptural grounds to leave him. What are you going to tell the church?"

"Lanny, what do you think I should tell them? I don't want to tell them any more than I have to; even most of the elders don't know what's going on."

"I know. The Bible gives you permission to tell them. First, Don refused Jerry, so you got me and Scott, and Don refused us, so you could tell the church next, but I don't think they are in the right shape to handle it."

"I know what you mean, Lanny. Don holds such a strong authoritarian role in most of their lives—he's their

THE TRUTH SHALL SET YOU FREE

idol, the final authority. He's not their servant, but a king of sorts, and their loyalty will dictate what they are willing to believe. At this point, I think it would only hurt them. I'll just tell them the truth about me. I'm moving out of the parsonage for my own emotional and spiritual well-being."

Jokingly, I added, "Actually, it's to keep me from chopping my husband up in little pieces and scratching the eyes out of some of these girls. I'm only kidding, even though I've felt like that at times." Getting serious, I said, "I may need you there to help me, Lanny, when the time comes."

"What are you going to tell Dan and Carolyn and David? Carolyn and Dan can handle it. They'll be real supportive. David? It'll be hard on David. Better that he hears it from you instead of somebody else."

"I know. I hope he never finds out who some of the girls are. It would kill him."

"Carolyn pretty much knows what's going on. Do you get to see Dan any more? Can you tell him in person?"

"Yeah, I'm meeting Daniel for lunch on Thursday."

Getting up to leave, Lanny says, "Good. Tell Dan 'hi' for me and let me know how it goes."

* * *

My son Daniel had a favorite restaurant in Bellevue, on the other side of Lake Washington, so I drove over there. Daniel is a distinguished-looking man. His bald head and graying temples made him look older than his thirty-three years, which was to his advantage being an investment broker. He had just established his own busi-

THE SCAPEGOAT

ness. With his soft, unimposing personality, he always fades out of the picture when his tolerance level has been reached. This had been the case regarding the church and past hurts from his father. He hadn't spoken with Don for sometime, nor did he have any desire to.

Over lunch, I quickly launched into my plan. With a sigh of relief, Daniel responded, "Good for you, Mom. It's about time."

Standing in the parking lot, we hugged one last time, and I said, "Goodbye, Daniel, have a nice life," as he backed away. I wondered when I would get to see my son again. When would I get to see my two grandsons? It was to be seven long years.

Unlike Daniel, David asked questions, "How do you know for sure? Could the girls be lying? Has anyone talked to Dad about it? How many elders know?" I didn't leave until I was sure David was at peace with my decision. Together we prayed for Don, me, our family, and our church.

* * *

Returning to the office, Jerry greeted me with, "I have great news! But first tell me how it went with David."

"It was hard, Z. Hard for him and hard for me. He couldn't accept it until I told him Don had admitted it to us himself. He's okay, though. David's okay. I want to go see him as much as I can; he's failing fast." I couldn't keep the tears back. "I hated to tell him about his father, Z. I just hated it." Wiping my eyes, I added, "I'll go back over tomorrow to check on him."

THE TRUTH SHALL SET YOU FREE

"Hey!" Jerry shouted in an effort to cheer me up, "Do you want to hear the good news?"

With a little smile, I responded, "Sure."

"Your lawyer called. You know, the one handling the Tacoma case. Guess what? You don't have to testify. You don't have to go to any depositions either. You're totally off the hook. How does that make you feel, huh? Isn't that great?"

I lied, "I feel great."

Jerry continued, "Now the Seattle lawsuit—that's a different matter. He said he's not going to be able to get you out of that one."

I sighed, "Well, I don't have to worry about that one now. It's a few months off." With a shiver, I added, "It's the yucky one, it's the yucky one."

The ringing phone took Jerry's attention. Sobered, Jerry put his hand over the receiver and motioned for me to pick up my phone. "B, it's for you. Joan is calling from Tacoma. She says Don's mom has taken a turn for the worse."

* * *

"Hi, Joan . . . Yeah, I know, Don's out of town . . . No, I'll call his brothers . . . I'll be right over . . . Joan, thanks for all your help with mom. You've been a blessing to all of us."

Hanging up the phones, Jerry insisted, "I'm going with you. I'm not going to let you drive over there alone."

Within five minutes Jerry had notified the office staff and we were out the door. There was no way to call Don. He was some place up in Canada on a vacation with a

THE SCAPEGOAT

seventeen weeks out of the last 52? If he spends a thousand dollars a week on these girls, that's $17,000 a year!" Hopeless, I added, "The senior elders didn't know what they were doing when they approved that $8,000 loan."

Thinking ahead, I asked, "Are you in charge of the service tomorrow night, Lanny?"

"I don't know whom Don is going to appoint, but it could be me, because I have a sermon I'd like to preach. What are you going to say to the congregation?"

"Well, I'm just going to ask them to make allowances in their hearts for me if they think I'm wrong in my decision to move out of the parsonage, but it's something I have to do for my own spiritual and emotional well-being. I'm going to say I have one of my counselors' approval and the other one is away so I couldn't ask him. How does that sound?"

Both Jerry and Lanny chimed in, "You gotta be specific."

"Okay, okay, I'll try. I might need you guys to help me."

When Lanny went to the platform after music ministry completed the worship service, he announced that I had something to say. I felt calm and I knew I wasn't going to cry. I addressed the congregation and was on my way down the steps from the platform when both Jerry and Lanny rushed to me, "You didn't tell them," they whispered. "You didn't say what you were going to do."

Wide-eyed, I wondered, "I didn't?"

"No. You said all the rest without telling them you were moving out."

Covering my mouth, I declared, "Oh, dear."

Lanny said, "I'll tell them." As I took my seat on the front row, Lanny stated, "What Barbara is trying to say is that she's moving out of the parsonage tomorrow morning." You could have heard a pin drop. I felt sorry for the congregation. One girl came up and gave me a silent hug. Later I learned that many, in their hearts, were cheering for me.

* * *

Feeling strange and almost empty inside, I gathered some of my clothes and cleared my things out of the bathroom. I peered through the glass door that separated the shower and our 106° hot pool from the rest of the bathroom. "I'll miss you at bedtime," I whispered, brushing a tear off my cheek.

Sleeping alone was going to be a new experience. I'd never been on my own in the entire 57 years of my life. Today the idea held no excitement for me. I felt like I was on remote control as I assembled my clothes in the closet next to the bathroom that was to be mine downstairs in Jody's tri-level home a few miles north of the church.

Then I got in my car and headed straight to Nordstrom's. I said to myself, *If Don can spend all that money on those girls, then I deserve some new clothes.* I smiled when I saw the sale signs in the lingerie department at the top of the escalator. I bought the softest robe I could find, camisoles, two nighties, and best of all, a Christian Dior pinoiur set. The white filmy fabric was dripping with lace and ribbons. The gown's bodice had mini-pleats held in the center with a bow whose streamers touched the floor. Clutching it to my waist in front of the mirror, I promised myself, *I'll save this for when we get back together.* I charged the entire amount of nearly $500 on Don's VISA card and left the store, feeling not one bit guilty.

* * *

The pastor made no mention of my absence from the parsonage the following weekend when he returned to the services. It was two weeks before I received an angry letter, blaming me for shaming him in front of his congregation. His letter stated that I had jumped the gun and moved out just two weeks before he got things under control with his connection and that I should have known he would have it cut off in a couple weeks. His letter also declared that Lanny had no right to give me permission to move out without the pastor's concurrence.

> *To this day, he has never admitted to the fact that in the middle of August the girl came to David—Don's self-chosen counselor—and confessed to the affair, asking for help. It was October before she was finally able to end it. I had moved out on June 17th.*

I continued to take my place beside the pastor on the front pew, although I'll confess I got up and walked out a couple of times during the sermons. Even though the whole congregation could see me leave, I wasn't going to sit there and listen to him accuse me of not lifting a finger around the house and spending eighteen hours a day with my connection. But the fatal service for me and Jerry was during the fall camp meeting on Labor Day, 1987.

* * *

We were already three days into the fall Bible college semester when camp meeting started. The hottest new class was Perspectives on Christian Counseling, but it wasn't going to stay that way for long. The enrollment was close to three hundred, in spite of dwindling numbers in the services. God's love manifested through connections had caused everyone to want answers. John, one of the four teachers, made this statement that first day of class:

"We're teaching this class, because the circumstances in which we've found ourselves in the last two years has unleashed on us every aspect of human drama—fast! It's because our little society here—and we are a society with our own doctrines and ways of thinking—is in the process of having a re-definition of love. That's right. We've been pressed to the limits of our emotional ability to endure, and demons have been unleashed. We've seen jealousy, love, hate, bankruptcy, theft, violence, murder, suicide, apathy, legalism, fanaticism, insecurity, stubbornness, joy. The only thing we haven't seen is boredom, so thank God for small favors."

John was right. We were being tested to see if our little society that we called a church could live out the Word of God under the pressure and the exposure brought on by this love.

It was Jerry who had taken the bull by the horns, sacrificed his whole summer, and researched every source

THE SCAPEGOAT

he could get his hands on, so the class would supply some of the needed answers. Even though Jerry had laid out an informative outline which gained the pastor's approval, Don was still nervous. Unknown to me, Jerry's assistant in the Counseling Center had been lobbying against Jerry. On several occasions he had gone to the parsonage informing the pastor that Jerry was "getting much of his material from sources outside the Chapel."

The first devastating call came late in the afternoon, the day Jerry taught his fifth lesson where the class's response had been a resounding handclap. When I watched Jerry slowly replace the receiver, I knew something terrible had happened. All the life and joy suddenly drained out of his face. "What happened?" I asked. It was several minutes before he could answer.

"They just axed me out of my class."

"What do you mean, Z? This can't be true! I don't believe it. Why? Who told you? I'm calling Don!"

Jerry stopped me as I lunged for the phone, "No, B. That was the Dean's office. He said Don told him before he left for Hawaii to cut me out."

Jumping up in a helpless rage, I shouted, "He can't do this! It's not fair. It's not fair to you, it's not fair to the students. What's the problem here? Don saw your outline. I told him he could read your notes but he said he didn't want to. This is awful!"

Jerry sighed, "I know. He didn't even come to me. If there was a problem, why couldn't he come to me so we could correct it. The students were loving the class today. Nobody complained to me. He didn't even listen to the tapes. I think Don made up his mind to fire me because he's afraid of me. He's afraid of exposure and he's afraid he's going to lose the hearts of the remaining people. He's afraid of you, too, B. He accused you and Lanny and John of rebellion in the camp meeting Monday morning, and then forbade anyone to talk about the service."

"Yeah, I know, Z. He just couldn't handle it when Mike (a satellite pastor) tried to get him to submit to prayer. He felt he would lose control and the respect of the people. Instead, he accused us." I mused, "Lanny did the right thing, though, praying that prayer of repentance for all of us."

"Well," Jerry concluded, "There's nothing I can do now. The pastor is conveniently in Hawaii, so he doesn't have to face me." Grief-stricken, he added, "I wonder what they are going to tell the class."

I wondered, *How could Don do this, when he knows how it feels because it once happened to him?*

Letters poured in from the students in shocked disbelief at the turn of events, and Jerry's wife was traumatized when she heard the announcement. Still bewildered and hurt, I received call number two several days later.

* * *

The general manager wished to see me in his office at 4:00 p.m. He said he needed my advice. Ten minutes into the meeting, I learned the opposite was true. After informing me that Jerry was being laid off for financial reasons, he reached in his desk and brought out a chart which laid out the new positions in the Counseling Center. One glance showed me my position had been eliminated. When I pointed this out, he said, "Well, I couldn't fire you, Barbara. You can still sort the pastor's mail."

I responded, "You've left me no choice but to resign."

Quickly, he countered, "I'll put in the records that you're on a leave of absence. My secretary has notified Jerry to join us. I thought you should be here when I tell him. Oh, by the way, I spoke with the pastor in Hawaii this afternoon. He told me to tell you that effective immediately, you are not to minister publicly until further notice."

When Jerry joined us, Jack tried as hard as he could to convince us that Don had nothing to do with this action—the cut was purely for financial reasons—but we knew too much to be convinced. Walking up the back stairs to our office, numb with the turn of events, I turned to Jerry. "I made it over on the other side of the mountain beside that mountain goat five minutes before you did," I quipped with a sad grin.

The next morning, before I went to the prayer room to pray before teaching my college classes for the last time, I slipped a note on the Dean's desk. It read:

"Just late yesterday I was informed that the pastor has forbidden me, starting immediately, to minister publicly. In order to keep the classes from not having a teacher today, I am prepared to take the classes unless I hear from you beforehand. I will inform the students of the pastor's decision at the end of each class, so they will know what to expect tomorrow. Thank you for your love."

I learned later that my letter was a relief to the Dean, because he had been told by Don to fire me. This saved him that embarrassment.

By the time I reached our office after teaching for the last time, Jerry had already started packing. Too full of grief himself to find out how I was doing, Jerry asked, "What did you tell your classes, B?"

"Basically I told them what the pastor had said. Everyone looked really shocked, but I don't think it hit them until I said I'd just finished teaching them for the last time. Some cried. One raised her hand and asked what reason the pastor gave. I said he didn't give a reason. Other hands started going up, so I said they should get their questions answered in the Dean's office. Then I told them not to feel sorry for me, because I was going to use this time in my life to build my relationship with Jesus."

I looked up and saw my favorite picture of Don on my office wall. I walked over, took it down, and held it, thinking, *I can't stand to look at you, now, but I'm going to take you with me, because someday I may wish I had.*

None of the staff knew what to say to us, so they didn't say anything. Without purpose, we methodically sorted through our desks until they stood as bare and empty as we felt. As we closed the office door for the last time, we looked at each other and echoed, "Let's go to Plan B."

Plan B for Jerry was to find a job, which he did the very next day. The first new car dealership he walked into hired him on the spot. He said, "I've always wondered what it would be like to sell cars. Here's my chance." He won the salesman-of-the-month award for two consecutive months.

But what was Plan B for me? I didn't have a home to go to. My son Daniel had moved his family out of state. My daughter was struggling to keep food on the table, living in a little apartment with her two children, having lost her job in our Christian School because of her divorce. David was barely holding on to life itself, needing constant oxygen, so first I went straight to him. After assuring him that I was fine, I got into my car and started driving.

THE SCAPEGOAT

I don't know where I drove nor how long I drove, nor how I drove to wherever it was, when I finally realized I was somewhere and I didn't know where or how I had gotten there. All of a sudden I heard my voice ask, "Where are you?" I answered myself, "I don't know. Let's see. I'm on a freeway. How did I get here? I don't know where I am. Look, girl, you better get off this freeway and take a nap. When you wake up, you can figure out where you are. Good idea."

I remember feeling betrayed by everyone. Someone stepped in and took one of my college classes, and my prayer class was finished by listening to last year's tapes. Lanny had told me almost a year before that there would be a time when I'd feel betrayed. This was it. But Lanny said, "I can do more by staying on the inside, instead of joining you and Jerry on the outside. I know you've been unjustly treated, but it won't help if all of us resign. We need to stay here so we can do something about it."

I knew he was right, but it didn't help my mutilated soul. It wasn't long, however, until Jerry and I found out that no one was doing anything to deal with the problem. Jerry had tried to get the elders to do something, but he was told, "You can't buck the system, Z. That's just the way it is around here." When Jerry responded with, "But the ship is going to sink!" he was told, "Just keep your own cabin clean."

Chapter Twenty One

"Pastor, Please Practice What You Preach"

"...Lest that by any means, when I have preached to others, I myself should be a castaway."
(1 Corinthians 9:27)
"Behold I lay in Zion a chief corner stone. Unto you therefore which believe is precious; but unto them which be disobedient . . . a stone of stumbling, and a rock of offense."
(1 Peter 2:6,8)

    Now it was December. More people left the church. Even Jerry couldn't bear to go, because he felt betrayed by his own elders and smeared from the pulpit by his pastor, whom he had only tried to help. One night, with another letter in his hand from Don, Jerry came to see me. After reading the first paragraph, I commented, "Z, this is terrible. He's doing the very same thing to you that he's done to me. For years Don did it; first he'd devastate me, then he'd experience all this love and compassion for me. I can't believe this!"

THE TRUTH SHALL SET YOU FREE

"I know what I must do, B," Jerry said without rancor. Together we sifted through the letters received from Don, then Jerry wrote:

"Don,
   Based on the following quotes from recent letters I've received from you, I'm prayerfully and thoughtfully responding to give you opportunity to do as you have stated..."

Jerry's letter to Don included over twenty quotes from Don, in which he stated he would do anything to restore Jerry; then Jerry listed 31 actions by Don which had destroyed their relationship and Don's and my marriage. Jerry concluded with the following paragraph:

"...I realize that you typically would prefer to make full explanation for these points. But because this is for my benefit, I'm insisting that you only respond with a Sheet of paper numbered 1-31 and follow each question with a yes or no answer. I'm insisting on this not to demean you but to get a preliminary indication of your ability to accept reality and deal with it accordingly. I need to be convinced that the same old patterns of defensiveness, justification and denial are gone before I make myself willing to discuss to any further degree the questions I've raised.

A copy of this will be sent to David [Don's self-appointed counselor]. I am expecting the desired reply soon.
               In Jesus,
               Jerry Zwack

The letter was mailed on December 9th. The pastor's taped reply was such a violent outrage that his secretary refused to type it. "I have my answer, B" Jerry said after receiving the message on tape. "Tomorrow I'll write a

"PASTOR, PLEASE PRACTICE WHAT YOU PREACH"

letter to all the elders. I'll tell them what's been going on for the past two years—not all the details, but enough so they can see what I've been up against. Then I'll ask them to do something about it, and if they don't, I'm taking it outside the church." Overcome with emotion, he added, "It's a shame that it's come to this, but I know I'm following Scripture. I just should have done it a long time ago. I was trying to protect Don. Now it's the only thing that can save this church and your marriage."

I whispered, "I admire your courage, Z. You're the only one who's been willing to see me all the way through this. I'm sorry for all the wounds you've received."

Jerry patted my hand. "That's what connections are for, B. That's what this move of God is all about."

Getting back to the problem at hand, I asked, "What if Don orders the elders not to read a letter from you. He's afraid you're going to write one to the whole church. He's probably going to tell them on Sunday not to read any letters from you."

"You're right. Okay, here's what we can do. We can personally deliver the letter to each elder on Christmas Eve, early, like 6:30 when most of them will be home. Then we'll mail Don a copy so he'll get it right after Christmas before he leaves for Hawaii."

"Yeah. This way the elders will have it before the weekend services. Don won't have a chance to warn them."

That's the only thing I remember about that Christmas. I know it started to snow a little just as we delivered the last letter (all but one elder was home) and I dropped Jerry off at his home to be with his family, before I returned to Jody's empty house. She was gone on a flight.

Sure enough, as soon as the pastor got the letter, he called each elder and commanded them not to read it. It was too late!

The very next day (Christmas), Jerry got a hand-delivered letter from a senior elder that said, "I think a very complete investigation is in order, and I think the elders will want to hear in detail from both sides in the matter."[15]

After reading the letter, I said, "Jerry (he knew I was really serious when I called him Jerry instead of Z), you're not going to tell them about Las Vegas, are you? Oh, Z, I beg you not to. I beg you!"

Placing a hand on each of my shoulders, he answered softly, "I have to, B. The elders must know Don has a long-standing problem. They have to see that his problem didn't happen because of the move of God's love. God brought this love to expose our problems so we could deal with them."

"But Z, he's been delivered of that problem."

"No, B, he was delivered of that particular demon, but not the sexual problem—you know that."

"I know, I know. Oh Z, I just don't want to hurt him," I sobbed, "I don't want to hurt him."

"I'll be as careful as I can, B. I'm only doing this to try to save him. A surgeon has to cut in order to heal. I have to be free to say whatever I feel will help Don and the elders to see the whole picture so we can find solutions. Are you okay, B? I gotta do it."

* * *

Don was so relieved that Jerry hadn't written a letter to the whole church that he agreed to the hearing. Fur-

"PASTOR, PLEASE PRACTICE WHAT YOU PREACH"

thermore, he signed a document[16] agreeing that "the board of elders as a group shall exercise final authority over these meetings" and that he would "not exercise any authority over these hearings or the elders' exclusive review sessions"—a very necessary agreement, given the fact that the bylaws state that the pastor has final authority over all church matters.

Before the hearings began at the end of January, eleven rules of conduct were drawn up to govern them.[17] Everyone agreed that Russell, also a Bible college teacher, would act as moderator. Rule #6 stated that strict confidentiality would be maintained, with no taping or permanent records kept and any discussion of the hearings was not permitted outside the eldership. The rest is history.

* * *

Sixteen men, plus the pastor and Jerry, assembled in a conference room on campus. First Jerry spoke, for seven hours. Then Don spoke, for twenty-two hours. And me? I ate little and slept less, spending the time that I wasn't sitting at my dying son's bedside, on my face before God in the little prayer room where the angel had stood beside me twenty years ago. By now I was very familiar with that angel. It had visited me many times since then, bringing visions and revelations.

I remembered the time at an elders' retreat when I was shown how much I needed the elders to fill their God-given responsibilities, and now I realized this was it's fulfillment. I wondered, *What will these men think of me after they hear Jerry's presentation and then Don's side? Who will they believe? Will they have any respect for me after Don gets through accusing me?* "Oh, God," I prayed, "If they align with Don's thinking, help me!"

For thirty-seven years I'd tried to be what my husband wanted, but it didn't solve his problem. Surely the elders wouldn't require me to go back. But what if they did? I pushed the thought out of my mind.

Then I remembered a more recent experience that I'd had. While worshipping the Lord with Jerry, we were both suddenly slain in the Spirit, flat on the floor, with the exception of my left arm. From the elbow, it was straight up in the air, and I couldn't move it. Although not a word was spoken between us, we both knew that we represented the whole body of Christ (the church) and my left arm symbolized Community Chapel.

Suddenly I knew from the Lord that my left arm had to come down and lay flat on the floor with the rest of the body, but I couldn't move it! It was held in an upright position by a force that was literally so strong all the strength in me couldn't budge my arm. When Jerry saw me trying to push it over with my right hand, he joined me, but neither of us could move it. It was a strange feeling. I saw in the Spirit, demons come and gnaw on it, trying to get it to fall, but all they did was hurt and bruise it. They couldn't make it fall. Then all at once, with one mighty blow, an angel, swift as lightning, smacked it. My arm hit the floor with a thud!

Instantly I regretted it. I didn't want it to happen after all. I tried to pick it back up and put it on the mutilated stump that was my elbow, but the Lord said, "No, let it lay. It has to decompose." Then I saw another angel come and, with a pleasant look on his face, started cleaning off the stump. The vision ended after the angel got all the old residue whittled off and was polishing the stump, getting it ready to hold a new arm. *Were these hearings going to result in this vision's fulfillment,* I wondered.

* * *

Sixteen men, one by one, had to come to grips with their own position before God, as the idolatrous place they had put their pastor in was silently revealed. Their idol shattered, and each one's co-dependent role to their pastor crumbled and fell to the ground as the facts began piling up, first from Jerry's testimony and then from Don himself. The experience put them in shock and horrified disbelief, driving them to the Word of God to verify their individual responsibilities to the church as elders. Only one stopped to contemplate the anguish I was going through, and he sent me a note of reassurance. I cried.

To a man, everyone agreed Jerry's attitude of humility and love towards Don was flawless. Even Don remarked, "Jerry was so completely like the unruffled Christ, it must have been demonic." Even before the pastor finished his 22 hours of blame, accusations, and admissions, the three senior elders—who along with the pastor made up the corporation's board of directors—knew what they must do. The letter they had just received from the church's attorney[18] made it clear. It read, in part:

"If the board becomes aware of a pattern of conduct on the part of the corporation or it's employees which is either illegal or could subject the corporation to civil liability and, with that knowledge takes no steps to either stop the pattern or conduct or to discharge or discipline the corporate em-

ployee, the individual board member may be found to be individually liable for the civil damages that result from the action of the corporation or its employees."

On February 15th, they delivered a letter to the pastor,[19] which had the attorney's letters attached. When Don came to the fifth paragraph, he read:

"We believe it is our duty before God, our church, and the laws of the state of Washington to place you on 'Special Status.' The terms of this special status are:

1. Not be alone with any female not your wife in any non-public place. This includes your home and covers both your professional and private life. The only exceptions to this would be Bonnie, your secretary, and...

2. Not take any woman not your wife with you on any vacations or trips.

3. Not counsel any woman alone.

4. To confine any time spent in the company of women not your wife to group situations.

Duration: Indefinite."

Don's defiance to the request was evident the very next day—he left on yet another vacation with a woman and others.

The entire eldership sent their pastor a letter supporting the senior elders' decision.[20]

The pastor's response to these letters in a meeting with the elders on the following Thursday convinced all sixteen men to obey Matthew 18:17. Regarding this meeting, Don's counselor later told me, "If Don could have gotten his shoe off fast enough, he would have pounded it on the table."

* * *

"PASTOR, PLEASE PRACTICE WHAT YOU PREACH"

The congregation didn't expect to see their pastor in the Friday evening service, because he had flown to one of the satellite churches in a feeble effort to prevent a church split. But they were surprised when at the beginning of the service, Lanny walked up to the pulpit, choked back tears and stated, "The board of senior elders has called this meeting from this point on. Please hold all body ministry until the Sunday services."[21]

After informing the congregation, which now numbered only 1200, of the five-week long meetings with the pastor, Lanny concluded, "We are facing the biggest crisis in our church that we've ever faced. We could lose our pastor whom we all love. We could have a major church split. We could lose our whole church." You could feel the people trying to understand the gravity of the situation. Lanny's next statement brought it closer to home. "Because of how this will affect you who have loved this church, sacrificed for it, given tithes and offerings for years, and have children in our Christian school, your elders have agreed by unanimous decision that we must address the church at this time."

Lanny's grief was apparent. He stammered, "We wish the matter had not forced us to this point, but our responsibility to God and you compels us to inform you of the problem. We do not know what the future holds, but you need to be aware of what is happening, so you can make necessary decisions for your lives.

"The problem has reached explosive levels, and this is our only chance to tell you what is happening. We have no desire to take over the pastorship or to take over this church. We don't know what the pastor's reaction to this meeting will be. When he returns tomorrow, there will be a tape of this meeting on his desk. No matter what he says on Sunday, we will not fight him for the microphone."

Lanny's slight frame trembled with emotion, "I deeply love Don Barnett. I have been blessed beyond measure sitting under his ministry since I came here in the spring of 1969. I have been here almost exactly nineteen years. I have loved him, I have supported him, I have agreed with him and felt totally one with him. It is with deep sorrow in my heart that events have transpired to a point that I have to do what I'm doing tonight. Our pastor has a gift of wisdom in the Word of God that surpasses any that I know of in the church world today. The devil is trying to destroy him and that gift."

After pausing to gain his composure, Lanny continued, "The problem is simply this: our pastor has been in sexual sin of substantial magnitude, and it has put our church and senior elders in legal jeopardy. We are in lawsuits right now over this. We foresee, within two months, the entire matter becoming public worldwide."

When Lanny finished summarizing the events to this point, he added, "We have no desire to expose the pastor's sins, so we won't, but the problem is so great that he has threatened to fire us, take 90% of the congregation and run, take the money, etc. It is our unanimous opinion that our pastor is in deception and cannot be trusted. He has said the problem was solved even when he was sexually involved that very day, so we cannot trust his own word."

Before he turned the pulpit over to one of the senior elders to read the "Special Status" letter they sent to the pastor, Lanny admonished, "We want you to continue loving our pastor, we ask you to accept him and not leave

"PASTOR, PLEASE PRACTICE WHAT YOU PREACH"

the church. Let's stay and support this church and get through this." The congregation responded with resounding "Yes!" and "Amen!"

I sensed the congregation's hopefulness when they heard the Dean read the letters from the church's attorney and the one he and the other two senior elders had written to the pastor, stating the four easy-to-follow restrictions placed on him. They became bewildered, however, when they heard this retired marine colonel describe their pastor's unbiblical responses to confrontation.

The stunned congregation sat in silent disbelief, yet they knew their elders weren't lying. As the Dean sat down, Mark (a Bible college teacher) made his way to the pulpit. He didn't leap up the steps three at a time as he usually did when addressing the assembly. Sobbing with each word, he testified, "I pray to God this is the beginning of what I've longed for! I've longed to be one with Pastor Don. I've longed to be in his heart and have that free love and fellowship." Speaking of the elders, he said, "Through these past few weeks, your elders have been united as we haven't been before. It's been wonderful! God is opening this body and trying to make us one. We need one another; it's the only way we can make it in the future.

"God is breaking isolation. He's used this move of love to unite us. The devil came to deceive and hurt many. All the Scriptures that deal with uniting us in love talk about the whole body being united in love, and God wants it—desperately! God wants the barriers to come down. An important aspect of this move is exposing our lives to one another, but we seek to hide and shut ourselves off. God will not be satisfied with that. He'll press us, because He loves us. That's what's happening to our pastor, because of love, because we love him."

Mark stopped a minute and wept. He continued, "We realize the judgment of God has come to this church. It began with the leaders and is working its way down through the ranks."

Mark concluded, "I predict if this is received by Pastor Don, it's going to be hard. We're going to face some really tough things, but I hope we can do it together. If we do, there's going to be a release of God in our assembly concurrent with exposing of sin. Nobody will be on high horses, just the love of God pressing to purity, so we can be properly united."

It was a solemn and prayerful people who filed out of that memorable service. Each elder had sobbed out their grief and concern for Don. Never had the congregation seen their elders so broken and humble.

Even a sermon was preached by Russell to fortify the elders' actions with clear Scripture. During his sermon, Russell testified of the time back in June—before I had moved out of the parsonage—that the Spirit of the Lord had come upon him and told him to go to the parsonage and warn Don that if he didn't repent and stop his sinful behavior that day, God's judgment would fall on him. At the time, Russell knew nothing of his pastor's sins.

The elders knew they had done the right thing, as they watched the congregation leave one by one after the final prayer. It was hard to know all the emotions the people were experiencing. Some were relieved that their elders were finally doing something to stop the problem which had driven away so many. Others were afraid, afraid for their own spiritual lives if the pastor wouldn't

"PASTOR, PLEASE PRACTICE WHAT YOU PREACH"

submit to the restrictions. Could they make it without him? What would happen to their church that had become their whole life? Would they be strong enough to make decisions for themselves, or would they need to keep their pastor in his role of control over them, in order to feel secure? What would happen to the Christian school their children attended all their lives? How many would choose to believe the elders instead of whatever their pastor would say on Sunday?

They had been taught well on how to handle correction and discipline. For this reason, some left encouraged. Nevertheless, I wept for each one of them, including our two hundred teenagers, who had already been thrown into confusion by the imbalances in the move. There wasn't a one of us who hadn't yielded, to some extent, to the move of the devil that God had warned us would accompany His true move of love. Would anger and bitterness drive them away, before they had a chance to sort it all out?

* * *

Most of the congregation had been praying around the clock since Friday evening, but that didn't stop them from arriving at the church on Sunday morning, long before the Sunday School hour, to pray for their pastor and church. Some misguided souls had rushed to the pastor upon his return, aligned with him against the elders, and made it their business to influence anyone who would listen, to join in a revolt.

The hearts of the people for their pastor were apparent, as he stepped to the pulpit to begin his Sunday School lesson; everyone jumped to their feet in a standing ovation. As the clapping subsided, it seemed it was going to be Sunday School as usual. But once the lesson began, it became evident the pastor didn't agree with the elders.

Although I was sitting in the back half of the sanctuary, after the first sarcastic statement came out of Don's mouth, I knew why he had to do what he did. He said pityingly, "So, here in your view is your poor pastor caught in all these places and you are just loving him anyway." I thought, *He can't accept their love unless it's merited. He has to justify himself in order to receive their love. If he can't earn their love, he's a failure.* Through the whole sermon (which filled sixty-one typed pages), I felt only pity for the man who had been riddled by fear all his life.

After admitting the fear he had in losing their love by defending himself, he seemed to talk in riddles, saying we needed to know things we didn't know and the elders needed to know things they didn't know, and what he brought to them they rejected, but he knew things nobody else knew. Questioning minds were left with the opinion that neither they nor the elders could make the right judgments and needed him to make all decisions.

When the pastor said, "I'm going to start with statements Lanny made," it was as if this time he held the razor strap. His added, "I'm not mad at anybody; you need to hear the truth" didn't soften the blows. Everyone felt them. He tore into Lanny and all the elders, claiming they had false responsibility, hyper-legalism, hypocrisy, rebellion, anarchy, Laodicea, and a power play to control the pastor. He asserted, "They are using their judgment over mine, which they have no right to do. They are using their theology over mine, which they have no

"PASTOR, PLEASE PRACTICE WHAT YOU PREACH"

right to do." He scolded me for being the leaven that leavened the whole eldership in my effort to control him.

When he charged the elders with trying to out-think their pastor, you knew that in his mind they were still his "little boys in the Lord" who would always need him to teach and discipline them. If ever they moved out of that subordinate role, they threatened his control over them. It seemed as if he couldn't let them grow up and be men of God in their own right, contributing to the oversight of the church.

Even though he accused the elders of trying to ruin his reputation, he revealed far more details about his sexual misconduct, and in doing so broke the oath taken at the hearings. No matter how many blows the elders received from the razor strap, the pastor couldn't get them to cry, "I won't, Daddy, I won't , I won't." Perhaps that is why the meeting lasted so long.

The two inescapable points he made were 1) how he felt about the elders; i.e., they were deceitful and wanted to control him totally, and 2) he had been "clean for six months." The problem was there were too many women sitting in front of him who knew it wasn't true. The pastor ended by saying, "My wife tried to control me and when she couldn't, she moved out. Jerry tried to control me and when he couldn't, he left. Now the elders want to control me, and if they can't, they're going to put me out. Now that's not what you want, do you?"

A few jumped to their feet and shouted, "No! No, pastor! We're behind you!" As the clapping got louder, others stood and joined in. Confident now that he had the backing of the congregation, he invited the elders and any others to receive the grace of God, his forgiveness, get up, and go on. Cocky over his new victory, Don grabbed the blonde sitting in my place on the front row and began dancing with her as Stu sang *Beholden to You*.

Blinded by tears, I stumbled out the back door and hid behind the tool shed. The grief in my spirit was so great the convulsions my body experienced went unnoticed. I ached to feel the strength of my connections. I felt all alone. *What must the congregation think of me now?*

Don didn't see me crumpled up against the shed when he came out of the building hugging the blonde close as they walked to his car parked beside mine. Giddy with excitement, he exclaimed, "Oh, my wife must be here," as he put her in his car and sped away.

"Jesus," I sobbed, "I'm going to need Your grace to walk back into my church again." Jesus spoke to my mind, "You had to give up your home, but you won't have to give up your church." I hid it in my heart, not really understanding.

Chapter Twenty-Two

Shattered Dreams—Shattered Lives

"For the time is come that judgment must first begin at the house of God; and if it first begin at us, what shall the end be of them that obey not the gospel of God? Wherefore let them that suffer according to the will of God, commit the keeping of their souls to him in well doing, as unto a faithful creator."
(1 Peter 4:17,19)

"I need more than grace; I need a lawyer!" I said to the empty room on Tuesday, after hanging up the phone. Don's secretary had just informed me, "There is no money in your account. Don's given it all to the lawyers. He said the VISA card is full, too."

My mind raced ahead, *This means Don's hired his own lawyer; this couldn't involve the lawsuits because the insurance is covering our lawyers for those. Oh-oh, if he's got a lawyer to sue the elders, then he's probably going to grab our savings!*

I picked up the phone and dialed our stockbroker. When he heard my voice, he exclaimed, "Whew, Barbara,

I'm sure glad you called. You're right. Don has ordered me to liquidate all your stocks and I have to have the check in the mail to him on Thursday. You better get a lawyer, quick! Good luck."

Next I called a good friend, a retired district court judge, "Chuck, what shall I do?"

"You need to talk to a lawyer who handles divorce cases. You not only need a good lawyer, you need one who can act fast."

By 7:00 that evening, I was sitting across the desk from one of the best divorce court lawyers in the city. I was scared. "I need to get a restraining order so my husband can't take our savings to hire a lawyer to sue the elders."

With cold calculating eyes, he asked, "How do you know this?"

"Do you know who I am?" I asked timidly.

He nodded. "I've read the papers."

After I told him about the phone call from Don's secretary and my call to the stockbroker, he said, "That's the kind of proof I need. But you can't just put a restraining order on the money. You have to file either for a divorce or legal separation."

An involuntary tear slid down my cheek. "I can't? I don't want a divorce."

Jeff looked at his watch. "Well, we can file for a legal separation for now, because we have to do something quick if we're going to save that money. Okay? We'll work out the details later."

"Okay."

Jeff had all the necessary papers ready for me to sign by the next morning. He filed it in court that afternoon and had a courier deliver the court order to the stock broker. Don got the call Thursday morning from our broker, saying he couldn't put the check in the mail because it was frozen. Don was furious! I had guessed right. He had already signed a note giving it all to his lawyer.

Before Don could stop me, I went to the bank and maxed out our Mastercard with a cash advance. I reasoned, *If I don't, he will, and if he does, it will all go to his lawyer.* I had no intention of spending the money, but as it turned out, I had to pay my lawyer, I had to get an apartment, and I had to buy furniture. I was glad I had the necessary funds.

When Don received the notice of the legal separation, he learned there was also a restraining order against him. He was not to contact me except through the church office, nor was he allowed to come to my residence. To show that I wasn't trying to take unfair advantage of him, I was not allowed to come to the parsonage without his permission.

When I sat in Jeff's office the second time to work out a spousal maintenance plan for the hearing which was three weeks away, I began to understand why my lawyer was one of the best. He said, "To be a good lawyer, you have to put yourself in your opponent's shoes and think like he thinks so you can come up with the right arguments."

"Oh," I said, "That's why you oppose everything I say."

* * *

THE TRUTH SHALL SET YOU FREE

The elders' week wasn't any less hectic than mine. The pastor's declaration on Sunday had all but made their decision for them.

Lanny told me, "The elders resumed their meetings on Monday, wondering 'What do we do now?' After some initial responses, David (Don's self-appointed counselor) said the answer was obvious: Don must be disfellowshipped. The "bombshell" statement prompted hours of debate before everyone was satisfied that we had come to this point. Did God want the elders to leave or stay and disfellowship Don?

"An excellent debate followed with eloquent speakers on both sides of the issue. Some argued that we must leave Don to God, because our responsibility ended Friday night. The other side argued that God requires us to act responsibly and fulfill our calling as elders to protect the congregation from further harm.

"After several days, the second viewpoint prevailed, and we all felt that it was God's will for us to stay and take action. To this day, I know of no one among the sixteen men who has changed his mind."

The Senior Elders wrote the necessary amendments to bring the bylaws in line with state law, and called a meeting of the board—which had to include the pastor—to vote on the changes.

On Friday morning the three men walked into the parsonage where the meeting was scheduled, called it to order, introduced the subject, and asked for a vote. Immediately the pastor jumped up, refused to vote, cancelled the meeting, and dismissed the elders. Before the elders returned to the east campus to finish the meeting, they voted—majority rules. Scott jumped into his car, drove thirty miles to the capitol building in Olympia, filed the amendments with the clerk, raced back to the church, and signed a four-page letter addressed to Don, along with the other two senior elders. It read, in part (see Appendix for entire letter):

Dear Don,
We three Senior Elders, each individually, wish to again express our personal love, our compassion, and deepest concern for you, our brother and friend. We are grief stricken at the personal situation you are in....
We are also mindful of our responsibility and stewardship to the Word of God, to you our pastor, and to the flock over which <u>God</u> has ordained us as overseers. We are committed to the fact that the Holy Scriptures are the highest authority which we are responsible to follow. We have searched our hearts and consciences before God and are fully assured we are acting in accordance with our proper stewardship of this holy trust. We can do no less....
Effective immediately you are prohibited from entering church property, with the exception of the parsonage. We will enforce this if necessary.
Even though we must take this serious action, we still love you and desire to deal mercifully with you. We greatly appreciate the deep sacrifice you have made for the congregation for many years. We will show you fairness and be benevolent to you with regard to the parsonage, severance pay, and the automobile you use. The Senior Elders in conjunction with the Deacon Board will extend terms to you as soon as possible.
We will provide for you in order to allow time for personal repentance and prayer , personal deliverance, and

counseling. It is our prayer that waiting on God with an open heart will result in a deep renewing and healing for you....

We pray that you will humbly accept this action as a needed restorative and redemptive step and as God's mercy for the sake of your soul. We look to the future for what our great God and Savior is able and sufficient to do.

Even before Don got the letter, he and his fiery red-headed attorney marched into the courthouse to get an injunction against the elders barring them from the church services. The elders' lawyer arrived and explained to the Judge what the elders did, stating that the amended bylaws have already been filed in Olympia. The Judge's response? "I don't have enough information here to totally decide this issue. I will do so next Friday. Until then, because of the action of the Senior Elders you, Pastor, are not allowed on church property until this is heard in court."

David, Don's counselor, wrote Don a letter[22] also, in which the sixth paragraph stated, *I am now absolutely certain that you must be separated from your ministry to save your soul.* In the next paragraph, David declared, *I know, at this point, there is no turning back for you. Your repeated declaration that self will reign has set you up that the Rock must now fall on you since you have refused to fall on Him.*

At 5:00 p.m. with a police escort (one of Don's advocates carried a gun) David took these two letters, plus one from all the elders to the parsonage. The letters were on his desk when he arrived home from the courthouse.

* * *

SHATTERED DREAMS—SHATTERED LIVES

The congregation, emotionally torn and insecure after last weekend's services, didn't know what might happen as they gathered for the usual Friday evening service. Two Christian school teachers sat on the curb outside the main entrance, held one another and wept. As part of Don's underground team strode past them with defiant determination, they sobbed, "We're going to lose our church."

Danny, a short, stocky man who was once on staff and at this time was restricted from ministering, marched up and staunchly stood behind the pulpit, gripping it with both hands before it was even time for the service to begin.

The pianist went to the piano and started playing, but Danny didn't budge. He said, "I just want to pray." Mark, chosen by the elders to be in charge of the service, nodded his head from where he was sitting in the pastor's place. Danny prayed while the pianist continued to play. The people wondered what was going on, but they tried to enter in, not sure where Danny's prayer was leading. Finally he stopped, but didn't loosen his grip on the pulpit. The` pianist kept right on playing.

Danny said, apologetically, as if submitting to the leader, "I just want to give a little testimony of what God did in me while I was praying this week." He motioned for the pianist to stop. Acting like he was going to stop speaking any minute, Danny switched back and forth from being with the elders to being with Don, reassuring the congregation that he saw things from a different point of view because of his vast experience as a minister, teacher, pastor, counselor, and helping other pastors in church splits.

THE TRUTH SHALL SET YOU FREE

Mark, paralyzed with carefulness, didn't stop Danny even when he insisted that the elders stand and look at all the raised hands after Danny asked the congregation to "raise your hands if you've ever been hurt by me or an elder." Danny recited again and again that he was a peacemaker and only wanted to hold the church together. (*He reminded me of those con artists who came into the bowling alley where I worked when I was twenty-six years old and managed to cheat me out of ten bucks when they paid for a ten-cent cup of coffee with a twenty dollar bill.*)

Finally, after over a half-hour interspersed with yells and catcalls from Danny's plants in the congregation, his last words were, "This week your elders legally put your pastor out, and if this church has any guts, they will get up and walk out!" He threw up his arms, beckoned the congregation to follow, ran from the platform and out the door. Those who had been told of the plan jumped up, yelled, and headed for the door, as well. Others, full of panic, and afraid they would miss out on God, followed. Mark motioned for everyone to stand. As I stood and watched some leave, I said aloud to nobody in particular, "There goes my marriage, walking out that door."

One lady (the blonde) turned to her husband and asked, "Are you coming?" He said, "No, I'm staying to hear what the elders have to say." She turned, walked out, went straight home, packed and moved out. Her reason? She and her husband were no longer "spiritually compatible."[23]

Suddenly, I remembered my son David was in the service. He had insisted on coming, even though he hardly had the strength to sit in his wheelchair. I whirled around and caught his eye. He gave me a little smile and nodded, so I knew he was okay.

Some got as far as the foyer before they realized, "I don't want to be doing this. I need to hear what my elders have to say." They came back in and joined us still standing and praying. Quite a few got clear out to the parking lot before they turned around and came back. Nobody even tried to hold back their grief and hurt. We held one another, sobbed, and cried out to the Lord.

Mark's voice was heard in the foyer as he spoke into the sound system, "The Bible says 'to make a judgment before the matter is given will bring folly and shame.' My heart hurts, my heart hurts for Danny. Let's pray for Danny that God will break that schismatic spirit that was just displayed here...." Before Mark finished praying, more people returned to the sanctuary. The weeping continued.

Julie, a prayer warrior, took the mic and prayed. Mark reaffirmed his love for Don and stated he had prayed for him hour after hour, as well as hundreds of others. He begged us all to stick together so we could truly help Don. Don's counselor, David, stepped to the platform, placed his papers on the pulpit, prepared to read, but broke down and bawled like a baby. He tried again to speak, but he sobbed instead. Julie and others came up and prayed for him.

While David regained his composure, Lanny took the mic. "I just want to remind you that I have known about Don's problems for one-and-a-half years now, but I've still supported him in every way possible, stayed under his ministry, and submitted to him. I didn't blast him or preach at him. I haven't wanted to touch God's anointed and that is not our desire now. If leaving would have helped, I would have left a long time ago. The best way to help Don is for us to obey the Word of God as the elders have done and believe God to see us through."

David stammered, "I'm not an elder, as you know, but I have been Don's counselor for the past six months, and I am a minister." After pausing to dry his eyes again, David read the letter he sent to the pastor. David burst into tears again—we all did. David said he was going to read his presentation, because he had Don's entire sermon typed out, which numbered 61 pages in which there were 35 quotes of his six-month "clean" record. He said he would read many quotes and carefully respond to them with evidence and information available to him, because, he said, "You need a layout of evidence and background information to see clearly the pastor's life and why the service on Friday was timely and necessary."

After David read just four of the 35 quotes, he told of incidents that girls came and confessed to him which occurred throughout the past six-month period. He said, "I have signed affidavits from these women." He added, "Never have we received such a large number of complaints from such a large number of women regarding the activities of one man. These complaints cover many years, but worse than ever over the last two years." David confessed that he wasn't bringing the bulk of evidence because he didn't want to tell any more than was absolutely necessary to prove that the special status the elders placed on the pastor was necessary for both the protection of the congregation and the pastor. "Suffice to say, the poor man has a severe problem." David went on to explain that now the elders' primary complaint against Don was not his sexual sins, but his refusal to deal with it.

David continued by reading from a letter[24] the elders sent to Don listing the following thirteen reasons why they felt the disfellowship action taken by the Senior Elders was necessary:
1. *Refusal to hear reproof at any level.*
2. *Extensive misuse of pastoral authority.*
3. *Rebellion against the Scriptural church authority.*
4. *Extensive lying.*
5. *Continual display of unrepentant, defiant, and uncooperative attitude.*
6. *Refusal to follow special status.*
7. *Extensive sexual misconduct.*
8. *Minimizing the seriousness of your sins and their consequences.*
9. *Emotional abuse of your wife.*
10. *Causing division in the church.*
11. *Teaching heresy in the church.*
12. *Extensive stumbling of others by your sinful behavior.*
13. *Refusal to follow church standards.*

David read 1 Timothy 5:20, *"Those that sin are to be rebuked publicly that others may take warning."* He explained how the Scripture applied, because the context is speaking of elders. He read many more quotes from the 61-page speech, then told what really happened. The reality of the deep deception and denial their pastor was in began sinking in to the congregation, as silent tears stained their faces.

Next, Greg spoke. He was an elder and Bible college teacher who everyone had a special love for, because we all knew that at one time he had to be put out of the church after he had fallen into deep deception and couldn't be reached no matter how hard many of us, including the pastor, tried. His testimony gave the congregation hope as he expressed his gratitude to Don and all the leadership for being willing to go through the embarrassment of putting an elder and teacher out of the church, because, he said, "That was the only way God could reach me. I wouldn't listen to man, to the government of the church, or to any of you. But when I was all alone, Jesus spoke to me in that 'still small voice' in my spirit just as plain as if I could hear it with my natural ears. He showed me that I was deceived and what would happen to me if I didn't let Him deliver me."

With great emotion, Greg finished the story of how he became willing to do anything the pastor asked of him regarding his marriage and his life. Hope trickled back into hearts as the congregation tried to believe for the same results for their pastor.

It was 11:30 p.m. before Mark closed the service after the Dean read the letter the Senior Elders had given Don that day, and Scott told what happened in court just a few hours ago. The elders also allowed me to address the congregation. This time I had no message from the Lord to deliver with the help of an angel.

Speaking from my heart in racking sobs, I whispered, "I love my husband with all my heart, and I hope you can accept the fact that, right now, your pastor is sick in his mind. He needs a rest from the ministry." Referring to Danny splitting the church and those who walked out, I said, "I pray that they won't insist on having a pastor right now, because we need time to put our marriage back together. Please be strong enough to allow us that time. We've sacrificed for you for 22 years. If you can sacrifice for us for a year, I know the elders can take care of you, then we can all go on together to become all God wants us to be." Their standing ovation helped me to realize their love and acceptance.

Mark announced that services would continue as usual, as well as Bible college and Christian school. The service ended after Lanny read this prophecy the Lord gave late Friday night:

"My beloved people, you do not have it in yourselves to come through this time. As you are willing to humble yourselves before your Lord, I shall be faithful to speak unto you in that still small voice. I shall place before each one of you that are willing to follow My voice. I shall give you opportunities to choose for Me, to choose for self, or to choose for man. I shall be faithful unto you. Will you be faithful unto Me? I have been your Lord and I have sat upon My throne and you have been as a body before me. Think not that your God has been unfaithful to you. Think not that your God has forsaken you. Yea, I shall turn the enemy upon himself and as you choose Me I shall use you to bring his defeat. As you choose Me, I will impart unto you that which you need to get through these difficult days. I am with you. Stand on My Word. Open your ears to My Spirit within you. There are those among you that I have been putting Myself within in a very particular way, and you who have been willing to listen to the voice of My Spirit within you shall be able to hear. There are those among you who have resisted and you will not be able to hear, but My love is extended to every one of My lambs. And I shall work with each one of you individually, because you belong to Me and you are precious in my sight. If you could see all that I am seeing, you would know that there was nowhere to go but into the arms of your loving Lord. As you run into My

arms, beloved, I shall teach you what you need to have. Do not fear for I am your Lord."

Someone came to me after the service and asked, "What do you think the pastor is doing right now?"

I didn't have to think twice, "He's probably writing a letter to everyone."

* * *

Sure enough! By Monday afternoon Don had not one but two long letters in the mail, addressed to "Dear Sheepies of my flock," and "Dear flock of mine," plus a letter addressed to the elders that was mailed to the entire congregation. The letters, however, didn't have the effect hoped for by Don. He had trained his people too well. They knew they weren't supposed to read letters from persons who had been disfellowshipped, so many didn't. Finally, after almost two months of getting these types of letters full of accusations, the elders mailed a twenty-six-page rebuttal to every member of the Chapel.

Of course, Don wasted no time in finding a building to hold Sunday services in until the Judge made his ruling as to whether or not Don would get his position back. His hot-tempered lawyer also rushed right back down to the courts and filed a new claim against the elders, stating that the actions they took to amend the bylaws were illegal.

In the meantime, the news media had been informed of the whole mess. Although their photographers and newspersons could be kept off church property, they weren't barred from taking pictures at the bowling alley where Don held his Sunday services off-campus. Now the front pages of the newspapers and TV were not only full of the Chapel, but they had pictures as well.[25]

It was interesting to observe that for over a year now the news media had hounded Don for an interview. They were printing stories regarding all the lawsuits against the Chapel, so Don had established a policy that no one except Loren, the operations manager, could talk to any news reporter. But, with this event Don not only accepted interviews, but ran to the civil courts, too. It took no time for the news to spread across the nation and even into Europe.

At one point, the elders tried to get Don to go to a Christian Arbitration Board, but he refused. The nightmare was just beginning.

Chapter Twenty-Three

Oh, Donald, Donald!

"Dare any of you, having a matter against another go to law before the unjust...why do you not rather suffer ourselves to be defrauded? Nay, ye do wrong, and defraud, and that your brethren."
(1 Corinthians 6:1,7,8)

Poor Donald, I pondered, *He's being pressed from all angles. First he spends every dime on lawyers. Next he gets served with legal separation papers from me, freezing our small savings account. Then he loses his salary by being disfellowshipped. Now his lawyers are screaming at him for cash advances or they'll drop him.*

In his mind, none of these actions against him were justified, so he set himself to fight. He would get control of his church and get his wife back! He was confident the judge would agree that this was an "illegal coup" by the elders and none of his sexual conduct would even be considered, because "sex between consenting adults is not illegal." He was sure I would come back home when I saw the judge rule in his favor. He was certain his lawyer would convince the commissioner in our legal separation pre-trial that I shouldn't receive any spousal maintenance, because there was no reason why I shouldn't come home. If nothing else would persuade me to come back, then being without money would.

> *Oh, yes, it was easy for me to know how Don thought. Not only had I lived with him for thirty-seven years, but I have stacks of letters and boxes of tapes from him. Nevertheless, I couldn't help feeling sorry for the man. I didn't have time to feel sorry for myself.*

With the increased harassment against me and its effect on Jody, I located a small basement apartment and moved. The eggs spattered all over our cars and the obscene bumper stickers plastered on mine was bad enough, but when Jody came home and discovered someone crawling out of her bedroom window, I knew it wasn't fair for me to stay there any longer.

It wasn't all bad, however. One day I came home and Jody was sitting in the middle of the living room floor cradling a large box that was shaped like a man's black tuxedo. Inside was a dozen gorgeous long-stemmed red roses! Someone had them shipped all the way from California; they're called "black-tie roses." We cried, then laughed, then cried again. At least there was someone who didn't hate us.

Shopping for groceries for my new apartment was a bigger challenge than I had anticipated. I walked into the Safeway store where I'd shopped for the past thirty years, got a cart, burst into tears, turned around and ran out. I muttered to myself, "I don't know how to do this.

OH, DONALD, DONALD!

I've never shopped for 'just me' before." It was too painful to face the reality that I was alone.

My biggest concern right then was for my son. He took precedence over the civil lawsuits which required me to go to depositions. I'd even had subpoenas stuffed into my hands as I pulled into gas stations and parking lots. The pre-trial hearing for spousal maintenance, the lawsuits Don filed against the elders, and the part-time job I'd landed as a sales representative for a candy broker were unimportant—David was dying.

I gave up my job. I postponed the pre-trial hearing. I rescheduled all lawyer appointments, the depositions could wait. My world narrowed to just my son and me. I hated to leave him even to sleep, but I realized the other men in the dorm deserved their privacy. I wished his father would at least have called to ask how David was, but he didn't. He was too busy with the legal proceedings against the elders and trying to force his way back into pastoring the people who no longer accepted him as their pastor. His behavior had destroyed their respect, but not their love. They still loved him.

* * *

Kneeling beside his bed, holding David's head in my hands the last night of his life on this earth, my emotional pain seemed as great as his physical torture. Watching him suffer was unbearable, but David was more concerned for me than himself. He struggled to speak. "David," I said with my face pressed against his, "You're trying to tell me something. What is it? What do you need to tell me?"

His body wouldn't let him say it. The harder he tried, the more the wretched disease fought as he gasped for breath and strained for muscle control. College students, all his friends who had believed God with him for years and admired his faith, were everywhere in the room, sitting on the floor, standing, praying, supporting.

"It's okay, David," I encouraged, "Just relax for a minute. You'll be able to say it in a minute." One of the ladies David had a spiritual connection with patted his other cheek. It brought a smile to his lips and his body relaxed. But the look in his eyes told me he had to ask me something. I bent close, barely able to decipher what was so important to him. "Danny, have you forgiven Danny? He didn't mean to. I have to know?"

My wet cheek pressed against his as I assured him, "Yes, David, I've forgiven Danny. I know he thought he was doing the right thing, and I don't hold any blame for him." David managed to get his arms around my neck and I cried enough tears for both of us. My precious son wouldn't allow himself to leave for heaven until he knew I didn't have any unforgiveness in my heart. His tortured body relaxed as someone began to sing, *"Oh, that will be glory for me, when by His grace we shall look on His face, that will be glory, glory for me."* Jesus came and took David home the next day—March 23rd—just before noon.

In an attempt to have some kind of memorial service for David in those troublesome times for our church, I asked the elders for permission to take a few minutes in the Friday evening service to thank all those who had, over the years, faithfully cared for and supported David. I learned after it was too late that some of the elders had not been informed of the plan and were very upset. They

OH, DONALD, DONALD!

considered me a threat, even of becoming "Mrs. Pastor." That was the last time I spoke from the pulpit.

* * *

In less than a week after my son's death, I was thrust back into the court scene with all the trials and accompanying depositions, trying to dodge news reporters and cameras. My wise divorce court lawyer, Jeff, had asked for a sealed hearing, so no one was allowed in the courtroom other than Don and me. Don never showed up, so there was just me and the two lawyers, besides the lady commissioner and her court reporter. Even Judy and Alan, my two friends, had to wait in the hall. (You remember Judy? She's the one who, at the beginning of the Chapel, the Lord told me to go get her by the hand and lead her to the altar. She and her new husband, Alan, befriended me after I moved out of the parsonage. In fact, they're the ones who sent the "black tie roses." Judy and Alan are still my close friends.)

When I came out of the courtroom uncontrollably crying, Judy rushed to me, asking, "What happened?" They had just seen Don's red-headed lawyer stomp out and disappear into the elevator, followed by the news media, headed for the 9th floor where the hearing had already started in the battle between Don and the elders.

"What happened?" Judy repeated. "Was it bad?" I shook my head, still crying too hard to talk.

Jeff answered, "No, we won."

Judy asked, "Then why are you crying?"

"I'm so happy," I sobbed. Without thinking, I grabbed my lawyer and hugged him.

THE TRUTH SHALL SET YOU FREE

"Oh, good," Judy sighed, relieved.

"Thank you, Jeff," I said. "You were terrific in there."

Jeff said, "Hey, it's my job. We got everything you wanted, and I would have been surprised if you hadn't. It didn't take long for her [the commissioner] to see what has happened to you."

I burst into tears again. "I know. That's what meant the most to me—to have someone who doesn't know the story be able to see what the truth is. It really helped me." I grabbed my head, and added, "I really am thinking straight."

Chuckling, Jeff said, "Did you see Pierce (Don's lawyer)? Boy, he got so mad he threw his briefcase across the bar and yelled, 'Here, you might as well give her the whole thing!' I don't know another lawyer who likes that guy. I mean none of us like him as a person; he's mean."

"Oh, dear," Judy chimed in, thinking of the hearing upstairs.

After explaining to me the legal procedure to complete the paperwork, Jeff added, "You should be getting your spousal maintenance check real soon, unless Don appeals it."

"Oh, no!" I exclaimed. "Can he appeal it?"

"Yes, but do you think he will?" Jeff asked. All three of us—Judy, Alan, and me—nodded our heads at the same time, "Yup."

Sure enough, three weeks later we were back in court. This time Don used his other lawyer and we had a different commissioner, a man. It didn't take Jeff any time at all to whip out the fax he had received from Don that very morning, giving all the reasons why he couldn't afford to give me any spousal maintenance. The fax came

OH, DONALD, DONALD!

from Hawaii where Don was enjoying yet another vacation with a connection. The commissioner threw up his hands in disgust and cancelled the appeal, charging Don to pay my extra lawyer fee and court costs.

* * *

Alan, Judy, and I cautiously made our way up to the ninth floor, avoiding the news media, and slipped into the already crowded courtroom to hear the judge's decision concerning the church. I filled Alan and Judy in on what had happened so far. "First, Don went to judge Johnson and filed a suit against the senior elders for holding an 'illegal meeting.' Don claimed they didn't have his permission, and therefore he wanted a restraining order preventing them from meeting again. Our (the elders') lawyer told the Judge what happened in Olympia and that Don had been disfellowshipped, so the Judge slapped a restraining order on Don until the matter could be heard in one week. It turned out to be two weeks, and in the meantime Don filed a different suit, stating the disfellowship was illegal. Then the elders filed a counter suit stating they had legal grounds because of the pastor's conduct.

"Then Judge Bates heard it in his court. He reinstated Don as president of the corporation on the basis that the elders violated the bylaws regarding holding the meeting, but said the whole matter had to be heard at trial. Until then, however, Don was reinstated."

"It's been awful!" Judy whined. "None of us want him for our pastor."

"That's why," I continued, "the elders hurried back to court and got permission for both sides to hold services on the property. They tried to get us on the west campus in the sanctuary, because we have two-thirds of the people and Don has only one-third, but Don refused, so we have to have our services crammed into the Chapel."

Judy added, "It's really hard, because the mothers don't have any nursery facilities."

Alan threw up his hands and said, "Our pastor has lost his mind. If he really cared about the people as his letters say he does, then he would let us have the west campus."

"I know," I said, "But that isn't the worst part. The worst part is the 103 people on staff are stuck with carrying out his orders when they no longer accept him as their pastor. Don's preparing to fire the whole staff and put his own people in. He's already given some people keys that aren't authorized to have them."

Alan surmised, "That judge didn't know what he was doing when he put Don back in. If I was on staff, I wouldn't follow him. I couldn't. I'd be disobeying God Himself!"

"It's really hard," I sighed. "That's why Jack resigned."

"The general manager?" Alan asked. "He resigned? He's a senior elder. What's going to happen to the corporation's board? Can Don put one of his men in, so the vote will be tied?"

"No, he can't, because it takes a majority vote and we still have a majority vote with the Dean and Scott."

"The poor Christian School teachers," Judy lamented. "They're having a terrible time. Don's got his men marching up and down the halls demanding copies of all the curriculum. He's even accused Debbie of stealing, and now she's been subpoenaed to a deposition by Don's lawyer."

"You mean that red-headed guy who just stormed out of court?" Alan asked.

"Yes," whimpered Judy, "The poor students; they're the ones who'll be damaged the most, but do you know what Debbie did? She printed a bulletin and sent it to all the teachers. It's an outline of exactly how to handle all the fears and questions the students are having so they won't feel guilty and bury their emotions. It's really good."

I added, "I don't know what we would do without Debbie. She's a jewel. She'll do just fine in the deposition with Pierce. The Lord is on her side." Getting back to the subject, I said, "Anyway, in this court today, the Judge is going to hear all Don's complaints against the elders because our lawyer got a restraining order put on Don. Now neither side can fire or hire anybody except through normal channels, which is a majority vote of senior elders. But—here's the big problem—we are running out of money, fast!

"We can't pay all the salaries, maintenance costs, and meet our mortgage payment each month. Nor can we use any church funds to pay lawyer fees. Neither can Don. So here's what both sides have done. They take up two offerings. The judge required us to pass the offering bags to support the church, but the problem is our people won't give to support a church with a pastor they don't want, so they don't give in that offering. But we need money to pay our lawyers, so the elders established a "BLM fund."

"What's BLM stand for?" asked Alan.

"I'm not exactly sure," I answered. "I think it's Benevolence, Legal, and Ministerial Fund. Anyway, Don is in the same bind, except he doesn't have very many people. He's having them write checks directly to him, and his men are even asking the people to take out second mortgages, sell insurance policies, have garage sales, anything to raise money. Somebody told me he's promising to give their money back when he wins, but I don't know if that's true. Anyway, Don's lawyers are here today because the senior elders put him on the top of the 'lay-off' list and cut off his salary to help trim the budget. They also cut off all the phone lines from the parsonage to the church."

"Oh, dear," Judy sighed, and with a chuckle added, "Without phones, he can't hassle the staff."

I continued, "Jeff says if Don gets his salary back today, plus any retroactive pay, he will put a restraining order on it, because I'm entitled to half of it, so I have to call him as soon as this is over. Oh, you know another thing the elders did?"

"What?"

"Well, they could see what was coming down the pike, so they gave me the Cadillac and Don the Riviera, because they knew we would both be without cars if the church folded. Boy, am I thankful! The Cadillac needs a lot of work, so I'm going to sell it and Jerry can get me a good deal on a Ford. But Don—now this is crazy—he's asking the judge today to make the elders take his car back, because he says they only did it to keep from paying for his gas and maintenance."

"Man!" Alan exclaimed, "Don's not thinking straight. If the elders win this thing, he'll be without a car."

OH, DONALD, DONALD!

As we entered Judge Wartnik's courtroom, Don's other lawyer was speaking, because Pierce was still too shaken after losing downstairs.

Next, our lawyer spoke. We were all disappointed. Alan whispered, "Russell could do a better job than this. This guy acts like he's not prepared."

After a couple more go-arounds, the judge made his decision. Don got his salary back, plus retroactive pay; he got one phone line; and the elders got the car back. Don's lawyers asked for a $500,000 bond to be posted by the elders to offset Don not being able to fire anybody.

"That's ridiculous!" Alan whispered, "They're just trying to break us so we'll give up."

"Shhhh!"

The judge refused, but made us post a $10,000 bond, twice as much as Don had to post to get the restraining order on the elders. As the judge retired to his chambers, Pierce slammed his briefcase shut and walked past me to the door with hate pouring out of his eyes. Judy remarked, "Wow, he doesn't like you."

I said, "Oh, I think I just remind him of his defeat and he doesn't like to lose."

Alan said, "Let's get to a phone and call Jeff, because Don gets his salary back."

Grabbing my stomach because of the ache inside, I said, "I want to wait in here until those reporters out in the hall leave." I sat back down and Judy put her hand on my back. Both of our eyes filled with tears; she knew what I was thinking. *No matter which way this thing goes, I lose. Either my right arm gets cut off or my left. Sure, Don gets his salary so I'll get a little more money—maybe—but now it's going to cost the church more and we can't afford it.*

We dried our eyes. Alan came up with a plan, "The back stairway is out the door and to the right. We can dash down a couple flights of stairs and get on an elevator from there, so we'll miss the reporters."

Feeling hopeless anyway, I said, "Sure. Let's go for it."

We opened the door, and wham! The reporters broke away from interviewing the lawyers and yelled, "Mrs. Barnett, how do you feel about what happened today?" A cameraman held his camera high above everyone's head and clicked the shutter. Alan pushed me through the crowd. Judy shoved open the door marked "Emergency Exit Only' and we escaped down the stairs. Alan crept out the door on the seventh floor and beckoned, "All's clear." We stood in front of the elevator, waiting for the door to open. It opened and a camera flashed; it was full of reporters! "Mrs. Barnett...."

"Oh, no," Alan yelled as he pushed me back through the "Emergency Exit Only" door. Judy and Alan thought it was a riot. I sat on the cold cement floor and cried. Hugging myself, I rocked back and forth, proclaiming, "I'm going to call Jeff from home. And I'm not coming back down here unless I absolutely have to."

I did have to, because things went from bad to worse.

* * *

The elders' lawyer advised them to file for dissolution, which meant that everything would go into a court appointed receivership and it would decide how and to whom the money would go. I thought it was a huge mistake, but of course nobody asked me. Don was horrified

OH, DONALD, DONALD!

and hired three separate law firms to fight it. They filed a claim against the senior elders, stating they were in contempt, making them personally liable.

The court allowed an open hearing in which anyone Judge Burdell would listen to could speak. They permitted news media to be present along with one TV camera. Don's people were told to stay away; he didn't want them to hear any accusations against him. But the room was jammed with not only the elders' side, but people who had left the Chapel and were hurt and angry. Some of the footage from this court scene, including what Jerry said, was televised nationwide.

The more the people talked, the more convinced the judge became. He declared, "The courts are a particularly improper and difficult place to resolve religious dispute." Noting the corporation was still alive, Judge Burdell said, "Checks are being written and honored, and there has been no evidence presented that money is being misappropriated. There is no doubt in my mind... that this is a religious problem."

Jerry and I quietly slipped out the door ahead of the crowd and headed for the back stairs, but not before a newswoman handed me a note. It read, *I'm here for you if ever you want to talk. No pressure.* It was signed, Deborah.

We walked down a half-flight and sat down. "Was what I said okay, B?" Jerry asked. I didn't answer; he needed to talk about it. "I wanted to tell the judge why I couldn't support the court's ruling when they reinstated the pastor, because most of the people feel like I do. I wanted him to see why the courts have put us in an impossible position. I thought it would help if he knew I wasn't basing my stand on hearsay, but that I was the one who had worked with Don to resolve the problem. I had firsthand knowledge."

"You did well, Z. What you said was easy to understand and follow. It made sense."

"I felt I had to try one more time to save my church," Jerry said, holding his head between his hands.

Reaching my arm across his bowed back, I whispered, "Thanks, Z. You've done all you could. I know what's going to happen, now that the judge is leaving Don in until the trial, which could be a year or more. The people won't obey him, so they'll leave. Don's going to cut the salaries of the staff down to minimum wage, so they will leave. By the time it goes to trial, the elders won't have many people left and we'll lose the west campus, because we can't keep up the mortgage payments. We won't be able to meet the balloon payment, because we've already used up most of the $500,000 we had saved."

"Well," Jerry said, "Burdell is right. Civil court is no place to solve this. The Bible tells us that. Don went against the Word of God, so now God is letting them judge him."

We stood up, and to cheer each other up we raced down the nine flights of steps to the ground. "The elders need to get a new lawyer," I panted. When they learned the judge had frozen the BLM fund, they did. Rob Rohan was his name. He was a long-time friend of John's, one of our ministers, and was he ever good! The elders never lost a case after that.

Rob got the BLM fund unfrozen, kept Don from cutting wages, asked for and got a summary judgment (which means the judge makes a ruling on just the points of law). In other words, was it legal for the elders to amend

OH, DONALD, DONALD!

the bylaws to agree with the articles of incorporation so they would have the power to act if Don breached his fiduciary responsibilities.

"We wanted to save Don the embarrassment of a trial if we possible could," the elders said. The matter was heard in Judge Quinn's court. He ruled in favor of the elders. Before the ink from Judge Quinn's pen was dry, Don appealed to the Supreme Court and asked to remain in the pastorship until Supreme Court trial. Rob got a "stay pending trial" so Don was out and the senior elders had control of the corporation.

It took a whole year and a half for the case to be heard in Supreme Court, including the verdict. (Supreme Court is a panel of judges which listens to all the evidence from both sides, then anywhere from six months to two years reaches a verdict.)

* * *

As soon as Don was ousted pending the Supreme Court's judgment, he formed a new church, named it Church of Agape, registered it as a trust in the state of Oregon with him as the only trustee, making sure this time he has total control. He and his followers meet in a rented building about fifteen miles northeast of the Chapel.

Don also lost no time in filing another suit against the elders, demanding the $15,000 we had given to the church when we sold our home. The church had built the parsonage for us but he contended that we had given it for construction of the home and therefore, if he was no longer pastor he was entitled to the money. Sitting in

THE TRUTH SHALL SET YOU FREE

Rob's office prior to the hearing, he shook his head and empathized, "Barbara, either way you lose."

"I know, Rob," I responded, "but the truth is more important to me than the money. We claimed that money as a donation on our income tax with no intention of ever getting it back."

Rob said, "I want to put you on the witness stand. We will be in Judge Quinn's court, because we have obtained a 'Civil Track One.'"

"What's that?" I asked.

"That means we've been assigned one judge to hear everything dealing with the Chapel. It won't be tossed from one court to another anymore."

"Will Judge Quinn hear the other lawsuits against the Chapel, too?"

"No, not necessarily," he replied. "Civil Track One just applies to Don and the elders. Rob continued, "Now, when you take the stand, I'll qualify you. What I mean by that is I'll say, 'Mrs. Barnett, I'm not going to ask you to disclose any personal information that is confidential between you and your husband, because that is not allowed in a court of law. I only want you to tell the court what you remember happened when you gave this money to the church.' At this point, Don's lawyers will probably object to you being a witness. If they do, it'll be up to the judge to decide. Of course, I'll argue that it's not illegal for you to testify, but the judge may decide to not allow you to say anything. If he does, it's okay. I have enough proof without your testimony, so don't worry about it."

Rob was right. Don's lawyers did object and the judge turned to me and said, "I'm sure it would not be illegal for you to testify in this case, but just to be on the safe side, I'm going to ask you to step down."

OH, DONALD, DONALD!

I was relieved. Later, Rob said, "I'm sure the judge had already made up his mind before I put you on the stand. I purposely held you until last, so the fact that you were willing to testify gave more credence to everyone else's testimony. We didn't need you to say anything."

Of all the lawsuits, this was the only one where I was called to testify. My name had been removed from the Tacoma lawsuit. After two straight days of depositions for me alone in front of eight lawyers and a court reporter, the class action lawsuit in King County was settled out of court. The decision was made by our insurance company. There was no way, however, that we could meet the settlement. We'd have to sell the west campus.

It was June of 1990 before we received the Supreme Court decision. Everyone was disappointed and weary with the whole thing. The only ones coming out on top of the mess were the lawyers. At one point, there were a total of sixteen lawyers involved. Thankfully, most of them were paid by the insurance company.

Don was disappointed, because now all the reasons why the elders had removed their pastor had to be revealed in court.

The elders were disappointed because the Supreme Court had overridden Judge Quinn's verdict. They found there apparently is no law that specifically states that a corporation's bylaws have to agree with the articles of incorporation. It is assumed that board members would not sign something that gave them legal power in name only. They added, however, that the matter of whether or not the pastor had breached his fiduciary responsibilities needed to be decided by trial. This meant all the work the elders had done to get a summary judgment to keep the pastor's shame covered had been for nothing. This trail was open to the public.

* * *

Don was adamant! He refused to have Judge Quinn try the case. Finally, the court agreed to assign a new judge. His name was Chan. All of Don's lawyer's attempts to get a motion inlimine, which would eliminate all evidence of Don's misbehavior, was refused.

When, on the first day of trial, Don saw the elders' first witness walk into the courtroom with her husband, he panicked. Frantically asking for a recess, he called for all the lawyers to meet in the jury room to plea bargain. The only avenue open to him now was binding arbitration. If both sides would agree, they could hire a judge to try the case in a closed court—Judicial Arbitration and Mediation Services—but his judgment would be final. Although it cost the elders thousands of dollars, they agreed to accept the offer for the sake of everyone involved, including the name of Jesus.

It took two months for Don to agree on a judge. Finally he settled on a kind grandfather type who had been a superior district court judge. David, who was there for every session and saw the thing through to the end, said, "I have never met a man who showed more kindness, consideration, and patience than Judge Derline. Even when Don, in his five-hour rebuttal at the end would go out on a limb and forget what his point was, Judge Derline would glance at his notes and help Don to remember."

After four months of discovery, where the lawyers ask questions of whomever they chose, the trial began. Because the contents of the trial are sealed, I cannot tell you the details except to say it lasted for three weeks with Don talking one-third of the time. I can also tell you such trivia as David's parking bill during this time was $250 a month, and the lawyer fees for the elders' side alone reached well over the half-million dollar mark with so much paperwork it had to be hauled into the courtroom in carts.

Even Judge Derline's patience grew thin, but he took two days to form his conclusions based on the evidence. With the state's top appellate attorney on the case, hired by Don, the judge didn't leave any loopholes. He took one and a half hours to read his conclusion which found Don guilty on twenty-five conclusions of law and 119 findings of facts.

Don was not granted a re-trial, so—you guessed it—he appealed it to Supreme Court. I know, he wasn't allowed to, but his lawyers tried it anyway. It wasn't until May 1992 that the decision of the Supreme Court was passed down. They cancelled the appeal, stating it was illegal. Judge Derline's decision stands. Don was forced to accept it, even though he was certain he was right. "The civil law cannot dictate the bylaws of a church, because of the separation of church and state," Don concluded.

* * *

By July of 1989, the Chapel was virtually broke. Most of the staff found other employment, elders left. In the spring, seeing the handwriting on the wall, the elders gained permission from the court to sell the west campus. After moving all the furniture and equipment to east campus as soon as Christian School was terminated, they held an auction, boarded up the windows of our beautifully red-carpeted sanctuary, and put it on the market. It looked just like the vision the Lord had given me a few years prior that was so hard to believe. The grief inside of me was so great I couldn't bear to even drive by the place, nor did I go to the auction.

Although Don lost getting back our $15,000, the church still needed to sell the parsonage. Scott came to me and asked, "Do you want to buy it, Barbara?"

Gripped with emotions that were racing up and down faster than a kid on a pogo stick, I cried, "I can't afford to say yes and I don't want to say no." I couldn't bear the thought of someone else living in it, neither could I imagine living there myself—alone.

How could I sleep in our bed that had been shared with other women, or ever lie on the floor in front of the fireplace, or be in our hot pool or on our private sun deck knowing who else had been there with my husband. On the other hand, there was the beautiful black satin bedspread made like an Austrian valance that I had designed myself and our daughter-in-law had made. There was the azalea plant outside my study window that was shaped into a heart just for me by the maintenance man, and the miniature rose bush by the back deck that someone had given me so I'd "always have flowers for my hair." My kitchen, full of gadgets, where I'd prepared dinner every Sunday for the whole family plus a few extras. All the good feelings about the house that we had designed and loved washed over me, but I knew I couldn't afford to buy it. I had tried to buy a little condo for $37k, just to get out of that basement apartment, but I couldn't get a loan. What bank would loan a sixty-year-old single woman with no established credit and no proven income $37,000—let alone $100,000+ to buy the parsonage?

Finally, I said to Scott, "No, but sell it to Don."

"Are you sure you want him to have it?" Scott asked.

"Yeah," I said, "As hard as it is for me not to have it, it's harder thinking about him having to give it up. I know how it feels. Besides, if he gets it, I may get to live there again someday, if ever he gets healed and restored."

Don's new church bought it for him for $110,000. The elders let him have all the pastor's library books, the office equipment, and the stereo system. I am glad he could keep the house we both loved so much.

It was more difficult, however, to find a buyer for the 36-acre west campus valued at $11 million. Fortunately, the judge let us lien the property to pay our lawyer. After almost a year, none of the offers made could be finalized. May 1st was the deadline before the bank could foreclose; we were in arrears by $22,500 a month. In the spring, we learned the state wanted to purchase it to use as a patrol training center, but no decision could be made until the legislature convened in September—too late. Besides the bank, we also had to fork over another huge amount[26] for the other lawsuits by the end of May.

Desperate, we sold in April to Equitable Capital Group who had the financial backing of a Chinese businessman. He put up the money without ever seeing the property. It was a smart move. In September, the legislature voted to purchase the property at market value, giving the investors more than $3 million in profit.

* * *

In the meantime, the whole ordeal had taken its toll on our wonderful Bible college Dean. Stricken with grief over the fact that the man he loved and had supported would sue him personally for following God's Word and fulfilling his God-given responsibilities as a corporate officer, was too much for this honorable man to bear. He suffered a stroke. A few months later, we lost our beloved Dean. Jesus took him home.

His memorial service, held at the Chapel, served as a blessed reunion for all the scattered flock as we grieved our loss, but celebrated his victory. Even our unsaved lawyer was overcome with emotion as he witnessed the compelling love we had for one another regardless of all the pain and agony we had caused by not properly handling the powerful love God had sent.

Chapter Twenty-Four

The Flawed Diamond

"The steps of a righteous man are ordered by the Lord, and he delighteth in His way. Though he fall, he shall not be utterly cast down; for the Lord upholdeth him with His right hand."
(Psalm 37:23,24)

Even before the church split, Don had rejected David as his counselor. New hope entered my heart, however, when Don agreed to get professional counsel. Alex was a Christian who was new to the area, so was not acquainted with the news reports about the Chapel. After one session, I knew Don would never go to Alex again. Within twenty minutes, he zeroed in on the problem and confronted Don. Three days later, there was a letter in my mailbox.

I called Jerry. "Guess what? I got a letter from Don."

"He won't go back to Alex, right?" Jerry guessed.

"Right," I said. "Listen to this, and I quote, *If Alex was this bad on the first try, I can expect nothing better of him in the future. I totally lost all confidence in the man. If he worked for me, I would fire him.*"

Jerry laughed, "We've heard that before."

I continued, "Don's next sentence says, *I can promise you that the problem had nothing to do with him picking something I needed to take care of—I feel thoroughly willing to admit any and all problems, and to be honest and open....*"

"Oh, B," Jerry interrupted, "It would be funny if it weren't so sad. You're wasting your time, B. He'll fire anyone who doesn't agree with him."

"Wait, Z," I interjected, "Don's already picked someone else he wants us to go to. Listen to this, you won't believe it. After he axed your class because of 'worldly psychology,' listen to what he says, *Furthermore, I have found out from my attorney that I need to get a man with a Ph.D., otherwise, the information may be subpoenaed in court. Although they charge close to double, they have doctor's degrees in clinical psychology. They have a lot more training in human behavior traits, they will be*—now, Z, listen to this—*they will be much more professional, accurate, and should be able to do a better job.*"

"Wow," Jerry laughed, "It's something for Don to admit that."

"Let me read the next paragraph to you, Z. Do you have time?"

"Sure, it's slow here today."

"Okay, here's what Don says next: *So Dr. (name omitted) is the man I have chosen, after much research. He has both a doctor of psychology degree and a doctor of psychiatry degree. He works in clinical psychology, and as such, he would be much more professional and much more capable having been trained in human response behavior and other psychological factors.*"

THE FLAWED DIAMOND

"Amazing!" Jerry quipped, "You should go, B, just to see what Don says about him after the doctor confronts Don on one tiny point like Alex did."

"Oh, Z," I whined, "I don't want to sit there and listen to Don accuse and blame me hour after hour while he tells his side."

"Well," Jerry suggested, "You could do this: you could tell Don to go first and tell the doctor everything he wants to without you there to interrupt. Then if the doctor wants to see you, you could go without Don. Is Don willing to pay for it?"

"He says he will if I'll go, but he wants us to go together."

"He might like the idea of being able to talk as long as he wants to without worrying about you cutting him off to tell what really happened. Oh-oh, I gotta go. A customer just drove up. I'll be praying for you. Go for it, B. One more time won't hurt. I'll call you later. 'Bye."

Don accepted my proposal. After he spent three hours with the doctor, I went. Near the end of my second hour, I asked, "Doctor, after listening to Don for three hours, surely you formed an opinion." He nodded. I continued, "Did your opinion change after hearing me, or could you tell what the problem is without my story."

The doctor answered, "I didn't need your story to see the problem, but your story caused me to see how severe it is."

The doctor went on to explain to me what I had discovered on my own at the University Medical library, while studying for the counseling class. I got to witness the theory given in the textbook in action when Don and I met together with the doctor.

THE TRUTH SHALL SET YOU FREE

Don gained permission from the doctor to ask me one question. Just the way Don settled down in his chair told me it was going to be a long question. When Don prefaced his question with accusations and blame, I wondered why the doctor didn't stop him. Couldn't he see what Don was doing? Finally, Don got to the black slip incident and then wanted to know if I would admit that it was my behavior that caused him to fall.

Turning to the doctor, I addressed my answer to him. "You can see, doctor, how impossible it is for me to answer Don's question. It's based on his version of what happened, and you have no way of knowing who is right. Don won't accept my version, or the version of anyone else who lived it, so we are at an impass. I can't be his scapegoat, because I'm not worthy. Only Jesus can erase his sin and guilt."

The doctor turned to Don and said, "Let's suppose, pastor, that everything you said about Barbara is true—I'm not saying it is, now, but just supposing it is—would that justify your actions?"

I watched Don, dressed in his black suit and silk tie slip into a superior pastor's pose and, putting his fingers together, he said, "Well, you see, doctor, the Bible clearly states there are actions and reactions. I've done a lot of studying on this subject, and I realize you probably haven't, but...."

I watched the doctor cross his legs and sit patiently waiting for Don to finish, and I screamed in my mind, *He's pulled rank on you, doctor. Why don't you call him on it? Why don't you ask him if he's here to teach you or learn from you? He's creaming me. Can't you see what's happening?*

The doctor, being wiser than I, knew it wouldn't do any good, and I knew I wasn't willing to take the abuse from Don any longer.

As soon as Don finished, I said, "With Don's theology, Doctor, there is no way for this to get resolved unless he would set you up as the judge and you interview all the witnesses to see who's story is right. Of course, Don has already rejected the verdict of a sixteen-man elder board, plus a county judge, but if he's willing to pay you to be the judge and he'll abide by your decision, then call me when you need me." I stood up and walked out.

Two weeks later, I called the doctor and asked, "Did Don ever ask you for your evaluation of the problem?"

"No, he didn't."

Earlier in one of our sessions together, I told the doctor what I'd learned at the University of Washington medical library while studying for the counseling class about a paranoid personality disorder in the journal DSM.[27] The doctor told me he didn't like to use labels for people's problems. Then he explained to me what usually happens in a case like Don's. "First a rapport between me and the patient has to be established—a mutual respect—because, if he feels I'm beneath him in any way, he won't respect what I say. Or, if he feels I'm superior, I become a threat. If he is pushed at all, he only becomes more rigid in his thinking."

I told the doctor, "Boy, that's what I've done, huh?"

He smiled and continued, "The problem is, there is nothing to hold him here; he can leave whenever he chooses, so as soon as I confront him on any point, he will take the superior position and leave. He needs to be lifted out of his environment, but as long as he has fol-

THE TRUTH SHALL SET YOU FREE

lowers, there is no way he can be helped, unless he is legally forced to."

I added, "And none of the lawsuits will do that, because they are civil suits. The only way that could happen is if one of the girls would have him prosecuted, then the judge could order him to get treatment."

"That's right," agreed the doctor.

I wrote Don a letter suggesting that he ask our doctor for his evaluation of the sessions, because, I said, "After all, you paid to get his opinion, so you certainly should find out what it is. Please ask him to send me a copy as well." I never heard from Don on the matter.

Now on the phone, I asked, "Doctor, what can you tell me about myself? What is your evaluation of me? What can I do to improve myself?"

The doctor, "You got married young and you've really never had a chance to know who you are until these last three years. I think you see things more accurately than Don; you're more honest and more aware of people's feelings and human behavior than he. You've come out of the mold [of co-dependence] and you can never fit back into it. For the first time in your life, you're becoming a whole person. I have no advice for you except to say 'Keep on going.'"

"Doctor," I asked, with tear-filled eyes, "What chance do you give my marriage?"

"Barbara," the doctor responded softly, "I don't give your marriage any chance at all, no chance." Hearing me crying on the phone, he added, "Dear, the Lord is not requiring you to go back into that marriage; in order to do so, you would have to cut out part of your brain."

* * *

THE FLAWED DIAMOND

Jesus knew I was hurting too much that day, sitting on Alki Beach on August 5th, on what would have been my 44th wedding anniversary, for Him to show me how my flaws had affected others, so He waited until the morning after a glorious worship service, in which He manifested Himself to me through a man name Stu who had been on staff in the Counseling Center for the sole purpose of praying with counselees. Stu still has a remarkable relationship with Jesus.

It was almost time to leave the building, which had to be closed at 10:00 p.m., when it happened. Suddenly, as a song of worship began, our spirits were drawn to dance together. Our eyes met, but it wasn't Stu who was looking at me—it was Jesus, Who makes His abode in him (John 14:23). Tears streamed down my face as Jesus' love, acceptance, and compassion permeated my soul. I knew I was His beloved, in spite of all that had happened.

Early the next morning, I was awakened by the Lord. He was speaking to me in what I'll tell as a parable. The story went like this:

Once upon a time there was a family with many children in which the father became an alcoholic. As a result, his wife and children suffered much abuse. The eldest son found himself being his siblings' protector and his mother's confidant and advocate. The poor father had no idea what he was putting his family through, because he was always drunk. By and by, after most of the children were grown, the father, through sweat and struggles, broke his addiction. Now that he was well, he wanted his family to be proud of him, without giving a thought to the suffering his behavior caused them.

THE TRUTH SHALL SET YOU FREE

Like a flash of lightning, I saw myself. I wept and wept. *Oh, Jesus,* I cried... *I've hurt many of your children because of the co-dependent mold I was in. I can see the flaw in the diamond. I understand why You manifested Yourself to me through others and why You put Jerry in my life. I needed him. I needed it all to get free, to get well, to get whole—but in the process, I've hurt the children."* I sobbed over and over...*I'm sorry. I'm so sorry. No wonder I got eggs thrown at my car and angry letters. No wonder they are bitter and hurt. Jesus, I'm so sorry. Please help them to forgive me. Please forgive me, Jesus.*

The Spirit of the Lord took me back to the vision of the lush green field that represented our salvation by grace, with the fruit arbor that typified all the ministry gifts, and the exquisite regal white chamber which was our love relationship with Jesus. This time, however, it was after the storm. There were ashes everywhere. The fruit arbor was gone. The lush green field was still there, but tattered and torn, covered with ashes and rubble. The love chamber was ripped and smudgy. It was empty, except for the people who had made it into the cave. There we were, wrapped in the love of Jesus like a blanket, with only our faces, full of sorrow and uncertainty, showing.

Suddenly, I saw Jesus, dressed in a white garment that came down to His ankles. He was out in the field among all the rubble and ashes, hunting for something. I watched as He shuffled through the debris, bent over, picked up something, wiped it clean of dust, and held it up to His Father. Instantly, the glory of God beamed upon it. It was a beautiful jewel, perfectly shaped to reflect all the glory the beam from heaven was shining on it!

THE FLAWED DIAMOND

I wish you could have seen the look on Jesus' face as He found the jewels and showed them to His Father. He was more radiant than a man putting an engagement ring on the finger of his fiancée and more proud than a father looking into the face of his first baby. He didn't mind that His hands and white garment were getting dusty from all the ashes. He turned and looked at us who were watching from the cave, too fearful to venture out again lest we would get dirty. His smile told us it was okay—wouldn't we come out and help Him find the jewels? He showed us how the dust brushed off, so we didn't have to worry about getting damaged again.

Then I saw what would happen if we would come out of the cave and help Jesus find and restore the jewels: suddenly the whole cave turned inside out. Like a huge balloon, it stretched over everything, including all the fruit that we held, all the Word of God we knew. All God's children were being covered with this wonderful love from Jesus that we at the Chapel had experienced! *"Now abideth faith, hope, and love; these three; but the greatest of these is love"* 1 Corinthians 13:13.

Appendix

Dear Don,

We three Senior Elders, each individually, wish to again express our personal love, our compassion, and deepest concern for you, our brother and friend. We are grief stricken at the personal situation you are in. We are diligently praying for you that our Lord and Savior Jesus Christ whom we all serve will do a restoring work in you. We want to again assure you that we have no ill will toward you, nor do we have any motive or desire to hurt you. You are beloved of us. We are, so to speak, your children in the faith of the Gospel of our Lord Jesus. We love you fervently and will continue to do so.

We are also mindful of our responsibility and stewardship to the Word of God, to you our pastor, and to the flock over which God has ordained us as overseers. We are committed to the fact that the Holy Scriptures are the highest authority which we are responsible to follow. We have searched our hearts and consciences before God and are fully assured we are acting in accordance with our proper stewardship of this holy trust. We can do no less....

We have sought to extend as much love and personal consideration to you as possible in our former letters read before the congregation. In those we intentionally avoided being specific about your misconduct in the hope that you would cooperate with our action and to minimize personal embarrassment for you. Instead, last Sunday you escalated the issue, and you gave specific revelations of your sins yourself, which we had hoped for your sake would not be told publicly.

The special status we placed you on was not intended to be the final judgment of the elders of this board. As of the date of the special status letter, we had much more than sufficient, substantial information, plus your own admissions to us, to take that action. Since that date the eldership has continued in lengthy, very careful, investigative meetings, and extensive further misconduct, present and past, has been substantiated.

Sad to say, your attempted rebuttals last Sunday to the congregation escalated the issue and now puts us in the position of having to reveal more facts to show that you are trying to perpetrate dishonest views of your actions.

The statements you made to the entire eldership, the congregation, and others have positively established that you refuse to abide by the special status imposed upon you February 15 by us for the protection of the flock. On February 16, one day later, you went on vacation with another woman and others in violation of that special status and you have continued to violate it in other respects since. You refuse even minimal and appropriate accountability to the government of this church and the Word of God. By your own clear statements you have place yourself above accountability to anyone for anything. We affirm that this is contrary to Scripture and that it is an exceedingly dangerous precept, both for you and our flock. Before God, we cannot submit to such an unholy, self-serving, and frightening demand. In the full eldership letter of February 24 to you

, which was read to the congregation last Friday, we demonstrated by the clear text of many Scriptures that the eldership does have the authority and responsibility to take such action. In your rebuttals to the eldership last Thursday and to the congregation last Sunday, you made virtually <u>no</u> appeal to Scriptures, and instead offered arguments that are dogmatic and self-serving. You did not try to see if our statements were true, you only attempted to justify yourself.

For well over two years now, you have steadfastly rebuffed and refused to cooperate with the many who have sought to work with you to help solve your habitual sexual immorality problems. Your continuing sinful attitude toward this whole issue is, in fact, worse yet than your sexual sins. It is obvious that you have never confessed or repented of your continued self-serving justification, lying, dishonesty, defensiveness, misuse of pastoral authority, making light of sin, and defiance of Holy Scripture. These sins are deep seated, adamant, and continuing. We agree that this is ungodly, anti-scriptural, sinful, and dishonoring to Christ and the Christian testimony of our church.

You have continually lied in the past and are currently lying about your sexual misconduct to counselors, the entire eldership, and the congregation. You have sworn on oath before God to the entire eldership that you have <u>not</u> committed any sexual immorality in the last six months. You stated the same before the entire congregation last Sunday when this was manifestly false. You recently admitted privately to your failure in the last six months but added that the elders do not know it.

You are currently lying about the number of women you have been involved in immorality with and the extent of it. There are numerous other ongoing lies which we know about, many from your defenses given last Sunday. We believe your word is in no wise to be trusted in respect to your sins.

There have been many repeated and flagrant abuses of pastoral authority. You have coerced women and even threatened to disfellowship unless they lied about your sexual misconduct to counselors, elders, and the courts. For over a year you have used your pulpit to blame and accuse your wife and others.

You have used your position of trust to enact policies which help shield you and prevent the discovery of your habitual sexual problems and you have preached these from the pulpit multiplied times. Further, you have for some time been preaching the defense of these tactics to the congregation. Your eldership, including all the theology teachers, are unanimous in this judgment. You have intertwined these teachings with correct theology and undiscerning people have doubtless accepted the full teaching as Scriptural. But we know that a large portion of the congregation sees this grievous error and are deeply concerned. We, the Senior Elders, are grieved and sorely distressed, as well as all of the eldership, to a man. Further, you have publicly attempted to split the church asking the congregation to take sides against the entire eldership. This is condemned in Scripture. Whereas the eldership last Friday evening admonished everyone to stay together, pray, forgive, love, and accept the pastor and all those involved. In addition to the above, the eldership has evidence of much additional sinful conduct which is shocking. We, the Board of Senior Elders, and every member of the entire eldership have the deepest of conviction before God that we cannot allow our pastorship and pulpit to be used this way.

It is our judgment that your habitual sexual misconduct problem is far from solved. It is our further judgment that this, plus all of the above continuing unchristian actions and attitudes, disqualify you for the office of pastor or elder of any church of God according to Scripture. We believe that you are presently a discredit and reproach to us and to the Name of Jesus. As such, we feel compelled to remove you from your position as pastor, Senior Elder, all of your other offices, and as a member of this church. We deeply regret that we did not find out about many of these things sooner. This disfellowship is not contrary to any provision of our Articles of Incorporation or bylaws as currently amended. Previous limitations in the bylaws to your dismissal have been removed by legally adopted amendments as of today.

Effective immediately you are prohibited from entering church property, with the exception of the parsonage. We will enforce this if necessary.

Even though we must take this serious action, we still love you and desire to deal mercifully with you. We greatly appreciate the deep sacrifice you have made for the congregation for many years. We will show you fairness and be benevolent to you with regard to the parsonage, severance pay, and the automobile you use. The Senior Elders in conjunction with the Deacon Board will extend terms to you as soon as possible.

We will provide for you in order to allow time for personal repentance and prayer , personal deliverance, and counseling. It is our prayer that waiting on God with an open heart will result in a deep renewing and healing for you.

We also want you to continue spiritual counseling with David Motherwell. We believe he will be an asset of the Lord for you. After a substantial season, ample and proven witness to your restoration, your full cooperation, and recommendation of your counselors, we may consider your application for reinstatement as a member if you desire at that time. We firmly believe that removing you from your ministry is intended by Scripture and us to be a necessary part of the redemptive work of your spiritual life.

We want you to know that our action is in no way vindictive or arising out of personal hurts. We love you as a person and friend, Don, and Jesus loves you. We want the very best for your soul in eternity. We want what God wants for you. Really, this is mercy and grace for you. We also want to see your marriage restored and this will give an opportunity for that.

We pray that you will humbly accept this action as a needed restorative and redemptive step and as God's mercy for the sake of your soul. We look to the future for what our great God and Savior is able and sufficient to do.

End Notes

1. *Born Again*; Charles Colson.
2. Documented testimony, available through Community Chapel & Bible Training Center.
3. Sermon tapes on legalism available through Community Chapel & Bible Training Center.
4. Sermon tapes available through Community Chapel & Bible Training Center.
5. Available through Community Chapel & Bible Training Center.
6. Available through Community Chapel & Bible Training Center.
7. Sermon tapes available through Community Chapel & Bible Training Center.
8. Sermon tapes available through Community Chapel & Bible Training Center.
9. Tape available through Community Chapel & Bible Training Center.
10. Tape available through Community Chapel & Bible Training Center.
11. Copyright Buz Goertzen.
12. Available through Community Chapel & Bible Training Center.
13. Tape available through Community Chapel & Bible Training Center.
14. News articles and videos available through Community Chapel & Bible Training Center.

15. Letter available through Community Chapel & Bible Training Center.
16. Document available through Community Chapel & Bible Training Center.
17. Document available through Community Chapel & Bible Training Center.
18. Letter available through Community Chapel & Bible Training Center.
19. Letter available through Community Chapel & Bible Training Center.
20. Letter available through Community Chapel & Bible Training Center.
21. Tape available through Community Chapel & Bible Training Center.
22. Letter available through Community Chapel & Bible Training Center.
23. Reported to me by the husband.
24. Letter available through Community Chapel & Bible Training Center.
25. News articles and videos available through Community Chapel & Bible Training Center.
26. The settlement amount was sealed by court order.
27. Table 5 DSM-111-R Criteria For Narcissistic Personality Disorder; page 633; Textbook of Psychiatry; The American Psychiatric Press; edited by John A Talbot, MD, Robert E.Hales, MD, and Stuart C. Yudopky. Table 3 DSM-111-R Chiteria for Paranoid Personality Disorder; 631.

To order addtional copies of

The Truth Shall Set You Free

please send $19.95* plus $3.50 shipping and handling (WA state residents add 8.2% sales tax) to:

Renewal Ministries
PO Box 66376
Burien, WA 98166-6376

(Single copy total is $25.09 including tax and shipping)

To order by phone, have your credit card ready, and call 1-800-917-BOOK.

*Quantity Discounts Available